HEARTLAND

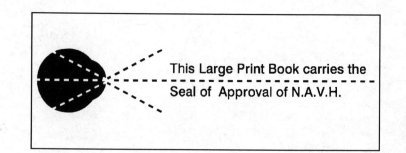

This Large Print Book carries the
Seal of Approval of N.A.V.H.

HEARTLAND

A MEMOIR OF WORKING HARD AND BEING BROKE IN THE RICHEST COUNTRY ON EARTH

SARAH SMARSH

THORNDIKE PRESS

A part of Gale, a Cengage Company

GALE
A Cengage Company

Farmington Hills, Mich • San Francisco • New York • Waterville, Maine
Meriden, Conn • Mason, Ohio • Chicago

GALE
A Cengage Company

Copyright © 2018 by Sarah Smarsh.
Portions of the work herein have appeared in different form in the following publications: *Flint Hills Review* ("The Firecracker Stand," Issue 16, 2011), *The Common* ("Death of the Farm Family," Issue 8, 2014), and *Longreads* ("The Case for More Female Cops," 2016).
Thorndike Press, a part of Gale, a Cengage Company.

ALL RIGHTS RESERVED
Thorndike Press® Large Print Biographies and Memoirs.
The text of this Large Print edition is unabridged.
Other aspects of the book may vary from the original edition.
Set in 16 pt. Plantin.

LIBRARY OF CONGRESS CIP DATA ON FILE.
CATALOGUING IN PUBLICATION FOR THIS BOOK
IS AVAILABLE FROM THE LIBRARY OF CONGRESS

ISBN-13: 978-1-4328-5956-5 (hardcover)

Published in 2018 by arrangement with Scribner, an imprint of Simon & Schuster, Inc.

Printed in Mexico
1 2 3 4 5 6 7 22 21 20 19 18

For Mom

CONTENTS

AUTHOR'S NOTE

I researched and wrote this book over the course of fifteen years. My initial task was to construct a family timeline of dates, addresses, and events, which I first undertook as a student at the University of Kansas with two small research grants in 2002. Throughout the drafting process that followed, I combed through public records, old newspapers, letters, photographs, and other archives to piece together a family history from the ill-documented chaos that poverty begets.

For the family perspectives and anecdotes recounted here, especially those I was not alive or present to witness, over the years I conducted uncounted hours of interviews with many of the people involved. Much of the story was drawn from their memories and perceptions. Events I witnessed myself were written mostly from my own memory, sometimes with sought input from family members.

Points on United States and world history, politics, public policy, and other matters beyond the private experience are based on news stories, studies, and books I deemed accurate and reliable in my capacity as a journalist. They are conveyed with my perspective.

In a small number of instances, I have changed or omitted the names of living people.

DEAR AUGUST

I heard a voice unlike the ones in my house or on the news that told me my place in the world.

It was your voice: a quiet and constant presence, felt more often than heard. You were like those stars that, for some reason, a person can see only by looking to the side of them. I was just a kid, but I knew the other voices were wrong and yours was right because my body felt like a calm hollow when you echoed in it.

I didn't try to figure out what you were. I just knew you. Often, what grown-ups say is mysterious, children readily understand. Eventually, in my mind, you took the form of a baby that I either would or wouldn't have.

You were far more than what a baby is. My connection to you was the deepest kind of knowing — hard to explain because it swooshed around in my mind and took dif-

11

ferent shapes and meanings over the years. But there was a moment, before I was even old enough to have kids, when I was fretting about the sort of decision that in another household might have gotten help from parents. Those moments usually sent me praying to some God outside myself. Instead, I thought, *What would I tell my daughter to do?*

I've never been pregnant, but I became a mother very young — to myself, to my little brother, to my own young mother, even — and that required digging very deep. So deep down to the quick of being that I found not just my own power but your unborn spirit, which maybe are one and the same. I can't tell you how that happened. But I can tell you why, for me, it had to.

America didn't talk about class when I was growing up. I had no idea why my life looked the way it did, why my parents' young bodies ached, why some opportunities were closed off to me. I suppose we never completely do know, even with hindsight. But the hard economies of a family, a town, a region, a country, a world were shaping my relationship to creation — to my womb, yes, but also to what I would or wouldn't have a chance to make of myself.

I was on a mission toward a life unlike the

one I was handed, and things worked out as I intended. I'm glad you never ended up as a physical reality in my life. But we talked for so many years that I don't guess I'll ever stop talking to you — not the you that would have been but the you that exists right now. There are two of you, as with all of us: the specific form and the energy that enlivens it. I only ever knew you as the latter, the formless power that I rode out of a hard place.

Probabilities and statistics predicted a different outcome for me — a poor rural kid born the year her country began a sharp turn toward greater economic inequality. Chances were that I would stay in that hard life, and that you would be born into it, too.

You have nothing to do with probabilities or statistics, of course, which are flimsy at best. But those were real, often devastating forces in my life and in the lives of so many children. I'd like to honor you by trying to articulate what no one articulated for me: what it means to be a poor child in a rich country founded on the promise of equality.

How can you talk about the poor child without addressing the country that let her be so? It's a relatively new way of thinking for me. I was raised to put all responsibility on the individual, on the bootstraps with which she ought pull herself up. But it's the way of things that environment changes outcomes.

Or, to put it in my first language:

The crop depends on the weather, dudnit? A good seed'll do 'er job 'n' sprout, but come hail 'n' yer plumb outta luck regardless.

1
A PENNY IN A PURSE

The farm was thirty miles west of Wichita on the silty loam of southern Kansas that never asked for more than prairie grass. The area had three nicknames: "the breadbasket of the world" for its government-subsidized grain production, "the air capital of the world" for its airplane-manufacturing industry, and "tornado alley" for its natural offerings. Warm, moist air from the Gulf to the south clashes with dry, cool air from the Rocky Mountains to the west. In the springtime, the thunderstorms are so big you can smell them before you see or hear them.

Arnie, a man I would later call my grandpa, bought the farmhouse during the 1950s to raise a young family. He spent days sowing, tending, and harvesting wheat. He eventually owned about 160 acres, which is a quarter of a square mile, and farmed another quarter he didn't own. That might sound big-time in places where crops like grapes are prized in small bunches. But for a wheat farmer in the twentieth century, when the price per bushel had been pushed down by the market even as yields had been pushed up by technology, it was just enough to earn a small living.

When a wheat crop was lost to storm damage or volunteer rye, sometimes milo went in. Arnie raised alfalfa, too, to bale for his fifty head of cattle. He also kept pigs, chickens, the odd goat or horse. He had one hired hand, and his sons and daughters pitched in at harvest. For extra money during the winter, when the fields were frozen, he butchered for a meat locker down the highway toward Wichita and sold aluminum cans he collected in barrels near a trash pile west of his pole shed.

When the old house turned quiet after his divorce, Arnie drank a lot of whiskey. On weekends, he liked to put on his good cowboy boots and go dancing in Wichita honky-tonks like the Cotillion, a small concert hall with a midcentury sign on Highway 54.

There, one night in 1976, country music played while widows and divorcées danced in Wranglers and big collars under a mirror ball. Sitting at a table with a butcher named Charlie and a farmer they called Four Eyes,

Arnie noticed a skinny woman with short blond hair at another table. She and her friend wore the paper rose corsages given to all the women at the door.

"She's not gonna dance with you," Four Eyes told Arnie. "You're too damn fat and ugly."

Four Eyes himself got up and asked the blond woman to dance. She said no. So Arnie walked over. His hair was a feathery brown comb-over, and he wore carefully groomed muttonchops on his square jaw. His round belly jutted over his belt buckle. The woman, Betty, had overheard his friends making fun of him. So when he asked, Betty said yes.

She would be my grandma, and I would have loved for you to know her. Betty's whole life amounted to variations on that moment at the Cotillion: doing something kind for an underdog. That's the kind of love I would have wanted to surround you with: indiscriminate and generous, from people like Betty who had every excuse to harden their hearts but never did. She was no saint, never pretended to be. But she would have loved you not just because you were mine but because you existed in a world she knew wasn't easy for anybody.

Betty and Arnie danced two or three

songs. He smelled like Old Spice aftershave, and she liked his happy laugh. They agreed that every Johnny Cash song was the same damn tune with different words. Arnie thought she was a looker. Funny, too. He got her phone number. But when the band packed up and the dance floor cleared, she wouldn't let him take her out for breakfast at Sambo's down the highway. She'd stick with her friend and buy her own pancakes.

In the coming weeks, Arnie called her trailer a few times, but she didn't answer. Then the operator said the number was disconnected. Arnie went back to farming the land.

Betty wasn't the farming kind. She'd spent her adult life moving among urban areas in the middle of the country — Wichita, Chicago, Denver, Dallas — and neighboring towns. She and her daughter, Jeannie, who would be my mom, first hit the road when Betty was a teenager. Their whole family, which consisted mostly of single moms and their daughters, was hard to pin down. By the time Jeannie started high school, they had changed their address forty-eight times, best I can count. They didn't count. They just went.

About a year after Betty and Arnie met, his pickup and her Corvette pulled up to the same highway intersection just west of Wichita. They waved at each other, rolled down their windows, and pulled into a nearby truck stop to get a hot drink. Arnie's life was the same, but Betty had gotten married and divorced in the months since they'd last seen each other. She had a wildness — not so much a streak but a core — that other middle-aged farmers might have found off-putting, even scandalous. But he fell in love and treated her better than she'd ever been treated. For one thing, he didn't beat her up. He didn't even complain about what she cooked for dinner or did with her life in general.

"*Mox nix* to me," he told her.

She stuck around.

During the wheat harvest of 1977, when Betty was thirty-two and Arnie forty-five, Betty drove every evening from her full-time job as a subpoena officer at the Sedgwick County courthouse in downtown Wichita to Arnie's farm. She took over the house, cooking for Arnie and his field help, driving tubs of fried chicken, paper plates, and jugs of iced tea to fields where yellow dust followed red combines. She learned the blowing dirt of the country summer, when teeth turn gritty in the wind and shower water turns brown between shoulders and toes. She rode the combine with Arnie, a rite of passage for any would-be farmer's wife, and woke up the next morning with clogged sinuses. She sweated through the harvest nights of midsummer, when fans blow hot air through hot bedrooms and sleep is possible only because of how hard you worked.

Jeannie was fifteen and going to high school in Wichita, old enough by our family's standards to take care of herself while Betty was at work or at Arnie's farm. She'd finally gotten into a social groove after changing schools twice a year for most of her life. She didn't want to move this time, especially not to a farm in the middle of nowhere. Now that she'd been in one place long enough to turn in her homework, she was getting good grades and enjoying school. She preferred hanging out at Wichita's little outdoor mall to fishing in pasture ponds. Her hobbies were reading and fashion, which she studied in magazines before sewing her own clothes. Fabric stores and public libraries would be in short supply on the Kansas prairie. Jeannie groaned. But her mom had decided they were going. They packed up yet again and moved west to Arnie's farm.

After a few months, Arnie asked Betty to marry him. Betty thought she was done with all that, and anyway, Arnie was Catholic. She'd heard the Church didn't take people who'd been divorced, let alone six times.

Father John, the priest of a nearby parish, assured her that none of those marriages counted since they weren't in the Church. She figured she had to count the first two husbands, since they'd fathered her children, but otherwise she liked the idea of disavowing every one of the bastards.

She and Arnie ended up marrying outside the Church anyway, in September 1977, at a little chapel on a highway next to a trailer park.

The newlyweds had constant company at the farm. Their pickup engines could be heard down the road, followed by the sound of tires rolling slow on the gravel driveway, usually around dinnertime. Betty peeled untold pounds of potatoes, baked pies, fried meat, and stewed vegetables that grew outside the front door. She learned the isolation of rural life through a batch of cookies — she had everything she needed but the brown sugar. What was she supposed to do, drive ten miles west to Kingman just to get one damn ingredient?

"It wasn't like when you lived in town, you'd bebop down to the QuikTrip," she told me years later.

She learned to keep the basement over-stocked with discount canned food, the deep-freeze packed with every cut of meat, the cupboards filled with double-coupon deals. She and Arnie were the sort of poor who, whether by spirit or circumstance, found a way to feed themselves and whoever else needed a meal.

Betty's city friends drove west to see her new country life. Arnie's friends showed up to see his wild city woman. They partied at Cheney Lake, a few miles away along straight dirt roads and a curving two-lane blacktop. They fished and swam in Arnie's pond with its water snakes and leeches, the crusty earthen dam dimpled where cow hooves had sunk in mud after rain. They camped next to fires in pastures with hot dogs, Coors, and s'mores. They drove mopeds through fields and crashed three-wheelers into trees. They had butchering parties in the detached wooden garage that housed a meat grinder, a sink, hooks hanging from rafters, and a bloodstained cement floor. Everyone got drunk enough to eat mountain oysters, and everyone who helped went home with a cooler of meat wrapped in white paper. They laughed when a pile of aluminum cans brought five times its worth at the scrap lot after Arnie, pulling them in a net behind his tractor, inadvertently filled the cans with sand and tipped the weight scales.

During one liquor-store run to Kingman, after skidding across an icy country bridge and rolling down an embankment in a small Toyota, Betty made her younger sister Pud mad by lighting a cigarette inside the upside-down car while she thought about how to get out. Pud named the place Camp Fun Farm.

It wasn't long before Pud's older daughter, Candy, moved into the farmhouse to escape some sorry situation. Next came Pud herself and her younger daughter, Shelly, after the inevitable divorce. Thus began a nearly thirty-year stretch of Betty's nomadic, cash-strapped family members taking refuge there by necessity.

When Betty wasn't cooking for people at the farm, she was working at the courthouse in Wichita. Or she was pulling weeds in the vegetable garden east of the house, cleaning, planting flowers, or digging for tools on the back porch that housed the washer and dryer and shotguns.

Betty was only ten years older than Arnie's firstborn, a surly, long-haired twentysomething who was often drunk. During the summer, he played on a slow-pitch softball team of area farm boys who liked to drink beer at Arnie's farm after games. One of them was Nick Smarsh.

That's how teenage Jeannie met Nick, the farmer and carpenter who would be my dad. He had grown up working the fields and hammering roofs in hot sun and cold wind. In the summer, his thick arms were tanned a deep red-brown, darker than the brown in his plaid snap-up shirts with the sleeves cut off. He drove a white 1966 Chevy Caprice, which he kept clean as a whistle inside and out, with air shocks lifting the back end. Sometimes he shot road signs through pickup windows.

He was always smiling, though, never critical or violent, unlike so many of the men she'd known. Nick turned out to be the one thing Jeannie didn't mind about the country.

Even though Arnie wasn't my blood relation, he played that big a role in my life — Jeannie and Nick never would have met if Arnie hadn't asked Betty to two-step. He was such a bright light for us that, after he died, it occurred to me that I would call you after his middle name: August. I knew you were a girl, but I never thought to make it Augustine. Your name was August.

It was a special name in that Grandpa Arnie and I were both born that month. The same sign, my mom would want me to point out. Grandpa and I used to butt heads something awful when I was in high school. That happens between teenagers and their family regardless of their birthdays. But I'd find out years later that he did see something of himself in me — a point he never would have told me himself and a sure recipe for friction. I wonder now whether he might have been hard on me as I got older because he was sad knowing that I was about to leave the farm.

Arnie was not one to act sad or complain. He had the gifts I would have wanted most for you: humor and generosity. He didn't register his own goodness, which was effortless and reliable. Grandma Betty used to get upset thinking he let people take advantage of him. What someone asked for, he gave if he could. And it wasn't because he was some salt-of-the-earth farmer. Plenty of farmers are jerks, and many favors went unreturned from the ten square miles or so that was our farming community. But Arnie didn't keep score. He just did his best every day, and the laugh that Betty liked that night on the Cotillion dance floor was a healing sound. He'd laugh so hard, his eyes squinted shut and filling with tears, that his whole

25

big, bald head would turn red. It makes me laugh right now just to picture it.

I saw that laugh many times. When I was a little girl, I loved following him around the farm. There are quite a few pictures of me back then wearing frayed denim overalls and the look of a seasoned farmer on my face, staring straight into the camera with my shoulders squared and my feet planted apart in a way that used to make my prim mother laugh. "Sturdy Gertie," she'd say and crack up.

I was small for my age but strong, and I rarely smiled at the camera — not because I was unhappy but because I didn't know that little girls were supposed to perform like that, I guess. Nobody in my family told me to act dainty. Plus, it was before all the digital screens that show people pictures of themselves in an instant. You could grow up relatively innocent of your own image. I see now that I looked like the spirit of an old man in the shape of a little girl.

Maybe that's another reason I liked Grandpa Arnie's middle name for you. The adjective form of the word means "digni-fied," "respected" — ideas we more often associate with old men than with little girls. I didn't realize it at the time, but they're also words we're more likely to associate with privileged classes of society.

Being born female and poor were the marks against my claim on respect, in the world's eyes, and I must have sensed it. Your name represents a corrective, or at least a defiance, on both counts.

I didn't even know "august" was a descriptive word and had no idea what it meant. People where I'm from don't use adjectives like "august." They don't use many adjectives at all. They speak a firm sort of poetry, made of things and actions.

Once I learned what "august" means, it was quite a few more years before I knew how to pronounce it. Like so much of my vocabulary, I learned it alone with a book but didn't hear it spoken aloud. In my head, I said it like the month.

It would be unwise for me to claim I know how much growing up in a poor family shaped my words. My mother's strong vocabulary, itself learned alone from books, probably has more to do with my language than any college degree I got. We can't really know what made us who we are. We can come to understand, though, what the world says we are.

When I found your name, in my early adulthood, I don't think I'd ever heard the term "white working class." The experience it describes contains both racial privilege and economic disadvantage, which can exist simultaneously. This was an obvious, apolitical fact for those of us who lived that juxtaposition every day. But it seemed to make some people uneasy, as though our grievance put us in competition with poor people of other races. Wealthy white people, in particular, seemed to want to distance themselves from our place and our truth. Our struggles forced a question about America that many were not willing to face: If a person could go to work every day and still not be able to pay the bills and the reason wasn't racism, what less articulated problem was afoot?

When I was growing up, the United States had convinced itself that class didn't exist here. I'm not sure I even encountered the concept until I read some old British novel in high school. This lack of acknowledgment at once invalidated what we were experiencing and shamed us if we tried to express it. Class was not discussed, let alone understood. This meant that, for a child of my disposition — given to prodding every family secret, to sifting through old drawers for clues about the mysterious people I loved — every day had the quiet underpinning of frustration. The defining feeling of my childhood was that of being told there wasn't a problem when I knew damn well there was.

I started to wake up to the gulf between my origins and the seats of American power when I left home at eighteen. Something about my family was peculiar and willfully ignored in the modern story of our country. My best attempt at explaining it was, "I grew up on a farm." But it was much more than that. It was income, culture, access, language, work, education, food — the stuff of life itself.

The middle-class-white stories we read in the news and saw in movies might as well have taken place on Mars. We lived, worked, and shopped among people whose race and ethnicity were different from ours, but we didn't know any "rich people." We scarcely knew anyone who was truly "middle class."

We were "below the poverty line," I'd later understand — distasteful to better-off whites, I think, for having failed economically in the context of their own race. And we were of a place, the Great Plains, spurned by more powerful corners of the country as a monolithic cultural wasteland. "Flyover country," people called it, like walking there might be dangerous. Its people were "backward," "rednecks." Maybe even "trash."

Somehow, without yet understanding any of that consciously, I picked for you a name about dignity and respect. I used to say it over and over in my head, the way some girls wrote boys' names in notebooks. I never even pictured a father for you — knowing on some level, I guess, that you wouldn't need one. I pictured only you. I knew how to say your name: Grandpa Arnie's middle name and the month I was born. A wealthy month for wheat farmers. August.

Betty was sixteen when she got pregnant with Jeannie. If I had to pick a fact of our family history that most shaped my relationship to you, it would probably be that one: Every woman who helped raise me, on my mom's side of the family, had been a teenage mother who brought a baby into a dangerous place.

The father of Betty's baby was a twenty-year-old Wichita street thug named Ray, whom she'd known since they were kids together on the bad side of town. I met this biological grandfather of mine only once, and he looked just like everyone had said — like a gangster. He had black hair, slicked back, and wore a suit. He usually had a look on his face that Grandma described as "arrogant."

Ray was the opposite of Grandpa Arnie. He routinely hit Betty, pinned her down, punched her. She would fight back until he knocked her unconscious or kicked her in the ribs and left her bruised and bleeding.

Betty knew Ray could murder her. So when Jeannie was just a few months old, she decided to get out of Wichita for both of their sakes. She would need money to do it. She couldn't ask her mom, Dorothy, for help; they were fighting, and Dorothy didn't have a dime to spare anyway. She asked her grandparents across the street, Dorothy's parents, to lend her $75, the cost of a divorce at the county courthouse. They told her, "You made your bed, now you lay in it." Betty told herself that if someday, somehow, she ended up in a position to help somebody in a bind, she would do it, without judgment.

She came up with twenty-five bucks, went to the public car auction, and bought an old Plymouth. Or maybe it was a Dodge. Her sister Pud helped her spray-paint it black in their mother's driveway so it wouldn't look so rusty and awful. Whether she could afford a divorce or not, she was leaving town.

"I packed my car with what little shit I

had, and my baby, and I took off," Betty told me. "And I had no idea where in the hell I was going. Chicago's where I stopped."

Every kid in our family moved more times than they could remember without getting out a pen and notepad. If you're wild enough to enjoy it, poverty can contain a sort of freedom — no careers or properties to maintain, no community meetings or social status to be responsible to. If there was a car that ran and a bit of gas money, we could just leave. Like my grandmother and my mother, you and I probably would have done a lot of that sort of rambling together.

Sometimes it's a worthwhile gamble for the poor to drift. Having no money looks and feels different in different places. Are your neighbors helpful? Is the landlord raising the rent? Can you walk to work if the car goes out? For a child, are the kids and teachers at school welcoming? Do you have to walk past a drug house to get there? Among the poor, the potential risks of starting over are more severe for women, people of color, and other disadvantaged groups. But often, by moving, there is little to lose and at least a chance at finding something better.

People without money today might be less transient, for a lot of socioeconomic reasons. But when Betty left Wichita in 1963, she could just about count on finding a job and a cheap apartment wherever she went, so long as she had the will to work for it. And Betty had will in spades.

Chicago was the biggest place she had ever seen, but she was unimpressed. "The Windy City," she told me, skeptical as one who was raised in Tornado Alley. "Shit. They never seen wind."

The day she arrived, she found an apartment for $20 a week. The same place might have cost half as much in Wichita, but there was a lot of work to be found in Chicago. The next day, she bought a newspaper and answered an ad for a job at a factory that made clock radios and other electronics.

She got the job and thought it paid well. She was used to earning the federal minimum wage of $1.15. The factory paid three times as much. Her landlady, a Puerto Rican woman Betty befriended despite their language barrier, babysat Jeannie all day while Betty sat on a stool at work drilling three screws into blocks of wood, over and over, and at night while she worked at the deli down the road.

She didn't care to find a new crowd to

party with. Back home, she'd done speed with Ray because everyone else did, but she didn't like it. Now Betty was seventeen and alone with a baby. Her entertainment was to push Jeannie in a stroller next to Lake Michigan. She couldn't afford to see a movie, but she visited the Chicago Natural History Museum, which must have had free admission.

Each month, after she paid the rent and utilities, and the landlady for watching Jeannie, Betty had $27 left. She budgeted some of it for cigarettes and gas. The rest went to groceries from the little store around the corner. The store sold frozen pot pies, five for a dollar. She'd buy twenty-five of them, beef and chicken flavor, and that would be her dinner all month. Every day, a candy bar for lunch at work and a frozen pot pie for dinner at home.

After winter passed, she left the factory for a filing job at a life insurance company closer to her apartment. She could walk to the office, then from the office to her job at the deli, then from the deli to home. She even had a stint at a chocolate factory, picking candy off the conveyor belt, just like in the *I Love Lucy* episode.

Once Betty came home from work and saw a skinny kid crawling out her apartment window onto the fire escape. She chased him up the metal ladder and across the roof, where she tripped and blackened the knees of her pedal pushers, which really pissed her off, especially since she had already dropped her cigarette. She followed him down a dirty hallway and beat on a door until a big woman with black hair opened it.

Betty told her what had happened. The woman dragged the boy to the door and yelled at him in Spanish. He dug in his pockets to hand Betty the costume jewelry he had taken. The woman was giving him a beating before she even closed the door. Betty felt bad for the kid. But she had her jewelry back.

Back in Kansas, according to Betty many years later, Ray had gone AWOL from the Army. He figured out where Betty lived, most likely from her mom. He showed up in Chicago saying he wanted to start over. Betty knew he would be trouble again. But she was scared of him, and she let him in.

Ray found a job, played pool for money, and sold drugs on the side, Betty told me. They moved into a bigger apartment. Soon Betty's lawless crew from Wichita was streaming in and out. Betty sent a letter to her mom and little sister. Baby Jeannie's scribbles fill the space at the end, and it looks like a kid wrote the letter itself — loopy cursive slanting backward, bubbles dotting the *i*'s. It was all about money. How much did things cost? Who was working? What were the losses to report?

June 24, 1963
1365 Sunnyside
Chicago, Ill.

Dear Mom & Pud,
Hi, how ya doing?
Okay, I hope. We are all okay. Still working, but I only work four hours a day so I'm gona look for another job. Ray's working anywhere from 12 to 17 hrs a day. But the checks will be good. He get's paid day after tomorrow & I get paid Thursday.
Well there's no new's to write about. Oh the car blowed out. The Brakes went out completely, we lost the front brake cyninder first, then the back & now the master cylinder. But we dont drive it at all. We moved again now we have a three bedroom apartment. 35.00 a week, it's a hell of a lot better.
No bug's or mice.
And everyone has there own privacy.

36

Lynda's ole man's sister is living with us now.

Were all working now so there wont be any money troubles. Well I guess I better close for now.

Jeannie is okay, she is crying so she can write a letter too. We got a baby sitter for her, she treat's her real good. Well we miss you all. Will write more often now.

Love alway's
Betty, Jeannie & Ray

Have we got any important mail like Ray's discharge?

Plans changed quickly with a volatile character like Ray around. The beatings got bad again. One night, when Ray left to go out partying, he padlocked the apartment from the outside, in case Betty had a mind to leave.

"If the place had caught fire, we'd have been screwed," she told me. "The fire escape would've been difficult carrying a kid with ya, but if you were doin' it for your life, I guess you'd try."

The next day, when Ray had come and gone again with the car, and the padlock was off the door, Betty packed what she could in a suitcase and split. She and Jeannie rode a train back to Kansas.

"Jeannie had a pet monkey, a little stuffed toy. She hung on to that, ya know, like some babies carry blankets and stuff," Betty told me, holding back tears. "This was her security, this stuffed monkey. And it got lost. I guess we left it on the train."

It wasn't the lost stuffed animal that made Betty cry, of course, but knowing how miserable her daughter's childhood had been — even her security blanket, of sorts, got lost in the chaos — and interpreting this as her having been a bad mother. Jeannie's childhood traumas had more to do with the generational poverty she was born to than with her mom's love and capability. But, like most poor people I know whose lives appear riddled with failure, Betty saw it as her own fault.

Nick, my father, was born on Labor Day in 1955. That's a poetic birthday for a carpenter, but I didn't realize it until I was well into adulthood. Labor Day was, for us, a day the country took a break, but that carried no political significance. No one in my close family belonged to a union — most of the men being self-employed as farmers or tradesmen and most of the women doing work that was poorly unionized.

Plus, being out in the country kept us separate from that sort of organizing. Farmers don't work for hourly wages negotiated between unions and company bosses. Fields need tilled and cattle need fed whether it's a federal holiday or not. Nick's little German Catholic farming enclave had a community picnic outside the church every Labor Day to mark the end of summer, but they still did chores before and after.

Nick was the youngest of six children — three boys and three girls. He was given his dad's full name, Nicholas Clarence, even though he was the third-born son, like his parents had run out of ideas. When he came along, his dad was forty-six and his mother, Teresa, was forty-one. He was probably a bit of a surprise. But his parents were both Catholic and farm people, groups that had different but intertwining reasons for producing a lot of children — the former thinking birth control sinful, the latter needing help raising wheat.

True to his birthday, Nick turned out to be a worker among workers. His productivity and money saving impressed even his stingy parents, who had come of age during the Great Depression. Before he was old enough to drive, he owned more head of cattle than his dad did. At age nineteen, he started a foundation-laying business. When he met Jeannie in his early twenties, he already had five employees and a few thousand dollars in the bank.

Jeannie had book smarts and was a talented artist, but, like Nick, her handiest sort of intelligence was with life, with money. She could always find her way out of a bind, hustling cash with odd jobs, making money stretch the furthest it could. She came from a long line of women whose lives amounted to getting out of a bind, often by working harder than their men. Nothing disgusted Jeannie more than a man sitting on his butt all day expecting to be taken care of. She respected how Nick worked and said "please" and "thank you."

Jeannie and Nick looked good together. She was small and fair-skinned with long, straight brown hair parted down the middle. He had blue eyes and a bushy, sand-colored beard. They smashed around farm parties and Wichita dance halls, where underage Jeannie carried her head so high no one dared ask for an ID. In a raffle at a party thrown by a Wichita lumber-supply company in 1978, they even won a trip to Paris. Besides the men who left to fight wars, no one in their families had ever been overseas.

As the 1970s drew to a close, discussion

in the United States was all about scarcity of resources, both real and perceived. In 1979 came the second oil crisis of the decade, a petroleum shortage related to trade with the Middle East and America's appetite for the world's fossil fuels. Cars lined up for blocks to fill their tanks while gas stations raised their prices, as the global supply-and-demand economy dictated.

People in our corner of society were far removed from the national political discussion. Their eyes were on immediate concerns: Was the hot combine shaking beneath them running right for the wheat harvest? Was there gas in the car to get to work? Had the cattle been fed? Who would pick up children from babysitters?

That's what my early life felt like, and it's how yours would have felt, too — like some invisible hand was making decisions that affected us in ways we didn't have the knowledge to describe or the access to fight.

In July 1979, amid a national panic over fossil-fuel shortages, President Carter visited Kansas City to promote his new energy program. The night before, he had given a televised speech about the oil panic from the Oval Office. Americans were weary and cynical after a couple decades of civil unrest, he said: the assassinations of moral and political leaders, a shameful and bloody war in Vietnam, public revelations about a dirty White House. Carter said the country was experiencing not just an energy crisis but a moral one.

"It's clear that the true problems of our nation are much deeper," he said in his Georgia accent, "deeper than gasoline lines or energy shortages, deeper even than inflation or recession."

The real trouble was with materialism, he said. He had grown up working his family's peanut farm, the sort of experience that doesn't mean you're a good person but does impart lessons about money and resources.

"Too many of us now tend to worship self-indulgence and consumption," Carter said, his pale eyes full of worry. ". . . But we've discovered that owning things and consuming things does not satisfy our longing for meaning."

That's where he was wrong. The country had not discovered those truths, not in the slightest. In fact, on the eve of the garish 1980s, our lesson was just beginning.

That's not to say people couldn't see economic trouble brewing. Carter's speech cited a poll suggesting that, for the first time in the country's history, most people thought the next five years would be worse than the last. Ten years of inflation had shrunk the value of a dollar and, with it, people's hard-earned savings. Natural resources once presumed limitless were being recognized as precious and finite.

We were at a fork in the road, Carter told millions of people through their living room television sets, and had to choose a path: remain fearful and selfish, grasping for economic advantage over other countries and even our own neighbors, or embrace unity.

"This is not a message of happiness or reassurance," Carter said, "but it is the truth, and it is a warning."

It was a warning the country would not heed. Carter's poll numbers went up, but the country didn't change. That America couldn't hear his message about worshiping the false idol of wealth is a public fact that would be felt privately for decades to come. No one would feel it more than the poor.

A few months after Carter's "crisis of confidence" speech, Jeannie and Nick got engaged. She had gotten her GED, and Nick had bought a spread of land near the lake for $350 an acre when it came up for auction. The wedding was set for January 1980.

But as the autumn leaves fell in 1979, Jeannie had second thoughts. She was seventeen, Nick twenty-four, but she often felt she was more mature than he was. She was thinking about calling off the wedding until, on Halloween night, they were messing around in Nick's parents' basement.

"Don't come in me," Jeannie told him.

Nick came in her anyway.

"I said 'don't come in me'!" she said.

"I thought you said, 'come in me,' " he said.

As Jeannie went up the stairs from the basement, out the door and into the dark, to turn a cold car engine under the big sky of a flat landscape, she felt different.

"I *knew* I was pregnant," she told me. Unlike most of our family, she usually disliked vulgarity. I was embarrassed, when she told me the story after drinking a great deal of boxed wine, to hear her say "come." I wasn't at all surprised by the point of her story, though — that a poor teenage girl in rural Kansas might experience pregnancy as an inevitable life sentence. A family cycle so old and deep tends to go unexamined and unquestioned but is always felt.

Your presence in my life both helped and worried me. When I was in junior high, I already knew that the spirit I felt beside me would be either my downfall or my redemption — that you would be either an unwanted fate crying in my arms or a pattern that I had ended by my own will.

Jeannie never took that sort of mission for herself, I guess, and neither did Betty. It's lucky for me that they didn't. But two things can be true at the same time. I'm grateful for my early life, and I wouldn't wish it on any child.

On a windy, cold day at the outset of 1980, Jeannie and Nick married at St. Rose, a small, white clapboard church built at the turn of the century. Still in her first trimester, Jeannie looked slim in her white lace dress, and no one was the wiser. After the ceremony, their friends and family from surrounding farms and busted corners of Wichita gathered at a big dance hall called The Keg in the small town of Colwich. It was thirty miles away but had a stage and space for a proper Catholic wedding dance. They ate brisket, drank cans of Coors beer, and danced to a country band. Nick shaved off his beard for the occasion, and Jeannie looked even younger than she was.

Betty was that way, too. When people looked at her, they couldn't believe her actual age. I'd grow up to hear I had those same "good genes." What people didn't see

45

was all the invisible "bad" we inherited, cycles handed down for what I have a feeling was centuries and maybe millennia. They were the negative cycles of poverty. One of them was to be a veritable child and have a baby inside you.

Jeannie wouldn't be able to keep hers a secret for long. Soon after the wedding, she and Nick stopped by a party at Betty and Arnie's farmhouse. Jeannie was one month married and three months pregnant, starting to show a bump. Betty and Arnie were drinking with their friends, the raucous bunch that as a child I would spy on through clouds of cigarette smoke in the dining room: Thin women wearing frosted lipstick and tight jeans. Thick men wearing sideburns and big collars, speaking bits of German without realizing it. On the dining table, more than likely: beer, whiskey, potato chips, a card game called ten-point pitch.

Jeannie stood in the dining room leaning against the wall of built-in oak cabinets that housed china, brittle photo albums, batteries, hammers, poker chips. She tried to cover her belly with her coat.

Betty looked over at her daughter and noticed.

"Are you pregnant?" she shouted. "Oh my God, you're pregnant!" Betty pushed away from the table and shrieked over her embarrassed daughter's belly.

The party sprang into full gear. They were drunk, yelling at Betty, "You're gonna be a grandma!" She was thirty-four years old.

When Betty sobered up, she was upset about the news. Did Jeannie want to get an abortion? It was even legal now.

She did not.

I thus was the proverbial teen pregnancy, my very existence the mark of poverty. I was in a poor girl's lining like a penny in a purse — not worth much, according to the economy, but kept in production.

Jeannie's third trimester carrying me was the hottest summer since the Dust Bowl. The Wichita area reached a hundred degrees for forty-two out of fifty-five days. The heat wave killed seventeen hundred people across the Great Plains — one of the worst natural disasters in U.S. history. But farmers might be the ones most likely to remember it. The drought shriveled crops and caused $20 billion in agricultural losses.

For Jeannie, the summer was one hell of a time to be pregnant. Air-conditioning was a luxury she didn't have.

That August of 1980, my parents brought me home to a tiny red shack they had rented in the same little community where I'd been conceived — a rural cluster of houses separated by wheat fields and long driveways. Mom stayed with me while Dad went back to work farming and building.

Mom and I were alone then, with a rotary phone, a cat, and a black-and-white television. On the TV, local news anchors surely talked about the weather, which my family followed closely, and the upcoming presidential election, about which my family was less concerned. Many of them didn't bother to vote, feeling themselves powerless in a system they suspected was rigged. Mom had recently turned eighteen, though, and intended to wield her new right.

For now, she wielded the cigarettes she had smoked right through her pregnancy, a laundry hamper full of cloth diapers, and a bottle of baby formula. It would have been cheaper to breastfeed, but that would have been the lowest shame of poverty. Mom didn't feel the maternal pangs she'd been assured she would anyhow. She scraped together change for formula. Betty had done the same in the '60s. I might have done the same if I'd had you when I was a teenager, before a mainstream cultural return to breastfeeding reached our place and class. I see so many things differently now. But we did as we had learned.

Grandma Betty was driving back and forth to work in Wichita every day but helped with baby care when she could, like the day I choked on formula and she shook me by the ankles while Mom napped.

"Your face turned red as a beet," Grandma would say, laughing and half-apologetic, whenever she retold the story. "Shit, I didn't know what to do."

In a few months, when the election rolled around, Mom would align with one-third of Kansas voters and cast her first ballot for Carter's reelection. But Ronald Reagan won, of course, and got to work cutting taxes.

Reagan said that big, private money would "trickle down" to us through the economy, as though we were standing outside with our mouths open praying for money to rain. Reagan was big on states' rights and deregulation, which appealed to the government-wary streak of my people. Back then, conservatism made some fair claims about keeping government out of people's lives, a noble enough idea in a country that won its independence from an oppressive monarchy.

But keeping government out of the private sector could lead to a different sort of oppression, it would turn out. Federal policies that had created a middle class in the twentieth century were giving way to corporate rule in which billionaires with political influence could be kings behind the scenes.

That same year, 1980, a country singer first recorded a song about the Great Depression with the lyrics, "Somebody told us Wall Street fell, but we were so poor that we couldn't tell." It wasn't the 1930s anymore, but even in my childhood before cable television and the internet, we lacked understanding of our place in the economy. We were so unaware of our own station that, in the rare instance that the concept of class arose, we thought we were middle class. That term occasionally got thrown around in the news, and we recognized it to mean "not poor, but not rich." Since we had enough to eat, that's how we thought of ourselves.

Being conceived a few months after Carter's foreboding speech and born a few months before Reagan's inauguration meant that my life and the economic demise of American workers would unfold in tandem. But we couldn't see it yet out in the Kansas fields.

That we could live on a patch of Kansas dirt with a tub of Crisco lard and a $1 rebate coupon in an envelope on the kitchen counter and call ourselves middle class was at once a triumph of contentedness and a sad comment on our country's lack of awareness about its own economic structure. Class didn't exist in a democracy like ours, as far as most Americans were concerned, at least not as a destiny or an excuse. You got what you worked for, we believed. There was some truth to that. But it was not the whole truth.

Dad had to fold his foundation-laying business a couple years before I was born. You can't pour concrete when the temperature is below freezing, and the record-setting winter of 1978 left Dad without work for his employees. He went back to doing carpentry with his dad, uncles, and two older brothers, known in the area as Smarsh Brothers Construction. He plowed his and other people's fields and took side jobs as a handyman.

When I was still an infant, Mom, Dad, and I left the little red house for a trailer that Betty and Arnie had parked next to their farmhouse. Arnie hooked the trailer behind his tractor and pulled it to our land, a flat stretch of grass and dirt between the tall dam of a state reservoir and the flat wheat fields Dad had worked his whole life.

I had my first birthday party in the trailer. Dad kept working and saving money, and I became a white-haired toddler. Mom cooked supper in the tiny kitchen that had black-and-white wallpaper printed with turn-of-the-century advertisements for corsets and shaving cream.

More often than not, Mom had a job outside our home, too. It almost always involved selling something. She decided to get a state real estate license to sell houses in Wichita. To be closer to work for both her and Dad, I guess — there being more structures to construct and sell in cities, of course — we moved east to Wichita, first to an apartment for less than a year, then to a rented house in a modest but quiet, treed neighborhood. On weekends, Dad worked on our house in the country.

Things were looking up. We got a cocker spaniel. I had Flintstones vitamins and a pink canopy bed. On Friday nights, Mom and Dad told me goodbye at the door and walked into the night dressed up — Mom with big, curled hair and bright blush on her cheeks, Dad wearing his snakeskin boots and smelling like Irish Spring soap and aftershave. They went out to dance halls, where Dad drank Canadian whiskey and Mom drank diet pop. During the days, while the two of them went to work, I briefly attended a preschool. I was three years old and had already lived in four places, enough to know that a canopy bed and vitamins was high on the hog.

When Dad had paid off the bit of land he bought for our house, he used it as collateral for a bank loan to buy building materials. It was early 1983, and the construction industry could feel a recession coming on. His father warned him against borrowing money when the economy didn't look stable. But Dad told him he had faith in the United States. He believed that things would get better.

The small-town banker wanted to know how he'd pay back the loan if work didn't pick up.

"I'll chop and sell wood if I have to," Dad told him.

He signed for the loan, and we headed back to the country.

By then, the trailer on our land had been moved back to Betty and Arnie's farm for some other relatives. So we moved into their farmhouse. My parents and I shared a bed upstairs that autumn.

Twelve miles down the road, before the air got too cold for cement-pouring, Dad laid the foundation for our new house. As the earth around us hardened into winter, Dad did the electric wiring himself. He hired a man from Mount Hope, a nearby small town, to do the plumbing and the air conditioner. The bricklayer would have to wait. The cold had come fast and hard, and mortar would freeze before he could smear it.

Arnie lent his posthole digger for Dad to put up a new pole barn. They dug the holes, loaded huge poles into the back of a wheat truck, and dropped each one into a hole, tamping dirt and pouring concrete from pole to pole. They nailed two-by-fours horizontally between the poles and hoisted the trusses with a tractor scoop. Male friends, their legs tightly wrapped around the tops of the poles, grabbed for the swinging trusses. When the frame was done, they slid sheets of tin up, up, and over.

The pole barn seemed to me a great, mysterious place, where men were dirty and spoke a language of measurements — bushels of wheat, kernels per head, miles per gallon, acres of milo, points on a buck, yards to the eight-point buck. I loved when they brought me along on chores or to cattle auctions.

I've heard stories that Grandpa Arnie was a violent, blustery dad to his own kids a couple decades prior. If so, he had changed by the time I came along, as often happens on the way from parenting to grandparenting. He would zoom me around on his three-wheeler to help feed the cows, keep me on his lap while he drove the tractor, tell me what tool to hand him in the work shed. He thought I was hilarious. He took to calling me "Sarah Lou," for some reason, even though my middle name was Jean, after my mom. Before long he and Grandma Betty just called me "Lou."

It makes me laugh now, seeing that many of the women I knew had what amounted to one-syllable trucker handles for nicknames. Betty was Sis. Her sister Dorothy was called Pud — short for "Puddin' " — so she wouldn't be confused with their mother. Because of Grandpa Arnie, I was Lou.

Like most of the men I grew up around, Arnie's surfaces were rough: enormous brown, chapped hands with bruised fingernails like my dad's; heavy, pointy-toed leather boots; wiry sideburns; a scratchy brimmed cap of mesh plastic and the logo for the meat locker where he butchered. I knew him as a tender person, though. He showed me how to pull a xylophone by a string and, years later, a hayrack by a truck with a manual transmission. He cried when he accidentally tipped over the three-wheeler we were riding and I broke my arm.

In the evenings, Arnie returned from the shed with oil handprints on his jeans. Betty returned from her job at the Wichita courthouse wearing Kmart business suits. Dad returned from construction sites with sawdust in his beard. Mom returned from the Wichita airport, where she'd taken a job at an airline check-in counter, wearing a uniform skirt and a name pin with little wings on it.

All four bedrooms at the farm were upstairs. They had wood floors and the original, single-pane 1910 windows that smelled like dust and had ice on the inside of them. Dad and I would sit in bed eating cereal out of the box until the crumbs in the sheets made Mom mad. We all snuggled against the cold. I'd never been happier than I was sleeping on a full-size mattress between my parents, with my grandparents just beyond the wood-paneled wall.

In the spring of 1984, Dad and his friends finished our house. They put up sheetrock, laid shingles, poured cement in front of the attached garage. A hired man dug a pond with a dozer. Dad built a wooden dock before the big hole was filled with water. A family friend who raised catfish a couple miles down the road stocked the pond. Mom and Dad moved our few things from Betty and Arnie's farm, along the two-lane blacktop that curved around Cheney Lake.

Mom decorated the house with things that to our eyes looked nice and to anyone else's eyes were at least well arranged: a shiny black vinyl sofa next to antique chairs from an auction, satiny rose-colored wallpaper in the formal entry that faced the pond. In the family room, burgundy paint and a print of men wearing riding habits and hunting foxes with their hounds, as though Mom meant to redefine what sort of "country" people we were.

She had a knack for making it appear that we had more money than we did. There was about her an audacious dignity. She said people hung art too high on walls. It really bothered her, as though she'd never had a real problem. She was bothered, too, by dirtiness — a necessary awareness, as there would be no visit by a cleaning lady. Her attention to cleanliness might have been defensive, as well, to avoid giving credence to ideas that people like us might be dirty. This inherited concern ran deep in us as females. *It's clean* would be Grandma Betty's first report after approving a new burger joint or roadside motel.

As for deeper problems, I knew Jeannie's with the unparalleled expertise of any mother's child. One of them, it seemed clear, was that I existed. Though I wouldn't know for years that I'd been an accident, I felt the knowledge at an atomic level. I'd materialized over one word that either wasn't heard or wasn't heeded, that night she told Nick not to come inside her: *don't.*

Maybe that's why, as a kid, I heard nothing but *don't* — don't speak, don't breathe, don't laugh, don't cry. The price of my existence — the food, the air, the water, the space — was made known, and my actions either did or didn't justify it. My life's merit was met with the same suspicion as my mother's and that of countless people before us.

I was determined that you would never know that feeling. It reached for you from far back in time, well before I existed, before my parents or grandparents existed. We were centuries-old peasant stock.

Mom's lineage was a mix of Scandinavian, German, and Scots-Irish, best I can figure out. I knew that side of my family as single mothers who moved like the wind and called themselves gypsies.

Dad's Catholic bunch — me representing

its fifth generation farming the windswept plains of Kansas — descended from foragers and farmers in what is now the German-Austrian border region, it appears. We ended up raising wheat and cattle, but our name, Smarsh, was for a much humbler food: mushrooms. In our ancestral homeland, I once read, poor people said mushrooms were holy fingers poking through the earth to nourish them.

That sort of alchemy, assigning a meaning — turning what some might view as the lowly act of foraging into a direct communion with God, for instance — is often the only sort of power a poor person has.

One thing Mom and I had in common was that we understood and respected the power of words and names. Her own mom said she had wanted to call her Jennifer, but Ray insisted they name the baby after Betty. That's how Betty later remembered it, anyway. So my mom was named Betty Jean and spent a lifetime explaining why she went by Jeannie.

My parents didn't know much about our lineage or even the meaning of our last name, but maybe Mom sensed it. She gave me a first name she knew meant "princess," as though someone who foraged to survive could still be regal or even rich in her own way. But it was my last name and its origins that decided the stuff of my life. Like poor immigrants not so far back in our bloodline, we were raised to not expect much and to ask for even less. It was a good thing, too. The house that Dad built wouldn't be ours for long.

I answered the question of whether I deserved to exist by working hard: folding laundry before I could read, reaching on my tiptoes to wipe off the bathroom counter while George Strait sang on the record player about rodeos and pretty women. I was raised to not be idle. Our hard work was how we had a roof and enough to eat.

What I did hunger for sharply, what my life lacked most sorely, was in my mother's heart — which had been scarred by the traumas of monetary poverty but carried a feeling of perpetual lack and discontent that knows no class.

The poverty I felt most, then, was a scarcity of the heart, a near-constant state of longing for the mother right in front of me yet out of reach. She withheld the immense love she had inside her like children of the Great Depression hoarded coins. Being her child, I had no choice but to be emotionally impoverished with her. I offered to rub her back every day so that I could touch her skin.

One develops a cunning to survive, whatever the shortage. My family excelled at creative improvisation: eating at Furr's Cafeteria on the rare food outing since it was all-you-can-eat and required no servers' tip; scanning garage sales for undervalued items that could be resold at higher prices; rigging our own broken things rather than calling an expensive repairman; racing to the grocery store to buy loads of potatoes at 5¢ per pound when the Wednesday newspaper ad had a typo that the company legally had to honor.

Similarly, I haunted hallways around the corner from where my mom sat reading Stephen King novels or watching soap operas as I tried to get up the courage to ask her if she loved me. It wasn't so much that I didn't know the answer as that I wanted to make her say it. Nothing was more painful to me than true things being denied.

When I asked, her answer had the right words but the same cruel tone as her silence. I wanted her affection, but more than anything, I wanted her to be happy. From what I've observed, a poor child's agony is just as often for her parents as it is for herself. You could say that is still a selfish impulse, because in order for a child to survive, her parents must survive, too. But I felt my family's burden as my own well past childhood.

You would have been born to creative, industrious people. That's what poverty requires.

Mom and Dad both were good at coming up with ways to make a fast dollar. During the summer of 1984, Dad got one of his more ambitious ideas when Sedgwick County banned the sale of high-powered fireworks — M-80s, bottle rockets, items known to blow people's hands off. Dad knew that Wichita people would have to go somewhere else to have some real fun on the Fourth of July.

We lived past the county line, in Kingman County, where no elected official would dream of banning any class of fireworks. The people of our county were farmers who drove enormous combines with giant, sharp blades that cut the wheat; carpenters who built their own giant sheds by swinging hammers while perched high on wooden rafters; and women who held down calves to inject vaccinations before they drove four-wheel-drive pickups to office jobs on the brick streets of small towns. They could handle their firecrackers.

In June, Mom drove to a wholesale warehouse on a blacktop road through the prairie. She wrote a check for hundreds of heavy boxes of various fireworks manufactured in China. Strings of Black Cats, TNT-brand variety packs, M-80s, M-60s, bottle rockets, children's sparklers and smoke bombs, little hens that shot glowing eggs out of their behinds, and cardboard columns that released quiet, pretty fountains of colorful sparks and had names like Springtime Sunrise.

Dad and Grandpa Arnie hammered together a vending stand with lumber out of a scrap pile Dad kept in our shed. They loaded the wooden stand onto a hayrack and pulled it down the county blacktop to the gravel parking lot of Kampling's Live Bait Shop, which stood at the entrance to Cheney Lake, a draw for people over the holiday weekend.

The fireworks stand was a narrow rectangle with a roof, a counter for customers to approach, and a visible rack of shelves on the back wall. Mom and Grandma Betty lined the shelves with merchandise, taking breaks to smoke Marlboros and stare at the horizon with weary looks. I was almost four years old and held red-white-and-blue bunting to the counter as they stapled it in place, the thick, smelly plastic blowing in the wind and sticking to our sweaty, dusty legs.

Dad hauled his power generator from our shed to the fireworks stand. It would run electricity to lightbulbs strung overhead, and to the blinking arrow sign he had rented and situated in the prairie grass next to the blacktop road. When the sun set, the sign's little bulbs flickered to life, and June bugs buzzed against them.

The morning we opened for business, the people of Wichita appeared from the east, pulling speedboats behind pickups and carrying wallets full of cash. They bought heaps of fireworks and headed off through the lake entrance for a long weekend. Grandma Betty, her short blond hair darkened by sweat at the neck, counted the growing pile of bills in our cash box.

Dad and Grandpa Arnie spent the days in the fields, cutting wheat with combines or, after harvest, plowing the stubble under. In the evening, they arrived to help at the fireworks stand. Sunburned, eyes tired, whiskers full of dust and bits of straw, they moved heavy boxes and drank beer and laughed.

My older cousin Shelly and I played with

bugs in the hot dirt and wrote fizzy sparklers across the dark sky until Shelly, who could be meaner than any boy and was tougher than most of them, shoved a firecracker up a frog's butt and lit the wick, which made me cry. Shelly's skinny teenage sister, Candy, stood near the ditch and waved in cars from the road, twirling a baton and wearing a stars-and-stripes bikini and garters. She had a paper Uncle Sam top hat over her short, sandy hair. Neighbor farmers waved when they passed. Everyone was covered in a thin film of dust.

When the stand closed around midnight, Dad spent the night sitting in his parked pickup, a loaded shotgun on the seat beside him, in case someone had a mind to rob us. There was security in guns for good reason where we lived. What we owned wasn't locked in a bank but sitting in a wooden stand with plastic bunting flapping in the prairie wind.

"You can't be too careful," he'd say, holding his gun with respect for the weapon but no pride about carrying it.

When it was all over, the morning after the Fourth, Mom and Dad counted and rubber-banded the bills. Once they paid off the wholesale supplier, the county permit, and the family help, they had a fortune of a few thousand dollars. It would come in handy, as Mom's belly was large with a baby that would be born in the fall.

Mom and Dad had their first fireworks stand the year Reagan was reelected — selling American pride in a field next to a two-lane blacktop while think tanks sold "trickle-down" economics. It's funny that both of their children were born weeks before an election that Reagan won. We would be able to map our lives against the destruction of the working class: the demise of the family farm, the dismantling of public health care, the defunding of public schools, wages so stagnant that full-time workers could no longer pay the bills. Historic wealth inequality was old news to us by the time it hit newspapers in the new millennium. That's the difference among the person selling the fireworks and the one watching them sparkle in the sky from a public park on a work holiday and the one watching them from a nice apartment in a city high-rise. You live in different Americas and thus have different understandings.

Dad didn't own any stocks or follow any market other than agricultural commodities. But he knew something about the economy wasn't right. Things were getting more expensive compared to how much money was coming in. That's a ratio felt acutely when you have to calculate budgets to the dime.

Dad saved coins in a giant glass bottle that had previously contained Canadian blended whiskey. One night he reckoned it was time to count them. He poured them onto a foldout card table in the living room near the brick fireplace. I watched the pennies, nickels, dimes, quarters trickle down into a pile. Touching the coins with great care, Dad separated them into stacks. He was not a materialistic man. I never knew him to buy anything for himself but work tools. But he lived in a materialistic world, a system of goods and services that required monetary compensation. He added figures on a notepad and a calculator. He left the family room for a while and returned to count the coins a second time. I walked past.

"Sarah, come here," Dad said.

"What?" I asked.

"Do you have something you want to tell me?"

"No."

"Are you sure?"

"Yes."

Dad sighed and looked at his coins.

"I know what you did," he said.

"What?"

"You took a nickel."

I hadn't.

"No, I didn't," I said.

"Sarah, don't lie to me."

"I didn't take it."

"Just be honest, and I won't get mad at you."

"I didn't!"

Dad sighed again and put his head in his hands, agonizing over what the moment meant to him: A nickel was unaccounted for, and every missing cent was his fault. I stood there looking at him and the stacks of coins on the wobbly foldout table feeling like I could cry. I hated being misunderstood, and I hated when my parents were unhappy. This moment was all of that at once, and the air smelled like dirty metal.

I realized the weight of those coins, then. The big, silver ones were worth the most, but the smaller ones mattered just as much when you needed every penny. It's a lesson I sometimes forgot. Grandma Betty scolded me once for throwing a few dirty, sticky pennies in the trash.

Her mom and grandma had worked on the Boeing assembly line during World War II. Once, a pay period shook out so that the company cut a check to her grandma for exactly one cent. After she died, the pay-check ended up among Betty's keepsakes.

"Here's a paycheck for one friggin' penny," Betty would say, holding it with reverence. "Can you imagine? But a penny is a penny. Every bit counts."

Currency values used to be based on a gold standard, Dad would explain when I was a little older, but now they were based on nothing tangible. It was just a game, really, the whole money system. Grandpa Arnie watched wheat prices go up and down in the local newspaper or on the price board that hung outside the grain co-op. At the courthouse in Wichita, Grandma Betty made less money than men who did the same job with less skill. We didn't own stocks, but the psychological underpinning of the market wasn't lost on us.

"Paying retail is for fools," Mom used to say. We could walk into a store and with one glance at a tag discern a showroom full of ridiculous markups. Mom would pick up a dish off a shelf, turn it over to read the number on the bottom. She'd raise her eyebrows and set it back down.

"I don't think so," she'd whisper.

Betty would raise her eyebrows, too.

"What a rip," she'd say once we were outside the store, walking back toward our car but not holding any bags.

Money was what made the world go around, I learned fast. I knew how to compare prices on tags before I knew how to read words. Yet money was a lie — pieces of paper and metal suggesting prices for goods, services, labor, and human beings themselves in a way that often had more to do with profit than with true value. We were on the losing end of that lie no matter how many acres of wheat we farmed.

In that way, my family and our class might have been the least fazed by America's obsession with wealth. As workers living at the taproot of the agricultural economy, we not only could grow and build our own necessities — we also understood the hard work a loaf of bread represented and thus put less faith in the money that bought it than in the bread itself.

Wealth and income inequality were nothing rare in global history. What was peculiar about the class system in the United States, though, is that for centuries we denied it existed. At every rung of the economic ladder, Americans believed that hard work and a little know-how were all a person needed to get ahead.

Unlike so many people of my generation, I did get a good life for my hard work and know-how. In addition to what I might have earned, there were strokes of grace along the way that I can't take any credit for. Somehow I ended up with a better situation than my parents had.

But the American Dream has a price tag on it. The cost changes depending on where you're born and to whom, with what color skin and with how much money in your parents' bank account. The poorer you are, the higher the price. You can pay an entire life in labor, it turns out, and have nothing to show for it. Less than nothing, even: debt, injury, abject need.

No matter who you are or what you started with, though, your fortunes are not assured. For decades, far more people fell down the ladder than climbed up it. The American economy is less like a dream supported by democracy than it is like an inconsistent god. Most of us, regardless of economic station, sacrifice a great deal to it.

That can be a satisfying agreement. Grandpa Arnie loved working the land not for the price of wheat per bushel but because smelling damp earth at sunrise felt like a holy experience. Dad loved building something beautiful out of good lumber not for the paycheck but for seeing his own creativity turned into a sturdy, useful structure. The pleasure that Mom got when she sold a little house in Wichita wasn't just for the small commission but for the tears in the family's eyes when she handed them the keys.

Work can be a true communion with resources, materials, other people. I have no issue with work.

Its relationship to the economy — whose work is assigned what value — is where the trouble comes in.

My family's labor was undervalued to such an extent that, while we never starved or went without shelter in a chronic way, we all knew what it felt like to need something essential — food, shoes, a safe place to live, a rent payment, a trip to the doctor — and go without it for lack of money. That's the sort of mess I wanted out of. That's the sort of mess I never wanted you to experience.

2
THE BODY OF A POOR GIRL

Our bodies were born into hard labor. To people who Grandma Betty would say "never had to lift a finger," that might sound like something to be pitied. But there was a beautiful efficiency to it — form in constant physical function with little energy left over. In some ways, I feel enriched rather than diminished for having lived it.

I know the strength of this body that helped hoist an air compressor into a truck, leveraged a sheet of drywall alone, carried buckets of feed against prairie wind. I know the quickness of my limbs that scaled a tall fence when a bull charged and that leapt when a ladder fell. But while I worked in those ways, like my mother and father I wrote poetry in my mind.

There's an idea that laborers end up in their role because it's all they're suited for. What put us there, though, was birth, family history — not lack of talent for something else. "Blue-collar workers" have jobs requiring just as much brainpower as "white-collar professionals." To run a family farm is to be a business owner in a complicated industry. But, unlike many jobs requiring smarts and creativity, working a farm summons the body's intelligence, too.

Sometimes it was miserable. Sometimes it was satisfying. The farmhouse living room where we spent evenings had a big wood-stove in it, and no fire will ever feel more glorious than the ones we sat next to after working outside in January sleet that clung to the metal fences as a coat of ice. I'm a little sorry you never got to feel that. But I am not sorry that you never experienced the dangers of being devalued outside those farmhouse walls.

The person who drives a garbage truck may himself be viewed as trash. The worse danger is not the job itself but the devaluing of those who do it. A society that considers your body dispensable will inflict a violence upon you. Working in a field is one thing; being misled by a corporation about the safety of a carcinogenic pesticide is another. Hammering on a roof is one thing; not being able to afford a doctor when you fall off it is another. Waiting tables is one thing; working for an employer whose sexual harassment you can't afford to fight and risk a night's worth of tips is another.

For black and brown bodies, a particular danger exists regardless of how much money is in a bank account. We were white bodies in peril specifically because we were laborers.

For those of us who were female, the body was also defined by its role as a potential mother. That's true in every class but becomes more problematic in the context of financial struggle. Poverty makes motherhood harder, and motherhood makes poverty harder. Single mothers and their children are, by far, the poorest type of family in the United States.

The frustration at the dangerous crossroads of gender and poverty was sharpened for my mom in a couple of ways, I think. She had a mind that wanted books, ideas, and sketch pads — things she sat with privately but didn't get to share with the world. And, because people considered her beautiful, she got a constant stream of attention about her body, at work and elsewhere. Being physically objectified that many times over — as a labor machine, a producer of children, and a decorative object — all while being aware of your own unexpressed talent can make the body feel like a prison.

My mom was beloved among her friends as a kind, funny, wise, and generous person, I'd learn as an adult. But there was a deep pain in her that only those closest to her saw. I think sometimes that she didn't really hate having children as a young woman; she hated her life, and the children who came into it would feel that.

There is a good chance you would have felt it, too. The anger she put on me, I would have put onto you. I can count on one hand the number of times someone has seen me in a moment of true rage; they would tell you my voice became quiet and my eyes stopped blinking. But I have felt the wild, ungrounded frustration of the women before me many more times than I have shown it. Not so much now. But very much when I was a teenager and into my twenties, during what would have been your most formative years. Back then it took every bit of strength in me to stop that energy running through my body like lightning, to refuse to be its conductor.

Anger was not Jeannie's true self, I'd learn as she aged. But, as tends to happen with people who are beaten down by daily circumstances, my young mother's core nature was glimpsed only in moments of life and death: the hospitalization of a loved one, her own water breaking. It was not a tender nature, but it wasn't mean, either. It was a severe serenity, doing whatever a moment required without complaint.

The day my brother arrived, she sat on the edge of my twin bed to wake me in the dark early-morning hours. She'd picked out my ruffled mauve bedding and kept it well laundered, but before that moment she had never sat on it, that I can recall. She had a habit of keeping her distance and flying off the handle at the smallest frustration. For this event that might actually warrant panic, though, she was calm as a priestess in the October moonlight.

"It's time," she said.

At the hospital more than thirty miles away in Wichita, Mom hemorrhaged during the labor. Her blood pressure dropped so low that the doctors said, "Stay with us."

Once she had recovered, someone put me in a blue smock and took me to meet Matthew, who was blotchy and black haired. The visitors' room had blue balloons and food on long tables; I'd never seen such a big spread of treats and drinks on a day that wasn't Thanksgiving or Christmas. Dad gave me a cup of sparkling grape juice, which I knew was expensive since it was in a big glass bottle involving bubbles and foil.

Mom wore a pink-and-black-striped cotton gown. She had curled and teased her long brown hair and put makeup on her twenty-two-year-old face, but her eyes were tired. They would stay tired for a long time.

My parents couldn't afford a babysitter and didn't live in a proper neighborhood where there might have been fellow mothers to help a woman recovering from childbirth. Both my grandmothers, Betty and Teresa, had promised to come by when they could. Dad was determined to get back to work. The Family and Medical Leave Act that might have protected Mom's job for a few weeks wouldn't be passed for another eight years; toward the end of her pregnancy, she'd been forced to quit whatever low-paying gig she had at the time.

So Mom would be on her own with a child not yet in school, an infant, a checkbook for a bank account with thirty bucks in it, and long miles between us and any town, any store.

With Matt's arrival just weeks before Ronald Reagan's reelection, Mom would soon cast her second vote in a national election. This time, though, her politics were different. While her teenage instincts had gone with losing incumbent Carter the year

I was born, by 1984 she had been won over by Reagan's charm or at least by the national consensus that he was a good president. Many others in our community would vote for him, too — if they voted at all.

"They're all crooks," I often heard about politicians. Mom never said that. She was not given to apathy and did her best to stay on top of the news. Based on what she could glean, Reagan was a good man.

The Republican party would hurt women like my mother in direct and indirect ways that decade: removing the Equal Rights Amendment from the party's platform, dismantling aid programs that helped poor women feed their children, eroding reproductive health rights. Unbeknownst to my mom, the Republican party was turning deeply socially conservative, different from the moderate, fiscally conservative party that people respected in my area. Mom didn't think women on welfare were lazy or that feminists were militant monsters. She voted for Reagan because a cultural tide told her it was the right thing to do, and she had little time or resources to question the wave of sentiment the country was riding.

The country was swinging right, and working people were changing party allegiance. My mom was one of them, part of a national trend that I have found says more about clever political messaging than about what people truly know or think about the issues. Meanwhile, poor rural mothers like her were receding from view in both political parties, if they'd ever been in view at all.

When she got home from the hospital, to our new house in the country, Mom was still bleeding through the stitches between her legs. She was exhausted in a way she'd never been and scared to have a four-year-old and a newborn under her care. Dad had to go back to work.

"Please don't go," Mom said to him. She was generally too proud to ask anyone for anything, including her own husband for support. But she pleaded. "I can't do this alone."

There were houses to build, though. My uncle was outside honking the horn, and Dad left — believing, to some extent, that it was his job to provide and her job to take care of the kids. There was no paid leave for him either in such a moment.

Once Dad was gone, Mom lay in their bed trying to sleep through her pain as Matt cried from his crib. I crawled up a chest of drawers in her bedroom and tipped it over. The dresser crushed me against the carpet.

Mom ran from her bed and somehow

lifted the chest off me, straining so hard she tore her stitches. Blood ran down her thighs.

I don't think we went back to the hospital. When she told me the story, it was about a day she barely survived because of my dad's absence. I see it now as a day she barely survived because society valued productivity and autonomy more than it valued women and children. Pregnancy slows you down, so pregnant women lost their jobs; mothers were alone in their nuclear households while fathers worked extra hours to make up the difference. For the poor and rural among them, the situation was keenly dangerous.

When Dad came home that night, Mom was quiet. She stayed quiet for weeks, until Dad made another announcement. He would be leaving for a construction job a long drive east of us. That meant weeks away from home. Mom thought he was finding excuses to be away from us.

"Please don't go, please don't go," she said, screaming and crying. She often screamed but almost never cried. It was like something had broken in her when the stitches between her legs tore.

But Dad packed up his tools and left again.

He was concerned about providing for his

family, he told me when I was grown, sitting next to him in his work truck and telling him how Mom remembered that day.

"I couldn't have turned down good money, even if I had to be gone for a long time," he said. His eyes filled with tears. "Look, maybe I was wrong."

How to handle the stress of it all when you don't even know that your life is stressful? Women saying "my nerves are shot" was the closest anyone came to examining the situation. What they didn't discuss, though, they felt. That's what substances were for.

Every adult I knew was addicted to something — mostly cigarettes or booze. Also pills, both prescribed and gotten by other means. The women of my mom's family, who had grown up in Wichita with doctors nearby during decades when health care was cheaper, were sold on the idea of prescriptions for symptoms rooted in psychological strife. Most of them were on "thyroid medicine" for exhaustion, "nerve pills" for anxiety.

Dad, however, didn't take even the most benign aspirin — not thinking it harmful or ineffective but suspecting it amounted to money spent on something your body and mind could do on their own, for free and without side effects. Dad had a quiet inner life as a self-healer. Once in a while he shared it with me, and in that way he was the most maternal force in my life.

He tucked me in most nights and helped me say my Catholic prayers to the Father, the Son, the Holy Ghost, Mary, and the guardian angels of me and all my family. This helped me relax at bedtime, but I had a horrible time falling asleep. I'd lie in my bed thinking through every problem and staring at my closed closet while my muscles were frozen in fear. One night I finally told Dad that I couldn't fall asleep for the longest time, even after the prayers. He listened. Then he put his hands around my toes through the comforter.

"Relax your feet," he said in a soft voice, and I did.

He said to relax my legs. I was amazed to find that I could and did.

"Now relax your tummy," he said. I did, knots and tension disappearing as though Dad had helped me wave them away. I felt like a warm blanket was being drawn over me, but on the inside.

"Now relax your arms and your fingers," he said. "Now your shoulders."

By the time the magic had reached my head, my eyebrows relaxed, and I fell asleep.

Dad knew how to help me quiet my mind because he had taught himself to quiet his own. No matter how hard a day was, he almost always treated me with respect, if only by keeping his distance when his own emotions were raging.

And he really listened to me. Even though Mom was the reader and writer of the two, Dad liked to claim I grew up to be good with words because he talked to me like a grown-up rather than in baby gibberish when I was an infant.

Conversations were different with the rest of my family. They often fell into trancelike repetition of nonsense once a kid had worn them out: "He needs a good pop upside the head," they'd say. Or "He's lazy," or "She don't mind when she's told." Even warm, loving Betty would brag about how she'd been beaten as a kid and it did her good. "She's up to something," grown adults would say about little kids — words of warning like an old fairy tale from a European forest, where a poor child was a burden unless she contributed to the household and obeyed the rules.

Dad never said things like that. He would have troubles with drinking and gambling over the years, but he carried an aura of peace even when our lives were chaotic. He brushed my knotted hair before the sun came up, before he went to work and I went to school. He jotted poetic little notes of wisdom on scraps of paper and put them in my bedroom. When I was older I realized how remarkable all that was in our culture where manliness had a specific definition.

"Writing poems and brushing your daughter's hair before school isn't something men brag about, where we're from," I told him, reflecting on how nurturing he was by nature.

"It ought to be," he said.

He was so good with little kids over the years that, even though he never said he wanted me to have my own, I sometimes felt simultaneously relieved I wasn't a mother and sad that he wasn't a grandpa to you.

Driving his truck, he would hang his left arm out an open window and let the smell of his wheat fields fill the cab. He barely pushed the gas pedal. The truck seemed to stand still, but through the large, flapping gash in the floorboard under my dangling feet I could see the dirt road moving past. Dad was quiet. The radio was off or tuned to AM. The fields were dirt or green sprouts or blond waves or tall stubble like Dad's beard. I'd crank my window down and do like Dad.

The place we lived was full of sharp objects, poisons, and frustrations, but there were moments — maybe most moments, on the whole — like in Dad's truck with the windows down, when the west wind that reached us all the way from the Rockies cleared the air, and I felt more free than I've felt in cleaner, safer places.

To find that feeling by myself, I developed a trick I called "doing the reflection." I'd crawl onto the bathroom countertop and press my face close to the mirror, my breath creating two little circles of fog that disappeared when I inhaled. I would stare into my own eyes. It was important not to blink, for some reason. Then I'd feel a shift inside my head, hear a little "swoosh" like the ocean inside a shell.

My face would suddenly look a little different, my vision was a fraction of a millimeter outside my own eyes. Then I felt calm, unlike the upset child I saw in the mirror.

The poverties that threatened my safety forced me to find that safest place. Eventually I would think of that realm as where we come from, and where we return when we die. That's where I heard you. That's the calm center where I received my most important assignment, as the body of a poor girl bound for a different life: to make sure you were never born.

I wasn't as poor as my mom or grandma growing up. In some ways, therefore, they faced more physical dangers than I did.

When Betty was a toddler, not long after her dad got back from overseas at the end of World War II, their small family lived on a gravel road at the western edge of Wichita. It was the kind of neighborhood whose sidewalks the city fixed last, if there were sidewalks to begin with.

The electric company was hanging the first power lines in the alleys between lots, and a worker left his tools at the end of their yard. Betty walked to the power lines lying on the ground, bent down, and touched them. Electricity ran through her. Dorothy dropped the wash on the porch and ran across the yard in her wet dress and pushed her daughter off the hot wire.

According to the story Betty remembered, Dorothy called the power company and took Betty to the hospital. When they got home, she found a uniformed man in the backyard inspecting the power line.

"That's no live wire," he told her. "Our people don't do that kind of work."

"If it's not live, why don't you pick the son of a bitch up then," Dorothy said.

The man licked his finger and touched the wire.

"Mom said it zapped the shit out of him," Betty told me and laughed.

Betty's father, Aaron, came home from the factory where he assembled Vornado fans and air conditioners. He wanted to sue the electric company because they didn't give a damn if their sloppy work killed a kid. But Dorothy didn't think they should sue. She was just thankful that Betty had lived, she said.

The poverty I knew as a child was less severe than Betty's and thus less perilous in some ways. But growing up with little supervision in an agricultural countryside came with unique dangers: big, snorting farm animals; even bigger farm equipment, sharp and rolling up and down the driveway; chemical fertilizer invisible in the air. What my childhood had in common with Betty's and everyone else's in my family was the space of neglect where adults were too busy working or too drunk afterward to look after me.

Mom was the only caretaker in our family who didn't drink when I was little. I didn't drink when I was a teenager and young adult, either. You would have had that going for you as a child — no small blessing. But even when Mom was sober, she seemed far away.

At our new brick house in the country, I tried to stay quiet and require nothing. I spent hours drawing with crayons, learning to fold towels, making myself useful. I was four and wanted Mom to hold me the way she had in an ear-piercing boutique at the mall in Wichita. I chose gold hearts and cried when the woman behind the counter shot holes into my ears like Dad's nail gun shot holes into wood beams. Mom carried me out of the store in her arms. It's the only time I remember her holding me.

During the long days alone, I wandered outside to find rocks and bugs in the dirt and prairie grass. Or I poked around Dad's work garage, which had bits of lumber on the floor and big metal saws plugged into extension cords. One day I found a new litter of kittens under the pegboard tool wall.

Mom said not to touch them because the mama cat would smell my scent and stop caring for them. This was agonizing for me. I saw myself as the protector of every baby animal born on our land. The cat was their mother, but I had seen many cats die violent deaths — mangled by hungry coyotes, chopped up when they found warmth under a car hood and someone turned the engine, shot from the road by some boy with a BB gun. I felt the metal shot lodged under the fur and wept.

As for cows, pigs, and chickens, the men were in charge of killing them, and I gratefully ate them. But while they were alive I fed and loved them. I watched them come out of their mothers as pink globs on the March snow and knew their mothers could only do so much.

To reach the kittens, I entered the work garage, which smelled like oil and sawdust. Dad had constructed the outbuilding where our trailer used to sit. I stepped around big circular blades and sawhorses as tall as I was, and crouched in the fine peels of wood that Dad hadn't yet swept with his push broom. I peered into the shadowy space under a shelf, boxed in by tools, where the mama cat kept her litter. They were tiny balls of squeaking fur coiled up like the roly polies in the soil near the house where Mom had planted tulip bulbs. I longed to pet them but remembered Mom's warning.

During one of my visits, the mama cat was gone hunting. The kittens seemed to be sleeping. I agonized again over whether to touch them. I'd watched them open their eyes for the first time, take their first steps with tiny tails stuck straight out and trembling. I decided that the mama cat knew me well enough to keep on nursing her babies whether my scent was on them or not.

I reached out and patted a furry head. The head rolled away from the small body, leaving a track of blood on the concrete floor. I felt a wave of heat rush through me as I realized that none of the kittens was moving.

Dad sometimes brought home big bleeding deer, pheasant, or quail, and peeled their skins off the muscle on the cement slab next to our front door. I wasn't scared of blood, but this blood was different: A baby bled out, and it hadn't even been eaten. When I looked closer in the dark space, I saw that all the kittens had been gnawed through at the neck. I heard a cry and turned to see the mama cat pacing behind me, out of her mind with confusion and grief.

I reported the event to my parents.

"A possum or a fox got 'em," Dad offered.

That was the hard truth of the wild place we lived: Parents left their children by necessity to hunt for food so they wouldn't starve to death, but those moments without protection offered plenty other ways to die.

The world was at once wondrous and lethal. The thunderstorms and funnel clouds that menaced us each spring and summer came from the most mesmerizing, sweet-smelling sky. The rare gray wolf with whom I loved to lock eyes at the edge of our land would hunt and kill the pets I also loved.

Along with the freedom and the space, that is a blessing you would have received from the feral way that children among us lived: seeing blood every day on a kitten's neck, a father's hand, the ground beneath a slaughtered hog hanging from a hook. Knowing in your own bones how fragile and fleeting a body is.

Our stretch of southern Kansas could be mapped by the Catholic saints that dotted the flat farmland as the names of churches and towns. He's from St. Joe, someone would say. Turn before you get to St. Louis. We're taking the pies up to the funeral at St. Vincent.

Ours was St. Rose, a parish located in Mount Vernon, which was homesteaded by Germans in 1870. By 1911, the place had a church with a steeple and a tiny Catholic schoolhouse. The priest's house during my childhood was where nuns lived in the early days. Three members of the Sisters of the Sorrowful Mother staffed the school, which my dad and all his siblings attended.

The church was the main community pillar for miles. When a June thunderstorm destroyed it with a bolt of lightning in 1921, the country Catholics rallied to rebuild and dedicated the new structure by the end of the summer. Like Saint Rose, a Peruvian woman who built a grotto with her own hands to pray in, our churches were things we literally built. When I was a teenager, my dad would help pour the concrete for the new baptismal pool at Wichita's grand Gothic downtown cathedral.

That is where his mother had gone to high school during the Dust Bowl. Teresa was raised on a vegetable farm south of Wichita, but as a teenager she moved in with a well-off family in town — cleaning their house, watching their kids, in exchange for room and board — so that she could attend high school. After graduation, she went to what they called secretary school. But she soon met a farmer with black hair named Nick, whom everyone called Chic. They married at nearby St. Anthony's. That was the end of her professional plans.

Chic was the sort of man who threw parties and made people laugh. During Prohibition, he made runs to the hidden stills of the Missouri Ozarks as a bootlegger, according to family — a story I'm inclined to believe because I didn't hear it until he'd been dead for thirty years. His parents gave him his nickname when as a little boy he tried to say a word for their ancestry: "Czech."

Chic and Teresa's wedding dance was in the country at Mount Vernon, where Chic's people were farmers and where Teresa would spend the rest of her life. All six of their children were baptized and had their first confession and communion at St. Rose, the Kansas wind whipping their skirts and ties after church. Three of them, including my dad, got married there.

In 1949, Grandpa Chic was commissioned to lead renovation of the St. Rose school. Church records say that parishioners did all the labor except furnace installation, keeping the cost down to $15,000. There was, from my observation in that community, a deeper bond through labor than through vaguely understood dogma. The Catholics I grew up with went to Mass every Sunday but were more concerned with saving money than with saving anyone's soul.

In fact, they were wild partiers. In Chic and Teresa's day, when the community still held the annual Labor Day picnic in the field across the road from St. Rose, they put beer in a big metal stock tank that usually watered cattle. They got drunk and ate homemade sausage, freshly ground outside Chic and Teresa's farmhouse. Grandma Teresa was always in charge of the pies since she bested the other women with her meticulous baking skills, but come party time the women showed up and hit the hooch, too. Some years, Grandpa Chic hammered together a wooden platform on the pasture to use as a dance floor. I don't know where the music came from — a Ford with the door hanging open and the radio turned up, maybe, or a real band — but they swing-danced right there on the prairie under the stars.

Since my dad was born on Labor Day, Chic and Teresa must have missed the picnic fun that year, 1955. Around that time, Chic and his brothers worked on the church again, this time rebuilding the steeple. Nick thus grew up praying to a heavenly father in a church whose steeple had been constructed by his actual dad. His big sister Jeanette was the religion teacher.

In 1966, though, when the state dug the reservoir that I grew up next to, the new water supply cut off access to St. Rose for farm kids to the north. Without them keeping enrollment up, the school closed. Dad finished grade school in Cheney about ten miles south, where I'd attend kindergarten through third grade. But Mount Vernon and its church called St. Rose remained our community touchstones, imparting a sense that we were connected in body, land, and soul.

The year I was born, Grandpa Chic carved a new communion rail from a walnut tree on his and Grandma Teresa's property and installed it at the edge of the church altar before my baptism. As a child, I knelt at it many times with the same fervent prayer I carried everywhere: that my family would be okay.

The inside of the church was decorated with images of blood, reflecting what life had taught us about our bodies. While we knelt in our pews, the Stations of the Cross encircled us — images of Jesus dragging his own torture device like a plow above the stained-glass windows my carpenter grandpa had replaced. Behind the altar hung the crucified Jesus, whose skin had been whitened to match ours. Near one of the rear pews, a small Pietà replica, perhaps ordered from some church-supply catalog in the 1920s, represented a mother's sorrow.

That same imagery existed in the richest Roman Catholic parish, of course. But what we found on the crucifix was not a metaphorical suffering represented by the body. We found the body itself. Dad knelt and prayed next to me, his cologne mixing with the priest's incense, his folded hands scabbed where real nails had pierced the skin when his hammer slipped.

All the genuflecting was hard on old farmers' knees, but they did it without complaint. People were not enjoying themselves, that was plain to see.

Our severe, old-fashioned priest didn't like that my mom let me wear pants and a tie to Sunday school. At Mass, his liturgy focused on sin.

But I loved going to church. As in hospitals, everyone was quiet and talking to God. It was a similar feeling to when I talked with you. I felt like you were the force that makes something alive, and even when I prayed Catholic prayers I was sensing you on the other end of them.

In a different Christian church, some Protestants were concerned with the idea of being born again. But my church rarely talked about such a joyful notion. Our fixation was on the sacrifice, the death, the martyrdom. Before communion, the priest spoke Jesus's words: "This is my body, which will be given up for you." It was an idea we understood.

My first memory of dancing is to Mom's 45 rpm single of Bruce Springsteen's "I'm on Fire" spinning in the family room, the beat constant and fast like an engine's pistons. The song is full of metaphors about longing, but I recognized the lyrics as literal things: the dull knife, big and shining, that tore the hide off a buck or a bumper sticker off a car bought used. The sweaty sheets of summer nights without air-conditioning, without sleep. The freight trains that moved through Kansas, unable to stop in time if something got stuck on the tracks. The intentional fire, controlled on the prairie, that glowed around us through the night and put ash in the air when farmers burned off stubble to wipe the slate of their cropland clean.

There is a notion of safety about childhood I've noted in my friends, the comfort they feel when they "go home" to sleep in a childhood bedroom under the same roof as their parents, which some children never know. It's what I would have wanted for you, but it's so hard for poor parents to give it — because they don't have safety themselves.

Every moment of my childhood required

vigilance. I felt true rest only when I couldn't keep my eyes open any longer and collapsed into deep sleep. As the child passenger in cars, I always felt like I was the one in charge of keeping the car on the road. Living in the country meant a lot of time on highways between here and there; I'd watch out the car window in a state of constant prayer and commune with the country sky. I wanted to lie down across the backseat and go to sleep, but I had to focus, to assert some control on the situation through my awareness. If I didn't, I thought, Dad would fall asleep at the wheel due to exhaustion from the long workweek, or Mom would drop her cigarette and bend to pick it up as we swerved into a ditch at top speed, or a drunk aunt would fail to stop at an intersection.

It was not an irrational concern. I couldn't list the number of wrecks I was in as a kid. Over beers, my family could map a rough timeline of their existence by car crashes and who was in them: "No, that's the time it was on the bridge over the crick." "You got that right, but it was a Buick, not a Lincoln." "Yes, Candy was a baby." "Was that the one where Jeannie was reading in a horse trailer and the hitch broke and it flipped into the ditch, or the one when the old woman come flying through the inter-section by the mall?"

Getting to and from school amounted to the same trouble because of our rural loca-tion. I was in three school bus wrecks by the time I finished high school; each time the bus tipped over into a muddy or snowy ditch on account of bad rural roads and hard Kansas weather. So I prayed and stayed vigilant on school buses, too.

One September afternoon at the start of second grade, at the end of the long school bus ride from the small town into the country, I saw a huge flame near my house. The bus driver was dropping me off at Grandma Teresa's a half mile to the south, as she often did since my parents worked. I saw the fire through the bus window. I ran down the rubber aisle, down the big steps with my bag, down the dirt road as fast as I could. I ran toward the fire as though I alone was going to put it out and save every-one in it. I got halfway down our driveway, which stretched a quarter mile from the dirt road, and saw with relief that it was our pole barn, not our house, that was burning.

Grandpa Chic had insisted they burn off some of the tall grass between the barn and the pond. Chic was an old man by then but still as cocky as when he was a young bootlegger. He was so cavalier about setting blazes to burn off fields or trash piles that Dad liked to joke he was a pyromaniac. That day, the wind wasn't on their side.

When the fire got ahold of a small bit of the barn close to the ground, Chic took an axe to the metal wall. That just gave the fire oxygen, and the flame roared all the way up the side of the barn.

When I got there, out of breath with ash in my hair, Dad and Grandpa Chic stood next to the fire with unimpressed faces as crisp pieces of the barn rained out of the sky.

The fire itself didn't scare them. They put their bodies on the line every day at work dangling from roof joists, operating giant electric saws, wearing plastic hard hats while bricks rained down from demolition projects. A shed blazing right next to our house was nothing to get excited about in terms of personal safety.

The pole barn on fire, though, was one of Dad's proudest feats of construction. He had framed the barn with wood he salvaged from the 1910 high school that Kingman had torn down to build a new one. He had spent $400 on new tin for its sides and roof. It was a lovely thing to him, a symbol of his hard work and skills. And inside it rested his Massey Harris combine, a farmer's biggest equipment investment. The Massey was a beautiful machine from the 1940s that he had bought at an auction in Pretty Prairie for $300. It worked better than his dad's combine or his older brother's down the road.

"It ran like a sewing machine," Dad recalled with a sad look, many years later.

He ran inside the burning barn and started the combine. Its tires were on fire as he backed it out onto the gravel between our house and the barn. He couldn't stop the flames from taking the whole machine, though.

Dad's shed and farming equipment weren't insured. He wasn't alone in railing against the insurance industry, whether agriculture or home or auto or health or life.

"Insurance is criminal," he would say. "One hundred percent rip-off." Everyone would nod.

We got a lucky break with the pole barn, though. The insurance agent said it was covered by the homeowner's policy in Mom's name. On the claim form, Dad listed what had been lost and added a few things that weren't in the fire for good measure.

But that was the beginning of a string of much worse fortune. Since Dad no longer had equipment to work what we called "the hill," a stretch of red jaw east of the lake that needed torn up with a plow, Grandpa Chic paid one of my uncles to do it instead. Meanwhile, home-loan interest rates had skyrocketed to almost 20 percent.

"That meant no one was calling Chicky or Nicky to build a house," Dad told me.

So Dad had to find some other way to make money. He did roof work with his oldest brother for a while; a hailstorm had hit Hutchinson that summer, and a lot of shingles needed torn off. Uncle Gary would pick him up in his Toyota Land Cruiser with a trailer behind it. But that work was temporary.

Meanwhile, Grandpa Chic was getting old. All his sons had inherited carpentry, but he had always been in charge. It was unsure whether the brothers would stick together after he died.

"Holy shit," Dad remembered thinking. "Smarsh Brothers Construction is going tits up." Between the loss of his farming equipment and the slowed demand for carpenters, he needed to find employment outside the family business for the first time in his life.

In the fall of 1987, at age thirty-two, he applied for a job managing the tear-off of factory roofs at Boeing in Wichita. They asked how much he wanted per hour. He said $18.

"That's pretty high," the Boeing guy said.

"And I'm pretty good," Dad replied. He lied and said he'd been in charge of twenty-five men before, that he had driven a semi, that he knew all the lingo the man was using.

It was a night job, so as not to interfere with the factory's daily functions. Each sawtooth roof was a forty-yard length of ridges, one side a steep pitch of glass letting light in for the airplane factory workers. Alone, Dad designed and built a rail track across the enormous jagged roofs to move the torn-off pieces. Once his crew showed up, they climbed a forty-foot ladder with no backstop in the darkness, stepping carefully across frost. When the crew left at 8 a.m., Dad still had to drive a semi full of tear-off to the dump. He often fell asleep while driving.

He was depressed and exhausted. Beyond the economic troubles, things weren't going good at home with Mom. When he wasn't at work, he drank a lot. He fell asleep at the wheel so many times when Matt and I were riding with him. I'd grab the wheel and slap his arm, and he'd veer us back off the shoulder to the other side of the painted line.

When the temporary job at Boeing ended, Dad found more work in Wichita, this time for a national company that supplied and disposed of industrial cleaning products. He drove a van around the city and surrounding small towns, delivering cleaning solvent and equipment to mechanics' shops. He then collected their spent chemicals, such as engine oil, into a large barrel in the back of the van to dump at a designated waste site.

He'd been working for them all of ten days when, driving alone along an interstate, things started moving in slow motion. By the time he got back to the company yard, saliva was frothing from his lips. Another employee drove him to the Minor Emergency Center at the mall where Mom sometimes worked holiday kiosks.

Dad knew he was dying. He got down on his knees outside the mall entrance and prayed to God while shoppers passed by and stared at him.

Emergency workers put him in a straitjacket and took him to a real hospital, the one where he and I had both been born. He had chemical poisoning.

I always heard it was from breathing fumes formed by reactions among toxic waste materials that his pickup sites had illegally dumped. Maybe the vapors had seeped into the cab of the work van due to improper ventilation and unsafe design.

Doctors put charcoal in his body to absorb the poison and waited to see if he'd make it. The hospital chaplain gave him last rites, the Catholic sacrament performed when death is near.

Dad never forgot the moment he decided to wake up and live: A nurse washed his hair, and the shampoo smelled like roses. It was the most beautiful peace he had ever felt. So he hung on. Mom took me and Matt to see him once, he told me, but I don't remember it. He wept in his wheelchair when he saw us at the end of the hospital hallway.

Doctors released him after six days, but he still wasn't right in the head. He was referred to a neurologist, from the University of Kansas Medical Center in Kansas City, who diagnosed him with toxic psychosis.

"It took three years to get my body, mind, and soul cleaned out," Dad told me. It was such a traumatic event that decades had passed before we ever discussed it.

That cleaning-solvent business — a billion-dollar corporation, when Dad worked for them — changed the design of their trucks because of him, he told me, but he couldn't say where or how he heard that. Maybe it's true. Maybe it was just a passing, hopeful, or misleading comment by an attorney, and Dad held on to it — giving some meaning to what he had gone through.

He settled with the company out of court. He walked away with about fifty grand after attorney fees and signed papers saying he wouldn't seek further damages. Through the Kansas Workers Compensation Act, he also collected disability payments for almost two years for a total of about $22,000. But he was back to work much of that time — messed up yet working anyhow — so the state cut him off.

When I was a young adult, it killed me to sit next to Dad in his work truck and hear him finally tell the story, insofar as a person might remember his own poisoning. It wasn't the inherent trauma of his experience that got to me but the lack of outrage he seemed to feel — like he knew damn well that dying on the job was his birthright, and his gratitude for having survived outweighed any well-deserved sense that he had been victimized.

We all knew people who had died working. When Dad was a kid in the 1960s, he found his favorite uncle pinned and dying beneath a tractor that slid off a dirt bridge near his family farm. I walked over that bridge just about every day and thought of Dad's painful memory.

We knew people who had been maimed but survived, too, some having lost limbs to combines during the wheat harvest. Every church or town across Kansas, it seemed, had a man with a glass eye replacing the one he lost in the railroad yard or a woman who limped from when her pant leg got caught in some moving part.

Around the same time Dad was poisoned at work, Grandma Betty had a farming-related brush with death.

One morning at her office in Wichita, she felt so weak that she visited her doctor during her lunch break. A primary reason she applied to work at the courthouse was the good state benefits, including health insurance. "State benefits" was a phrase that adults I knew said with reverence. Many of my uncles, aunts, and cousins worked the Wichita airplane factories, and their union benefits were spoken of like a coveted prize, too.

The doctor told Betty she was fine. Doctors have a way of not believing women about the pain they report, and I've observed that poor and working-class women are less apt to argue with medical experts. Maybe their lack of formal education makes them reluctant, if only because they speak different kinds of English and encountering an authoritative professional thus feels intimidating. In any case, Betty went back to work.

When she left the courthouse, before she headed west toward the farm, she stopped at her mother's little apartment in one of Wichita's poor neighborhoods. Dorothy was in her sixties and had been diagnosed with paranoid schizophrenia decades prior. She lived alone without consistent treatment, due in part to a distrust of medical professionals but also due to lack of money.

Dorothy needed help at the same moment state mental hospitals were losing their budgets and turning people away. In the 1960s, when she was middle-aged and newly diagnosed, government programs began excluding coverage for patients in state psychiatric hospitals, leaving the mentally ill at the mercy of local economies and private general hospitals. Over the last half of the twentieth century, the number of state psychiatric hospital beds in Kansas for every hundred thousand people dropped from a few hundred to fewer than two dozen. For those who couldn't afford private care, that left adult children — usually women — to become caregivers.

So that summer afternoon when Betty left the office feeling terrible herself, she stopped to check on her mom. When she waved goodbye and walked to her truck, the afternoon heat hit her. She felt funny. Her left shoulder slumped beneath her heavy purse.

She thought of going to the hospital, but her doctor had said there was nothing wrong. She continued toward the farm, pulling to the side of the road a couple times when she got dizzy and the highway blurred.

Forty miles later, she rolled up the farm's gravel driveway, got out of the truck, and fell down.

Arnie ran across the yard and carried her into the house. She was shivering. He wrapped her in quilts and hauled ass along the highway back to Wichita, to the hospital.

Betty had pneumonia and histoplasmosis, a rare infection where mold spores settle in the lungs and grow. It's most common in farmers, who go in and out of damp out-buildings full of moldy hay. A large abscess had collapsed Betty's left lung. Doctors hooked her to an IV and blasted her with antibiotics.

When Dad took me to visit her, I was surprised when we stopped in the gift shop to buy flowers. I was worried about how much everything cost. I had learned to sneak candy from the gas station into movie theaters because the concessions stand was unaffordable and to put a cooler of bologna sandwiches in the trunk when going to some event whose food vendors would charge an arm and a leg. I was sure we should have bought flowers anywhere but the hospital's own gift shop, but Dad thrilled me by letting me pick out a bouquet.

Riding the elevator was exciting for a kid from the country, where buildings have two levels at best. I walked slowly down the hallway so that I wouldn't drop the heavy vase. We found Grandpa Arnie and a few others quiet in a room where Grandma lay in a bed.

"Sarah Smurf, come here," she said.

I looked at the tubes and plastic on her skin. She touched my hand and smiled.

"Hey, Sarah Smurfenburger," Grandma Betty said, patting my hand. Sometimes she called me that when she wanted me to laugh. I liked a cartoon called *The Smurfs,* and Betty had turned it into a funny play on my last name. We didn't realize it, but the German was always close in our words.

Grandma Betty's voice was soft in the hospital, different from her usual buzzing energy. Mom was there and somehow soft, too, like when she bought me pink high-tops and taught me to tie the laces while I sat on her bed's floral comforter. I liked how hospitals made people well behaved, as did libraries, Sunday Mass, and funerals.

The hospital's smoking ban was a particular point of relief for me. Every morning when I woke up, the first thing I did was notice the smell of tobacco smoke. Having learned at school that it was bad for me, in cars and at home I often became worried and held my breath. I'd seen Great-Grandma Dorothy, who had emphysema, spend afternoons watching TV with an oxygen tank hooked into her nose and a cigarette hooked between her fingers.

I understood, from television talk shows and the things children said at school, that I was living in an environment full of what society had recently discovered was danger-ous: the smoke, the fried food, the unbuck-led seat belts. But I didn't know the half of it: sugary diets that led to cavities, noxious glue in the walls of cheap houses, nitrates from farm runoff in our drinking water, insecticides on the wind that shimmered down from crop-dusting airplanes like daytime comets. I could feel it in my body. I had frequent headaches, my heartbeat drumming against my skull.

When I grew up and made a different environment for myself, the headaches stopped. As children, though, we are help-less. Except in spirit. The way I healed myself back then was by talking to you.

When I was that little, I didn't quite think of you as a child I might have but as some-one protecting the child I was. In either case, there was a kid who needed shielding from something. The shield was an unrelent-ing awareness of my surroundings. It hurt not to go numb to the world around me, but talking to you kept me away from poison and danger. Talking to you kept me awake.

So much of childhood amounts to being awake in a grown-up's nightmare. Ours happened to be about poverty, which comes with not just psychological dangers but mortal ones, too.

My childhood happened to coincide with

the moment health insurance and drug companies veritably merged with the nation's for-profit hospital system, creating costs that were prohibitive for uninsured families like ours.

In our parts, health care was rare not just because of escalating costs but because of our remote location. We didn't put much faith into doctor visits, anyway. To make a health concern feel better, we told ourselves that we didn't need doctors. But the truth was that we couldn't afford them. If you had a real health emergency, you were liable to be dead before some small town's ambulance made it down the muddy, sandy ruts of our dirt roads. But a decade-old dropper of stinging red iodine would fix most cuts, so we went on like everything was fine.

By the time I was born, rural hospitals were closing and American health care had transformed into a slick, big business in urban centers. Being the youngest of six, my dad was the only baby Teresa gave birth to in a hospital rather than in the farmhouse where they were raised. But when I was a kid, the old ways of country doctors were still hanging on in places like ours — places, I would later learn, much of the country thought endured only in movies and books.

As an infant, one night I came down with a dangerously high fever. My parents rushed me miles along bumpy roads to the rural home of Joseph Stech, a small-town doctor who still sometimes made house calls. He had delivered me at a big Wichita hospital, but as I grew up he was still charging a modest fee for a visit at his nineteenth-century office on Main Street in nearby Andale. He gave me all my immunization shots and prescribed penicillin when I got strep throat.

We didn't have health insurance, but my parents could afford Dr. Stech's fees. When I came down with chicken pox the day before the Christmas play at school, I cried next to our kitchen telephone while he told Mom over our shared rural party line that I had to stay home.

Once in a while, we'd drive past what to my eyes was a grand mansion on a hill, and my parents would say, "That's where we took you when you were a baby and had a fever in the middle of the night." No one remembered what Dr. Stech did to save me. For my family, the more important takeaway was that I just wasn't meant to die that night.

"The good Lord will call you home when he's ready," Grandpa Arnie liked to say.

"When it's your time, it's your time," people repeated. The Lord wasn't ready, and it wasn't my time.

I would develop a habit of burning up, though. Until I was two or three, Dad told me years later, severe fevers came and went. They didn't rush me to Dr. Stech again or even to a Wichita hospital; the issue had ceased to seem an emergency, and every doctor visit costs money. Instead they put me in a small tub of cold water.

"We'd splash a little water on you, and every time you were good to go!" Dad said.

I had lived, and that was all that mattered. The medical industry worked by naming ailments and prescribing medicine, but the sort of healing we knew operated in mystery. We didn't know the word "placebo" but figured that's all survival ever was, until God called you home. Mind over matter.

But a few years down the road, people like us would face health epidemics that cried for professional care: obesity, diabetes, methamphetamine addiction, sepsis from what we called a "bad tooth" with infection at the root, abuse of opioids overprescribed by the same doctors who were supposed to help. When I was a young adult, I would see all those ailments on the bodies of extended family members: grooves and scabs on their faces, expanding waistlines, swollen feet, missing teeth, the erratic shakes of a body craving a Lortab fix. By then the same forces of privatization that had all but shuttered state mental-health hospitals had compromised an entire system of general care to such an extent that even the middle class couldn't afford treatment.

What was still preventable in the 1980s would, in a couple decades, become manifest; what once was treatable would become deadly. I'm not sure my immediate family's brushes with death when I was a kid — mom's hemorrhage in childbirth, Grandma's collapsed lung, Dad's chemical poisoning — would be survived today. Mom would have been less healthy going into labor, Grandma would have been sent home too soon for lack of insurance, Dad would have been given a cheaper and less effective treatment. The mortality rate for poor rural women, in particular, has risen sharply over my lifetime.

Health insurance had been around for a long time, of course, but the power of that industry had swelled up fast, transforming access to care and all the costs that come with it. Betty would forget a lot about giving birth to Jeannie, but she always remembered how much she owed when she left the hospital: $12.

"That was hard to come up with then," Betty told me. "I handed them the money and told her, 'You're all mine now.' "

That was at a military hospital in the 1960s. I can't imagine how I would have paid a private hospital to deliver you several decades later. When I was in my twenties, it took me two years to pay off an emergency-room visit, and I had employer-based health insurance at the time.

It's a hell of a thing to feel — to grow the food, serve the drinks, hammer the houses, and assemble the airplanes that bodies with more money eat and drink and occupy and board, while your own body can't go to the doctor. Even though no one complained or maybe even realized it, I could feel that the people around me knew they were viewed as dispensable.

A life full of peril and lacking in care leaves its mark not just on the body but on the brain. Under the surface, the amygdala — the brain's fight-or-flight center of primal fear — enlarges and remains that way, a physical reflection of the hypervigilance developed by necessity under chronic stress.

This isn't to say someone facing the daily dangers of poverty lives in a constant state of perceived fear. I didn't even register the emotion, because high alert was my constant state. I've learned that I still don't feel fear the way most people do. This has helped in some ways and hurt in others. For the ways it gets me in trouble, someone once gave me good advice.

"Would it be stressful for most people?" she asked.

"Yes," I said.

"Then assume it's stressful for you. It's just that you can't tell."

As a child, though, I could tell. Everything felt all wrong. In a rural home with my poverty-scarred mother, I felt her stress first.

Jeannie had a four-year-old daughter and a newborn son in the middle of a countryside she never wanted. The lake was on one side, the wheat was on the other, and Jeannie was in the middle. The narrow woods planted to the north of us as a windbreak couldn't stop the Kansas weather. The north wind blew hard there, gaining momentum as it passed across the lake and pummeled the house.

One night when Dad was on the road with some construction job, Mom heard something clawing at the window for so long that she put me and Matt in her bed, locked the door, and stayed up all night with a loaded gun in her hand.

During the day, Mom would close her bedroom door and take long naps. I'd open the door and crawl under the floral comforter, get close enough to smell the lotion on her skin and cigarette smoke in her hair. Usually she said nothing. Sometimes she'd feel my cold feet and offer to let me stick them between her legs for warmth, as if the emotional blocks that kept her from touching her child had been surmounted by practical purpose.

I'd shift around to get comfortable.

"Stop moving around," Mom would say.

I'd hold still, feel every muscle tighten, my body frozen as it was every night when I awoke from the nightmares and watched the door for intruders. She would sigh.

"Do you have to breathe so loud?" she would say.

I slowed my breath to make it quieter. I took tiny breaths of air through my nose, trying not to make sound or motion. My chest got heavy and tight.

"Stop," she would say with her jaw clenched. *"Stop breathing."*

I held my breath as long as I could. I already knew to make myself useful — the earliest lesson, perhaps, for the working class — but in those moments I learned, too, that a child's body was an active nuisance to an unhappy woman.

If I had to pick the second most important factor that shaped how I thought about you — after my lineage of poor teen moms — it would probably be that awareness of the misery motherhood brings some women and thus their children. I didn't have any choice about inheriting my mom's unhappiness — at least for a while — but when I got to be a teenager, I made a vow to not create a child in the midst of it.

Dad thought Mom was sad because he didn't make a good enough living. While Mom worked whenever she could, men still felt a duty to be the "providers."

Dad felt sure that their problems all went back to money — specifically, his uphill battle trying to earn enough of it and nearly being poisoned to death in the process.

"Just hang on and I'll get that settlement," Dad told Mom. "Just hang on." He said everything would be all right once the money came in.

But, maybe because he had long-term symptoms that needed to be documented to maximize the payout, he wouldn't receive the settlement money until three or four years after the injury. In the meantime, Dad had toxic psychosis, Mom was angry and depressed, and everything wasn't all right.

I would take Matt outside so that he couldn't hear. He was what the grown-ups criticized as "tenderhearted" and struggled worse than I did with the pressure in our house. That wasn't how a boy was supposed to be, where we lived, and he often got shamed for his tears. We all did, but I saw how it hurt Matt as a little boy.

I dragged him along on my explorations as soon as he could stay upright. His language was slow to develop some sounds, like the letters *r, l,* and *v,* so I translated for him to the adults. Isolated together, we developed a dialect between us, the way twins often do. Meanwhile, we didn't even look like siblings: me, tan with green eyes and fine, almost translucent hair down my back, and Matt, pale with gray eyes and thick black hair.

We were immensely different in nature, too. One of my goals at home was to not create a stir, but Matt made himself a large presence. Once Mom had a party, and Matt snuck out of his bedroom to walk among the guests with one hand up as though he were carrying a platter.

"Pâté?" he asked, probably repeating something he'd seen on television. The adults, who might not have been able to define pâté but knew it was for rich people, cracked up.

Matt would grow up to look like my mom's biological dad, Ray, and by all accounts he inherited Ray's manner. By the time he was a toddler, he was a violent whirlwind. In one moment of frustration he banged his head against a dining room wall so hard he left a dent in the Sheetrock.

Matt had the hardest time at night. In his sleep, he screamed for me to help him. His baby voice would awaken me through the wall that separated our bedrooms.

"Sissyyyy! Sawaaaah!"

I'd jump out of my bed and run to him. He was covered in sweat, sitting up in his twin-size bed and still screaming, tears and snot on his face, sobs stopping up his words. His dark hair was wet against his hot forehead. I'd try to comfort him, but he'd look past me and keep screaming, not seeing me. I'd slap and shake him. Finally, he'd come to and sob.

I'd tell him it would be okay and command that he go back to sleep. I wanted to hold him but had learned that's precisely when you should tell someone to toughen up.

The nighttime screams got more frequent. Mom found her way to a Wichita psychologist, who diagnosed Matt with "night terrors" — nightmares during which the physical body wakes up but the mind stays asleep.

Like the kittens whose necks were chewed through, we weren't even safe in our sleep.

I was fortunate to have a kind father in a place where women's bodies were vulnerable for being rural, for being poor, for being women. I grew up listening to Betty console my cousins, aunts, and family friends as they sat at the kitchen table after a beating. They might have a black eye from a fist or sticky hospital-tape residue on their forearms from an emergency-room visit after being knocked unconscious with a baseball bat. On my mom's side of the family, that sort of terror was a tradition.

"Talk about hotheads," Grandma Betty told me about her parents, Dorothy and Aaron. One evening when she was a kid, she was watching her dad and uncle work on a car in the driveway, and her mom opened the screen to tell them that dinner was ready.

They didn't come inside, so Dorothy yelled for Aaron to get his sorry ass to the table while his food was hot. Aaron got mad and threw a wrench through one of the car windows.

"It pissed Mom off, so she picked up another wrench and smashed out the headlights," Betty said with a laugh. "My mom was wilder than a peach-orchard boar."

Like Grandma Teresa on my dad's side of the family, Dorothy grew up during the Great Depression in Wichita, the biggest city in the state, with just over a hundred thousand people. She lived in a small house with her second-generation, German American parents. Her dad, Ed, was a tall butcher who processed cattle in the Wichita stockyards next to the great confluence of train tracks that moved cows in from the center of the country and moved packaged meat out to Chicago and New York. Ed and Irene, Dorothy's mom, had lived their whole lives there in southern Kansas, except for when Ed ran off to Mexico and brought back a disease from a prostitute. That was the talk, anyway. Dorothy escaped the tense household by running with a tough crowd. She fell in love with the toughest guy in it.

Aaron was the son of a wheat shocker near Pratt, a small prairie town at the center of southern Kansas. He quit school after sixth grade, at the start of the Depression, and spent the Dust Bowl years working fields with his dad. When he was a teenager, his mom died of cancer; he and his younger brother, Dee Roy, went to live with their "sister," Mae, and her husband. There was talk that Mae was actually their mother.

Among the big German men of the area, Aaron was short with toothpick bones and sinewy arms, fine blond hair, and milky blue eyes. He almost always wore a sneer with a Pall Mall cigarette hanging from it. As a teenager, in 1935, he went to Minnesota to work for President Franklin Roosevelt's Civilian Conservation Corps. When he came back, he found a girl who raised hell as well as he did.

Dorothy and Aaron married in February 1939, when she was seventeen and he was twenty-one. As a pair, they didn't match. He was pale and gaunt, and she had bulbous, olive cheeks and coarse, dark hair. Their first home together was a little white wooden house on Custer Street at the western edge of Wichita, where pavement turned to dirt, where corner stores and filling stations tapered and gave way to prairie.

The year after the wedding, Dorothy had their first child, Carl. By 1942, she had joined the women of Wichita in the airplane factories. During the war, Wichita was on its way to becoming "the air capital of the world," sprouting airplane factories on the flat, cheap land of its perimeter the way

Detroit had sprouted automobile factories. Dorothy found rivet work at Boeing. So did her middle-aged mother and teenage sister, Bert. Aaron wasn't drafted, but his brother Dee Roy survived combat overseas.

In the spring of 1945, Dorothy gave birth to a daughter, my grandmother, on Mother's Day. She and Aaron named her Betty Dee, after Aaron's soldier brother, Dee Roy.

By the time the United States dropped two atomic bombs that summer, when Betty was an infant, Aaron had been drafted. He got sent to the Philippines. He came back meaner and drunker than when he left, people said.

While Aaron drank, Dorothy worked multiple restaurant jobs to cover the bills, while also doing all the cleaning and child-rearing, putting supper on the table for Aaron, and getting a beating for her trouble.

In 1952, Betty contracted polio and was one of the few Kansas children who survived it without some form of paralysis. I don't know if that was a turning point for Dorothy, but the next year she left Aaron. Betty was eight and her little sister, Pud, was a baby. Carl was a teenager by then, making himself scarce.

Betty, too, would grow up to marry abusive men, and that chaos would shape Jeannie's early life. But when it was Jeannie's turn to become a wife and mother, she somehow managed to pick a man who respected her. The violence was in her. I felt it every day in words or slaps. But mostly she kept her distance. And, crucially, she didn't choose men who would physically torment her or her children.

Thus, for all the perils I remember about being little, within the context of my family I had relative safety in my own house. Not just that, but a gentle father who loved me deeply. That may well be the difference between Jeannie's life and mine, what allowed me to escape other family cycles she wouldn't — addiction, teen pregnancy, lack of a college degree.

I read somewhere, "What you don't transmute, you will transmit." That is how a person changes not just herself but the stuff of her life, including the trappings and outcomes of socioeconomic class. I know what it feels like to transmute the sorrow, anger, and fear of good-hearted people. It's usually at nighttime, alone and awake in bed. It feels like swallowing something bitter with your soul, where it hurts and then dissolves, and then you wake up a little more okay in the morning.

All that transmuting is why I didn't transmit a hard life to you, I think. But what could be seen as my success owes much to Betty and Jeannie. Betty broke the cycle of extreme financial destitution and reliance on men; as soon as Title IX legislation made way for her to demand a decent job, she got one and held on. And Jeannie gave me a dad my body didn't have to fear. Without those triumphs, my upbringing would have been harder, the outcomes probably worse for you and me both.

While we struggled to improve our situation with our intelligence, creativity, and grit, manual labor changed our bodies. Wrinkles and sun spots from years working in fields beneath an unobstructed sun in the big Midwestern sky; limbs or fingers bruised, scarred, or lost altogether to big, churning equipment; back problems from standing on factory floors making motions as repetitive as the conveyor belt.

The physical markers of our place and class were so normal and constant, from my vantage, that I never thought to question them: the deep, black bruises ever-present beneath my dad's fingernails, the smoker's rattle in Grandma Betty's lungs, the dentures she'd had since her late twenties, the painful sunburns I sometimes got on my young corneas working outside against a hard slant of light.

Occasionally, though, I detected something curious about my family's bodies. Once, concerned, I rubbed a bump on Grandma Teresa's nose. She explained it was where a doctor had cut off a bit of skin cancer, a common ailment among farmers out in the sun all day. Grandpa Chic's face, too, was a map of where the sun had been every day of his life. Like Teresa, he was skinny and long-limbed. His overalls, which Teresa had washed for decades until they were worn thin, hung from his body like a sheet on the clothesline.

Clothes didn't hang from Grandpa Arnie but rather stretched across him. He was as tanklike as his tractors and combines. He was of average height but had the shoulders of a lineman, a bovine torso, and a round belly that threatened the snaps on the thin, brown plaid shirts he wore to threads. His hands were tremendous clamps of callouses and bruised fingernails and seemed too large even for his powerful arms. His hands handled rope with no gloves and swatted wasps on his shoulders. He wore sideburns on his wide jaw, and a fine patch of brown-gray hair swept across an otherwise bald head connected to a neck so thick Grandma

Betty could never find collared dress shirts that fit around it. Most days he wore the top of his shirts undone to leave way for his neck, which I often studied.

It didn't look like other necks. Not like my mom's, pale and smooth beneath long brown hair, or even my dad's, darkened from work in the sun but still youthful. Grandpa Arnie's neck was something else: serrated on the back, reddish-brown, with deep grooves like rough sediment in creek embankments that revealed the geological strata of epochs. When he tilted his head back, his neck wrinkled into mounds of thick flesh.

I rubbed his shoulders when I was at their farmhouse and he came in from work to sit at the table with instant iced tea. Almost every evening, I dug my thumbs into his or Grandma's or my parents' shoulders, which always seemed to be aching. Once, while kneading the knots in Arnie's enormous back, I asked about his neck.

"Why does it look like that?"

"Like what?" Grandpa Arnie said.

"Like there are scars in it," I said.

Grandpa laughed and told me someone had accidentally hacked him on the back of the neck with an axe while chopping wood. I was so little that I didn't realize he was joking. The real cause of the deep, jagged ruts on the back of his neck, of course, was a lifetime on the Great Plains, pulling plows through fields in the hard sun and sand-filled wind or feeding cattle while stinging ice pellets rained down.

People today would call us "rednecks," but I didn't hear that word much growing up. When I did, I understood it as an insult — a city person calling a country person backward. Or, occasionally, a country person calling another country person trashy.

I had no idea about the word's origins back then, of course, and linguists still aren't certain. It likely refers to a white field worker's neck burned by the sun. In the early 1900s, striking coal miners took the term when they wore red bandannas around their necks in solidarity. And white-supremacist politicians in the South have used the word to pit poor whites against poor blacks.

Today, the term is leveraged to disparage an entire class and place. It is printed on baseball caps, even baby bibs sold at Walmart, and worn by people with seeming pride.

As with other terms that have derogatory histories, reclaiming "redneck," "trailer trash," "hillbilly," and so on is a sort of cultural self-defense, I guess. That is understandable enough. But I never would have put you in a shirt with any of those words on it. If such a trend had existed when I was little, Mom wouldn't have put me in one, either.

When I got to be a little bigger, there was a hit country song on the radio called "Trashy Women." Once, riding with Mom in her car, I sang along with the lyrics: "I like my women just a little on the trashy side." The male singer went on about how he was raised in a sophisticated, well-to-do household but was turned on by poor women, by waitresses in tight clothes and too much makeup. Mom winced and told me not to sing to that song. She changed the station.

We might have been born poor, and we might have been born female — two strikes against a body in the world. Mom might have looked like something that men wanted to possess, and I might have been an unwanted child — one more strike against each of us navigating an already perilous life. But Mom knew she wasn't trash. And she knew her daughter wasn't, either.

3

A STRETCH OF GRAVEL WITH WHEAT ON EITHER SIDE

What defined the relationship between you and me wasn't just the forces at work on my body but where my body stood on the earth.

It was an increasingly rare place to stand. By the middle of the twentieth century, most Americans didn't live in rural areas. Not even most Midwesterners. But I was born a fifth-generation Kansas farmer, roots so deep in the county where I was raised that I rode tractors on the same land where my ancestors rode wagons.

During the 1860s, the Homestead Act had invited any adult citizens or immigrants who had applied for citizenship — including, at least officially, single women and freed slaves — to occupy and "improve" an immense area west of the Mississippi River in exchange for up to 160 "free" acres.

That land had been inhabited for centuries by native peoples, of course. Those tribes had been harmed by European raiders long before the United States was formed. But the late nineteenth century marked the devastation of the Plains tribes as the federal government strategically and violently "removed" their people and annihilated the bison herds they followed for sustenance. Meanwhile, 1.6 million people, many of whom were poor whites, were welcomed west with the promise of land ownership.

That was profit-motivated propaganda; the United States had given massive swaths of land to private railroad companies with the idea that the development they promoted and enabled would commercially invigorate the country from one coast to the other. The concern was never about the people being summoned to farm the land. It was about turning land into a commodity and immigrants into its workers.

A handful of Smarshes came to the United States in the 1800s, stopped for a generation in Pennsylvania Dutch Country, and took on the Kansas prairie by the 1880s. They could have stayed in New York City, as so many did, after crossing the Atlantic. Instead, they ventured into the so-called frontier.

I grew up not knowing about that history, what would have been your history, because my family had a way of not discussing themselves or the past. The stories I know, I know because I asked again and again. But as a child I nonetheless absorbed the self-understanding that sustains a rural people who have grown and hunted their own food for a very long time. What I understood is that we were hard workers, and what we worked was the earth.

Many who tried that work as homesteaders didn't last more than a few years on the prairie. They shot themselves in the head while blizzards buried their sod houses in drifts. They pushed farther west toward more verdant places when drought starved their crops and therefore their children. They took a Pawnee's flint arrow to the thigh and died from infection. Intimate problems, all of them, but ones that stemmed from public policy: The federal government had given them land to work as though the arid plains were just like rich eastern soil, as though it was a great deal. By and large, it wasn't wealthy folks who took the offer.

Those who managed to profit or at least subsist on their land soon saw the population tide turn. After the Homestead Act, it was only a matter of decades until the American industrial revolution made cities into hotbeds of economic potential. Factory smokestacks beckoned from city skylines, and agriculture became an option rather than a requirement for the underclasses. For some of them, a new system of state universities and land-grant colleges held the promise of higher education and work in office chairs rather than on their feet.

So where once immigrants were told to go west as "pioneers" — complicit, in the process, in the government-sanctioned genocide of indigenous peoples — now their bodies were needed for urbanization's boom. Thus, 44 of Kansas's 105 counties had reached their peak population by 1910.

Flowing from that history of westward expansion, subsequent rural flight to cities, and the vast land that enabled it all, the United States still has a uniquely mobile population.

But once my family got to Kansas, they stayed. They worked the land too hard and too fast for the soil to keep up, and the prairie wind buried their houses in dirt. Many people fled the Great Plains then, amid the Great Depression and black, hellish, roiling clouds of dust in the 1930s. Still, my family stayed. Maybe they wanted to leave but didn't or couldn't. I don't know. But not even the Dust Bowl drove them out.

By the time Teresa gave birth to my dad in the 1950s, advancements in farming equipment finally allowed for the economic dream of something beyond mere subsistence. Farmers were working huge swaths of land, putting away a large surplus of grain that would be distributed around the world by way of new transportation infrastructure — ports, highways, and railroads the country had invested in. Dad grew up driving Depression-era tractors, since Chic was too tight to invest in new equipment, but workers like them had successfully turned the center of the country into a massive wheat operation.

Then came trouble with banks.

Land prices rose in the 1970s, and banks started granting farm mortgages using a farm's productivity as collateral, regardless of a family's ability to repay. When land prices fell during my 1980s childhood, collateral value did, too; interest rates spiked, and farms were foreclosed on in droves.

They called it "the farm crisis." Family operations went under in record numbers, and federal farm bills didn't stop the corporate and global forces that were devastating small farmers like us. During the first ten years of my life, from 1980 to 1990, rural Kansas lost about 40,000 residents, while

Kansas metro areas gained about 150,000.

That was the climate I came up in. All around us things were closing: the small-town department store, the hardware store with its tiny drawers stretching to the ceiling, the local restaurant. Lawyers took down their small-town shingles and doctors moved to cities. But we held on. So when I think of you, I think of a place. You would have been born, as I was, in a place people said was dying.

In that place, even planned pregnancies were expected to happen very young. I remember once shocking my friends I grew up with by telling them I didn't want to have a baby until I was twenty-six, a scandalously old age for a first child in some corners of rural America. I don't know why I settled on that number. I remember when I passed it, though. I didn't live in the country anymore then, and many of my friends who stayed already had more than one kid.

With those sorts of pressures shaping me, I would come to see my grandma Teresa — a farm girl who spent a few years hustling for her own education and job training in Wichita and then ended up a farmer's wife with six children — as a woman whose life was defined foremost by its ruralness. By the time I knew her, she was an old woman who was so cranky that even people who loved her laughed and called her a mean ol' bitch.

Teresa was thirty-one years older than my other grandma, Betty. She couldn't imagine where young Betty got her energy, she said. She wore polyester shorts, nurse shoes, and support hose for her varicose veins. She drove her and Grandpa Chic's long Chevrolet Impala to Cheney, where her children had gone to high school, to get her graying black hair "set" in a short, tight permanent or to the nearby farm where we gathered warm eggs out of the coop and left change in a coffee can.

Her mind was starting to go by the time I was a kid, and I didn't know how fiery she'd been throughout her life until I grew up and heard stories. I only knew that she loved me in a particular way that no one else did — like I was almost the only thing she loved. She had legions of other grandchildren, as Catholic women did back then, and many of them were terrified of her.

Jeannie and Teresa had a lot of friction between them but also a mutual respect as the type of good women who get called "bitch." Mom was vaguely proud that her cranky mother-in-law had found a soft spot for me.

The only makeup Teresa wore was a dusting of perfumed powder that was loose like flour. Her cheeks were soft, creased, and falling. My eyes were shaped like Teresa's, Mom used to say when I was very young. I didn't see it then, but now that I'm grown I can. Other than my lighter hair, I grew up to look just about exactly like someone had taken Teresa's eyes and put them on Mom's face. Mom was always right about that sort of thing.

Grandma Teresa would send me to get her rural-route mail delivery from the metal mailbox banged up by hail and her small-town newspaper from the plastic box next to it. It was a long walk up the driveway, a stretch of gravel with wheat on either side. I carried the mail past the cottonwood, maple, and peach trees that Grandma Teresa taught me to name, past the gazebo that Grandpa Chic built. Chic would be working in the shed at the other edge of the field, but Grandma Teresa was always there asking if I wanted an after-school snack: some canned cherry pie filling in a bowl, crackers, maybe ice cream from the Schwan's man who drove a refrigerated truck down bumpy dirt roads.

Teresa rarely left the three-bedroom house my dad had helped build when he was a teenager. The five older kids had married off, and Chic and Teresa had given the farmhouse they'd spent almost forty years in to one of their sons and his growing brood.

So there in her new house, all of a mile from her old one, she spent days pulling a heavy canister vacuum across the marble-brown deep-pile carpet I often pushed toys through, or cooking for Grandpa Chic. She cursed him from the stove while he sat in his recliner after a day working outside.

"Just sit in there, goddamnit, and watch your goddamn *Wheel of Fortune,*" she'd mumble, or sometimes yell, through the wall between kitchen and living room. Grandpa Chic was silent, smoking in his denim overalls and looking at a television screen set in a wooden console with golden speakers and a big knob that switched the channels.

Dad later said that Grandma Teresa and my mom had a lot in common, which seemed plausible since they'd disliked each other tremendously. They'd both been young, smart mothers unsung in houses their husbands built.

"She was a hard mother," Dad told me

about Teresa when I was grown. "She had woman problems that didn't get treated. But when she got older, she mellowed out, and you two hit it off."

I'm unaware of any diagnosis, but the "woman problems" might have been depression, creative energy stifled and imploding in an isolated wife and mother who went unseen and unheard. I often played with her scarves and jewelry left over from when she was middle-aged in the 1960s, the last decade when she was inclined to buy such things. Who was going to see her anyway? You can go a very long time in the country without being seen, which can be both a blessing and a problem.

When I drew pictures for her, she would tell me I should design greeting cards for Hallmark. The global greeting-card company had started north of us in Kansas City in 1915, a year after Teresa was born, and was still based there. In moving from Wichita back to the countryside in the 1930s, she had moved against the economic flow of a nation. But often she subtly hinted that her granddaughter should leave for Kansas City — a true urban center that for her had once represented jazz music, jobs for a woman who had gone to secretary school, an Art Deco skyline.

In every place, something is gained and something is lost. Out in the country, at the end of Teresa's life and the beginning of mine, I felt both the treasures of isolation for a strange girl and all the things an independent, thinking woman stood to lose.

In the quiet of her house, so quiet you could hear distant birds through the walls, I found Teresa's high school yearbooks in the bottom drawer of an old bureau. I asked whether I could look through them, and she stared at me without answering. I set them at the wobbly kitchen table with a plastic covering over it and paged through them for hours. They were full of handwritten notes from girlfriends in strange 1930s penmanship and slang, which I read over and over again. Still without saying a word, Grandma Teresa watched me paging through them with an unsettled look on her face, as though a little girl fascinated by her life was the most surprising thing that had happened in fifty years.

My mom and Grandma Betty were large characters who had done a lot of wild things and had a lot of adventures. Grandma Teresa was the only female caretaker in my life who seemed, on the surface, like a traditional "homemaker." Yet, of all of them, she was the only one who seemed concerned that I be known for my talent. She praised my report cards from school and asked what I was going to be when I grew up. She was also the only one who raised hell if someone forgot to feed me or pick me up at school, the only one who tore my dad up and down if no one was paying attention and I walked alone two miles up the road to the trailer full of kids and a man she didn't trust.

Unlike Betty and Jeannie, Teresa was a reserved woman who stayed married to the same man for fifty years and never "worked outside the home." But I have a feeling that she is the one who would have most deeply understood my connection to you — at once a maternal sense so profound that I refused to have you in a poor rural place and a selfish mission to never be trapped.

It wasn't all bad, that poor rural place. Though money was scarce, you would have had your basic needs met because we knew how to grow and build things.

Dad left farming behind when he moved to Wichita, but Betty and Arnie's farm was a constant operation in food production: an enormous vegetable and fruit garden that stretched from the dirt road to the house, the animals we killed and butchered our-selves, hens giving eggs, the peach and walnut trees, thickets of boysenberries, the fields of alfalfa, soybeans, and wheat. I sometimes missed meals in Wichita while my parents worked and I babysat Matt, or when I changed schools and was too embarrassed to tell an adult that my free-lunch paperwork hadn't transferred and I had nothing to eat. But at the farm we had more than we could eat ourselves. Grandma and I would spend an entire summer day putting up thirty quarts of tomatoes for making chili in the winter. Then we'd give a jar to every old farmer who stopped by for a beer.

The popular image of Kansas is a monotonous, level expanse. If you drive through without getting off the interstate highway, that might be all you see for hundreds of miles, but some corners of Kansas are made of modest hills, woods, red-rock formations, slight cliffs. Still, my family fit the stereotype as both a people and a place: farmers on flat earth.

Some of us saw a beauty in that earth that people heading west toward the Rocky Mountains seemed to miss. But the earth was more of a tactile experience than a view. We had it on us. Cars got stuck in muddy ditches after thunderstorms. My feet got stuck in the marshy edges of ponds full of cattails. Gravel got stuck in my knees when my bike tires slid on roads made of sand.

We pulled radishes out of the garden, rubbed them on our jeans, and ate them right there if we pleased because a little dirt was good for you. After a shower, it was still under our fingernails and in the grooves between our toes. Grandpa Arnie said you could grow potatoes in my ears on account of how dirty they were.

We rarely bothered to wash our cars and pickups because they went up and down muddy roads every day and what was the point. If someone came through in a sparkling vehicle, got out in clean clothes, and asked us how to get somewhere, when he drove off Grandpa Arnie would say he was a real dandy but then it takes all kinds.

What came out of the dirt went into the kitchen. Grandma Betty hadn't grown up that way, coming from Wichita, but it turned out she loved it. Her cigarette burned in an ashtray on the windowsill while she showed me how to chop vegetables, peel potatoes, pull guts out of chickens, and beat the eggs they laid. Her Supremes or Conway Twitty albums turned on the outdated record player, or soap operas played on the little black-and-white TV that sat on the kitchen counter. Grandma breaded pork chops

Grandpa had butchered and put them in a hot skillet while I stood on a kitchen chair in my underwear running a hand mixer through a bowl of boiled potatoes and milk.

The place had a comfortable rhythm and stability that Betty, my mom, and I had known nowhere else. Betty and Arnie had been together for a decade, her longest relationship by far. Cheap things had hung in the same place long enough to leave behind clean rectangles on walls that sunlight and cigarette smoke discolored over the years. It felt like home. When I came inside with cockleburs and tacklike stickers in my bare feet, Grandma helped me dig them out and kissed the bleeding holes they left in my skin.

On the weekends, the house brimmed with drunks and hard characters. When the sun went down, Grandpa Arnie was likely to hitch a long hayrack to his pickup and pull a mob of singing, beer-sloshing adults and dirty children through the humming night. The coyotes, bobcats, and chickens heard us sing, laugh, and scream. Grandpa's favorite trick was to pull the flat rack of wood and steel down the muddy waterway that funneled rain to the crops. He yanked us up and down the sides of the jagged canal. Someone invariably fell while the rest of us clung to corners and one another, legs dangling from the hayrack's rusted metal edge.

Or on Halloween, under a big moon and a clear sky, we'd climb onto the hayrack for a chilly midnight ride past the potato patch and among tall, fragrant rolls of wet hay. We'd howl with surprise when three of my uncles leapt from behind the bales with masks and flashlights.

At the first snow, Arnie would tie the inner tube from a tractor tire to the back of his three-wheeler and drag rosy-cheeked drunkards across the yard. Or he'd rope old wooden sleds to the back of the tractor and forge down the snowy road with squealing children behind him pulling at their wet ski masks. For great stretches of the Midwest, people have to get creative to have some fun after a blizzard — lots of snow, no hills. In situations like that, where you had plenty of one thing and not enough of another — say, plenty of acres but not enough money — Grandpa Arnie's ideas never quit.

Once, my cousin Shelly and I chased him across the snowy gravel toward the Big Shed, the large, easternmost outbuilding beyond the chicken coop and the Little Shed. The freezing air smelled of ash, which drifted in large chunks from the burn pile, anchored by an old cast-iron bathtub and a few crumbling barrels just past the pigpen. Somewhere between a broken antique band saw and an icebox covered in cobwebs, we found the four Radio Flyer sleds we dug out every winter. We dusted them off and lugged them toward the Big Shed with the rope Arnie had taken from his pickup bed.

"No, that ain't gonna be enough," Arnie said, looking at the sleds as he choked the Honda's cold engine. He clicked his tongue against his teeth as he counted people on his stout fingers. He shook his head and crawled off the humming three-wheeler.

"You *Katzenjammers* can help me dig something else out," he said, his boots stomping across the dusty shed floor to a corner that housed the defunct camper he and Betty had bought at a farm sale ten years earlier, in the late '70s, for a family road trip through the Ozarks to the east in Missouri.

We helped him yank an old, torn-up canoe from the camper's narrow metal door.

Arnie tested the bottom of the metal boat with his boot. The canoe had three seats, and the floor at one end had a hole in it. Arnie pulled two sandy floor mats from Old Brownie, the 1974 GMC pickup relegated to farm chores. He shook the mats and threw them over the torn canoe floor. He slid the boat forward a bit, and the bare frame between the mats and the ground was enough to keep everything in place.

It was almost five o'clock, and the slanting light under the roof of the open-air shed was stretching farther inside as the sun lowered. Shelly and I waited for Arnie to rope the canoe to Old Brownie's hitch, and we climbed into the boat. Arnie started the diesel truck engine and dragged us past the Little Shed to the house.

"You gotta be shittin' me," people yelled from the porch. They boarded the canoe with whiskey in plastic cups and beer cans wedged in foam koozies. Shelly and I sat over the hole at the back of the boat since we were kids and our bony little butts would be fine, they said.

"If this goddamned thing tips over, I quit," Aunt Pud said. We all remembered when she wrecked a three-wheeler into a snowdrift and laughed so hard she peed and sent steam into the air. Betty laughed as she squeezed in front of me, pulling my legs up around hers. Our thick coveralls made rustling noises when we moved.

Arnie revved the idling engine. We heard the truck switch into gear, and the canoe shifted forward.

"Oh, shit," Betty said. We all laughed with nervous joy.

Arnie turned east at the road and picked up speed.

Riding a canoe down a dirt road was just fine, we discovered. The people at the front were singing Christmas carols, and we were wedged so tightly that the biting wind was easily avoided with a dip of the head behind a pair of shoulders. Arnie turned north at the tree row to pass our dozens of hay bales, half-buried in drifts, and I looked at the impressive expanse of white fields that stretched to the orange and pink horizon. The wheat and alfalfa, sprouting beneath the snow, were young enough that they would survive.

The rope between the truck and the canoe grew slack as Arnie shifted gears. Old Brownie tilted sharply as it crested the dirt mound at the edge of a wheat field, and I whispered a prayer: *Please God, don't let us get hurt.*

"Hold on to your butts!" Grandma Betty yelled, her beer splashing as we broke out onto the open field and Grandpa hit the gas.

I pressed my face against Betty's back as Arnie sped us through another dip in the field that was so familiar to him. Betty's arms were wrapped around someone's, maybe her sister's. Shelly's arms were wrapped around my waist. To keep from falling out of the boat, we shifted our centers with every turn.

People pay for a version of that now. They pay for hayrack rides through pumpkin patches, a safe industry called "agritourism." They go to bars that use Mason jars for glasses. They even throw expensive weddings in barns. Somehow, I got the real thing, increasingly rare in an urbanizing world.

I would have passed all sorts of poverties to you. But some late night a tractor would have pulled you, well fed by what we grew, under a clear sky full of stars. That laughter — that freedom — would have been the fortune you inherited.

We were country people in the middle of the country, living in a way that, I gather from things they've said to me over the years, some middle-class people in cities and suburbs on coasts thought had died long ago. For someone who never worked a farm, for whom the bread and meat in deli sandwiches seemed to magically materialize without agricultural labor, the center of the country was a place flown over but not touched.

"I haven't heard of anything like that since *The Grapes of Wrath*," people with different backgrounds would say to me in all seriousness when I described life on the farm. They thought we didn't exist anymore, when in fact we just existed in places they never went. It was an easy way to think, I guess. I rarely saw the place I called home described or tended to in political discourse, the news media, or popular culture as anything but a stereotype or something that happened a hundred years ago.

We were so invisible as to be misrepresented even in caricature, lumped in with other sorts of poor whites, derogatory terms applied to us even if they didn't make sense.

We lived on the open prairie, so we weren't the "hillbillies" of the Smoky Mountains or the Ozarks. We weren't "roughnecks" in oil fields; Kansas had a humble tap on oil thousands of feet below the prairie, but nothing like Oklahoma or Texas to the south.

"Redneck" and "cracker" didn't quite translate, since their American usage was rooted in the slave South, against which Kansas had lit many of the fires that sparked the Civil War. After the Kansas-Nebraska Act of 1854 allowed those territories to decide for themselves whether to allow slavery, abolitionists fought border wars with slaveholders across the line in Missouri. "Bloody Kansas," historians call the period, and that blood ensured that Kansas would be established as a free state. Kansas and Missouri still have a cultural rivalry more than 150 years later. That's not to say white abolitionists were morally righteous on the matter of race or that black and brown Kansans were treated well. But it's a different history to come out of, as a poor white.

Slang terms for my plains ancestors who built dwellings there from sod, the only available material for lack of trees, didn't survive in common vernacular. We were so willfully forgotten in American culture that the most common slur toward us was one applied to poor whites anywhere: "white trash." Or, since we moved in and out of mobile homes, "trailer trash."

There's an image in popular culture of the poor white female version: a smoke hanging out of her mouth, a baby on one hip, and the screen door to her trailer propped open with the other. You could say my mother was that woman and I was that baby, and that you would have been that baby, too. But as members of all sorts of stereotyped groups know, the popular image — selected or fixated upon by someone more powerful than you — doesn't tell you much about the life.

For one thing, anyone who has lived it knows that what matters less than the trailer is where the trailer is parked. Ours was in the country by my father's choice, on the land where he later built our house. The place was thought boring for being grassland — mountains and forests being the landscapes that more often inspire awe — but without hills and trees we had a bigger sky than Montana, an unobstructed view of bright color between dark thunder clouds like nothing I've ever seen elsewhere. Those displays were so grand outside a single-wide metal dwelling on wheels that it felt less like us having a good view than like God having a view of us. I could feel how small we were.

I knew, so deeply that I wasn't even conscious of it, that my family was on the outside of something considered normal. That normalized thing was the city, suburbs, even little burgs of three thousand people. We called them all "town," even the small ones seeming to lord over us when we wore dirty jeans to visit a bank teller wearing a suit from Dillard's. Places with banks, schools, stores, and county courthouses — let alone skyscrapers — represented to us a sort of power we were removed from, a disenfranchisement not only by culture but by geographic distance.

This bred in us a distrust of just about anyone who held a power we didn't — even those who tried to help.

"I never seen a dime of it," Grandpa Arnie would say about Farm Aid, the concert fund-raiser begun in 1985 to save dying family farms. The founders were white singers from humble places: Willie Nelson, who was born the son of an auto mechanic during the Great Depression and spent the summers of his youth picking cotton in the Texas heat. John Cougar Mellencamp, who was born in small-town Indiana and became a grandfather at age thirty-seven. Neil Young — well, he was a middle-class hippie from Canada. Grandpa Arnie didn't know or care about any of that. All he knew was that he'd never been to a big concert in his life, and he wouldn't get to go to this one.

Whether or not famous singers in cowboy boots testified before Congress, public policy went on selling us right up the rivers of corporate monopolies and factory farming. It was hardly a new story but reached its sad climax under Reagan. All around us, farm loans were underwater. Old farmers died and their kids sold everything off; many of them had already moved to cities, which their parents often encouraged for their survival.

That economic collapse deepened a consensus within society that a talented person from the country would endeavor to "get out." Some did. They got scholarships to college, blew town, and — their politics and economic prospects having changed — never looked back. That "rural flight" made way for the idea that country people can't "make it" in a bustling metropolis. But the ability to measure distances for planting alfalfa and smell the right moment to cut it isn't so different from the ability to map out a subway trip and feel when a stop has been missed.

Like all industrialized countries, America started out country and turned city. My people didn't turn with it. Instead of striving toward glowing economic meccas, they stayed on tractors in fields, or in small towns where life struck many of them as not just good enough but preferable to bigger places. Often, it's not that country people can't hack the city but that they choose not to — or life just played out differently regardless of their desires.

The Kentucky farmer and activist Wendell Berry wrote for *The Atlantic* in 1991, "The only sustainable city — and this, to me, is the indispensable ideal and goal — is a city in balance with its countryside," one that would pay "all its ecological and human debts." Those human debts might be to the indigenous people pushed off the land where a Western city would rise, or to black slaves who worked Southern fields so that cotton and tobacco would be cheap to city whites wanting clothes and cigars.

It is harder to imagine a debt owed to members of the race that committed those horrors. And indeed my countryside was an overwhelmingly white one. A few thousand freed slaves started African American farming settlements in Kansas, one of which still survives, but most went to urban centers farther north. Around the same time, the federal government was killing and forcibly driving indigenous tribes to "Indian Territory," the border of which was fifty miles south of my family's land. A lot of Mexican American people settled throughout the state due to the cattle drives from Texas. But during the twentieth century, most of the state population was of European descent.

We thus benefited from our skin color in ways that are hard to perceive by three white people working a field together, no other human being, town, or structure in sight to the horizon — a complicated mix of privilege and disadvantage. I don't know what, if anything, is owed to that version of the countryside. I do know that, mostly neglected by state and federal power centers, much of it is now economically dead and abandoned or under the thumb of seed corporations, natural gas corporations, and factory farms.

Government programs pop up to offer financial incentives for businesses and homeowners to stay in or move to rural America, but they can't prevent infrastructure costs from rising when populations decline or home values from going down and, with them, local tax revenues and the schools they funded.

When I was a kid, the United States was a few decades away from reckoning with the reality that the next generation would be worse off, not better off, than the one before it. But my community had been facing dwindling odds for generations. They knew that children like me likely wouldn't and shouldn't aim for life on a farm. Few country kids were pressured to keep a farm going.

Well ahead of middle-class America, for all my family's emphasis on hard work, on some level we'd done away with the idea that it always paid off. Being as we got up before dawn to do chores and didn't quit until after dark, it was plain that the problem with our outcomes wasn't lack of hard work. The problem was with commodities markets, with big business, with Wall Street — things so far away and impenetrable to us that all we could do was shake our heads, hate the government, and get the combine into the shed before it started to hail.

We didn't know much about the policies and politics that were changing our environment and the food chain. We were proud that, from the exact geographic center of our country, we raised the wheat, the beef, the pork that got shipped around the world. Living in a relatively remote area, our work feeding strangers was our sole sense of connection to places we had never been. It was not, for us, a perceived political or even cultural identity but a way of life.

What it means to be "country," though, has changed in the few decades of my lifetime, I think, from an experience to a brand cultivated by conservative forces. Once, when I was about thirty, I saw a boy from a small town wearing a T-shirt that read PRO GOD, PRO GUNS, PRO LIFE. I was shocked. In my experience, there was no evangelism about my family's Catholic faith in the 1980s and little overt cross-pollination between our church and our politics. There was, that I can recall, no resentment toward people in cities with more formal education and money. I'm suspicious when I see these tropes trotted out proudly to represent the rural, working-class experience, often by people who have things my family never could have afforded.

I'd never heard of Carhartt, for instance, the popular work-wear brand sometimes worn as a class-conscious fashion statement, until I was well into adulthood. My choring coveralls were twenty years old with a big corduroy collar and holes in the lining, and I slopped the hogs while wearing old tennis shoes as often as I did in boots.

Grandpa Arnie's trucks were small Toyotas bought used, not big Fords or Chevrolets jacked up a foot above big tires to look tough. Those trucks tend to look too clean for a machine that's done any work. The big flags flying off the back of them would've scared our cattle. The people who drive them often live in suburbs and have big, clean garages full of all-terrain vehicles that they call "toys" next to a row of shiny helmets, a very good option I didn't have as I drove three-wheelers from one pasture to another with buckets of feed.

Someone could have gone without beer for a week to buy a helmet. It was culture and lack of education as much as it was empty bank accounts that explained many of our habits. I'm not saying our way of country living was right. But I can tell you that Grandpa Arnie would have chuckled at a man with a cattle guard on the front of his truck driving to and from an office job.

He would have laughed, too, about designer jeans yellowed with a wash meant to evoke the dirt that was under his fingernails or the "shabby chic" decorating trend of new furniture meant to look like it had weathered decades in our barn. My family found stuff like that funny rather than offensive, maybe because it was so poorly executed. When affluent urban men in plaid flannel shirts let their hair grow wild and unkempt across their face and necks to affect a laborer's style for doing laptop work in coffee shops, I think of my dad immaculately trimming his beard every morning before dawn to work on a construction site. The men closest to me took meticulous care with their appearance whenever they had the chance.

Mom, too, presented herself like her main job was to be photographed, when it was more likely to sort the inventory in the stockroom of a retail store. Her outfits were ensembles cobbled together from Wichita mall sale racks, but she always managed to look stylish. My favorite was a champagne-colored silk pantsuit that was cut loose and baggy. She wore it with a scarf that had big, lush roses on it like the satiny wallpaper she had glued and smoothed across our hallway. She had married a farm boy but had no interest in plaid shirts.

After she recovered from the hard delivery of her second child, Mom was relieved to get back to work in Wichita. She'd load Matt and me into her 1982 AMC Spirit to take us to the babysitter, stopping to fill up the gas tank and send me inside with some cash for five dollars' worth of unleaded and a pack of Marlboro Lights. If Dad's construction site was in town, sometimes Matt and I rode to the babysitter on the torn tapestry of his pickup seats and went to a McDonald's drive-through just as the sun was coming up — a treat since we lived so far from restaurants and fast food. I remember the first time I saw a pizza box, brought home for dinner from a family-run joint in Cheney when I was in second or third grade.

For me, country was not a look, a style, or even a conscious attitude but a physical place, its experience defined by distance from the forces of culture that would commodify it. That place meant long stretches of near-solitude broken up by long drives on highways to enter society and then exit again.

Our situation was different from that of people living in the farthest rural stretches of, say, western Kansas. That proximity heightened my awareness of the contrast between country and city while allowing me to feel at ease in both. We lived in quiet but could access opportunity with a forty-minute drive.

Dad liked it that way. Owning a small bit of the countryside brought him a deep satisfaction. The state had seized some of his dad's farmland through eminent domain in the 1960s to dig the reservoir and move water east in underground tunnels for the people of Wichita. Sometimes Dad would park his truck on the shoulder of the two-lane blacktop that ran along the lake dam and take Matt and me up the long, steep concrete steps to look at what would have been his and then our small inheritance, now literally underwater. We couldn't use the water ourselves; it was for Wichitans to access by turning on a faucet. We thus had dug a private well right next to a giant reservoir on what once was our land. It's an old story: pushing poor rural communities out of the way to tap natural resources for cities.

Witnessing this as a child had affected Dad deeply, and he shared Grandpa Arnie's attitude toward the value of land: "They don't make any more of it." He had plans to buy the bit of land north of the house and build an addition when Matt and I were older and needed more room.

Mom was less sure of these plans.

Some evenings, I'd watch her curl and tease her dark hair at the vanity mirror that my dad had built next to their master-suite bathroom. She smelled of hair spray and Calvin Klein Obsession perfume. She left in the darkness and turned her car wheels from our dirt road onto the highway for Wichita.

Dad would say to Mom, "Ever since you started running around with those girls at work, you're never home. Those girls aren't married."

"I'm going out," Mom growled.

While she was gone, Dad sometimes cried thinking about what she might be doing "in town," which is what you call it when you're country and someone has gone grocery shopping or to the bank.

When Mom went to a George Strait concert at the small Cowboy Club in Wichita, when George was newly famous, Dad sat at the stereo next to our brick fireplace, listening to a radio broadcast of the show on a country station. George would pick a woman from the audience to join him on stage, the man on the radio said. Dad held his breath, worried that Mom would be picked and swept away by a handsome celebrity in tight Wranglers and a cowboy hat. The men I knew more often wore ball caps stained through by the salt off their foreheads. Dad didn't even like country music. Too sad, he said.

When she wasn't in Wichita working or going out with girlfriends, Mom had one good use for the country: moneymaking schemes. Some rural women didn't get to town often, so knocking on their doors with a product to sell was a good bet. This was before the Internet and online shopping, of course. Matt and I rode in Mom's car as she drove far past the county line to peddle Avon cosmetics or a mail-order service that dipped baby shoes in precious metals as keepsakes. I'd sort her inventory or product samples in the front seat while Matt sat in the back with toys.

An Eagles tape would stop playing when

she pulled the keys out of her rusted little car. She would walk up a gravel driveway in high heels, and the woman who answered would ask if we were the family that had the firecracker stand by the lake last July.

My mother loved country music but didn't wear boots. She didn't announce who she was or give a shit what society thought of it. But whether you're a farmer in a field or a young mother opening a heavy car door against the Kansas wind, that's about as country as it gets: moving back and forth across the earth to catch a little opportunity.

At Betty and Arnie's farmhouse, just past the sliding glass door that led from the pool and cement patio into the dining room, sat an out-of-tune console piano. Somehow Grandma and Grandpa had come into it for free. When I touched the keys, I had such a strong feeling that it was a natural instrument for me that the frustration was almost physically painful in my hands. The swimming pool felt like that, too. I'd become a swimmer in adulthood, but as a kid I never had lessons, which would have been an ordeal for my family in both logistics and finances.

The frustrations of rural life were all about opportunity and proximity. In the pool, at the piano, I felt the agony of potential energy without the training that might release it into breaststrokes and melodies. It was something like the agony I sensed in my mother and Grandma Teresa.

School was my best bet for relieving that sort of frustration, even though it wasn't always a hospitable place for a poor kid whose mom wasn't in the PTA. Cheney, population fifteen hundred, was ten miles of dirt roads and two-lane blacktops to the south. It was where Dad graduated from high school in 1973 and where, a few years later, Mom was so miserable from the small-town cliquishness that she dropped out and got her GED not long before I came along.

Early in the morning, I walked down our dirt driveway, which was longer than a city block. I waited at the end of it and stared at the corner where our dirt road ended at the lake dam. That's where the bus would appear from behind the trees along the black-top.

If it was cold, I prayed for the bus to come and shoved sometimes ungloved hands wherever I had warmth. Once the bus arrived, being short, I struggled to climb its tall steps. I took an empty seat. The journey smelled of sweaty plastic, and it was a long one. I was at the edge of the route, the first to get on and last to get off. On account of so many stops along muddy roads full of ruts, often winding far off course to reach isolated rural homes, the ride took upwards of an hour each way.

I loved school for the learning, the activities, having things I made hung in hallways, the chance to be around other kids. But even as I excelled at all those things, Cheney had never accepted my scandalously young Wichita mom and therefore never accepted me. Yes, most women had kids at a young age where we lived. But the difference between doing it as a teenager who got her GED and a twenty-three-year-old recent college grad who came back to town from a small state university with a ring on her finger was the difference between unacceptable and encouraged. There are pecking orders within pecking orders.

The few times Mom showed up at school for "room mother" duty, the other mothers would murmur to one another about how young she was or who was she trying to impress with that outfit, or they'd raise their eyebrows about how unnatural she seemed with children. Once she brought a plastic bowling set for toddlers from Matt's toy box since that's all we had in the house that a group of kids might be able to do together, and she couldn't go buy something new. I could feel how embarrassed she was when the other moms laughed. It broke my heart worse than any embarrassment I'd ever felt myself.

Those realms of family and school rarely overlapped for me. My parents were often absent from this or that function due to work or not understanding its significance in my life, since it seemed to have proved insignificant in theirs. They didn't ask whether I'd done my homework; I always had, and I had no idea a parent was expected to be involved. I don't know if I was born that way or developed that way to fit my circumstances. But as far back as I can remember, there was an adult me inside the child me — which probably explains a lot about how I could sense you back then.

School was run by adults who seemed so different from the ones at home. They wore different kinds of clothes and spoke what was almost a different language. Even the logical order of daily operations seemed foreign to a child who so often knew chaos. I thrived there, whether anyone was rooting for me to do so or not. I wasn't from a family or background anyone seemed to be rooting for. Our small town was almost entirely white, and in that context economics decided the social order.

My first-grade teacher, a short woman with permed hair in the shape of a triangle and a tall poof of bangs at the top, singled me out to verbally pick on, probably because I was both the most likely to talk back and the least likely to have a parent show up raising hell about how her kid was treated. There was a boy in our class who had a mental disability, and once I saw her yank him up from the floor by his hair.

I'd say something to object when she was unfair or mean. She'd send me to the hallway and remember the offense later when chocolate milk cartons and graham crackers got handed out and I had to apologize to get mine.

When unfit teachers occupy classrooms, certain children are most vulnerable — those with disabilities, who can't convey mistreatment to their parents, and those whose parents are too negligent, too drunk, or too busy to ask how school is going.

Every day, the teacher gave me horrible looks that made me feel like I would die inside. If I was tired from no sleep and yawned, she'd leap at the chance to harass me.

"Sarah, does this bore you?"

"I was just yawning," I'd say, and I'd be

sent to the hallway for talking back. She sent me to the hallway just about every day in first grade, though I never had any trouble with other teachers and everyone always said I was a nice girl.

Once the teacher called me over during recess.

"Sarah, did you know you have a B in reading right now?"

This didn't make sense. I'd gotten an A on every worksheet I could remember. I always got A's and took nothing more seriously than my school assignments. I was worried and confused.

She was wearing big sunglasses and a trench coat in the cold. She had a little smile on her face. Sometimes when she pulled me aside, one of her eyes rolled back in her head like she was turning into a different person, which seemed about right because when parents were around she was nice as could be.

"I thought you were smarter than that, but you have a B," she said and stuck her chin out. "I want you to think about that."

While rural schools employed some fine teachers, in many cases they couldn't be too picky. For decades, those school districts had been consolidating, unable to keep the lights on without pooling resources. Even schools that remained separate often shared teachers, who would drive half an hour from school to school to teach, say, music to the sixth graders of three different small towns in one day.

I craved learning so much that my teacher's abuse never deterred me from trying my hardest on every assignment. In many ways related to my sensibilities, school was all I had. If it contained monsters, I would face them by necessity, without question. There was a sadness, though, in my so desperately needing something that could be gotten only in a difficult, even cruel way.

On long bus rides home from school, then, while other children played and screamed, I was quiet. I usually had one or two friends but had been established as a general outsider on the first day of kindergarten when I carried my school supplies in a paper grocery sack instead of a purple unicorn backpack. From that day on, while the other kids on the bus shouted and played and fought, I always sat alone and watched through the window: The mobile homes where, during the winter, children ran coatless to the bus's accordion door. The bigger homes with horse stables and entry gates where children waited with their mothers. The wheat fields that changed from frozen sod to ankle-high grass to waving coats of gold.

When I got home, I'd drop my bag and walk past the tree row, past the two-lane blacktop highway, to the large state lake. I'd climb up the dam to the spillway, a monstrous release valve for the water. I'd cling to the tall metal fence around it, waiting for it to open. When it did, an enormity of gushing, gnashing water ripped into the deep concrete spillway, spraying me through the fence and electrifying me with adrenaline.

I cherished the quiet pleasure of life close to nature but was developing the same sort of tension that Mom, Grandma Teresa, and so many rural people carried — a feeling of containment, a desire to somehow rip free.

By early 1987, Grandma Betty had tired of the long drive between the courthouse in Wichita and the farm in the middle of nowhere. Grandpa Arnie said she could quit her job, but she didn't want to quit. When had she not worked? She was proud of what she did at the courthouse.

"Plus," she said, "I got used to the big money."

She received a meager salary, accepted without negotiation, as were most women's salaries. But living at the farm, she paid no rent or mortgage. A lot of what she earned went into savings, for the first time in her life, or to bail out a friend who needed help the way Betty herself had needed it not so long ago. She was tired of the long daily commute from the farm, but it made more sense, she thought, to keep her job and find a house in Wichita, which could be a long-term property investment anyhow. For all the moving in her past, and even her many years on the farm, Wichita was still her home.

I went along as she visited open houses. I liked the brown brick house with the glass coffee table.

"They want sixty thousand dollars for it," Grandma Betty said. "That's too high."

Back home I told Mom, "We went to a house that costs sixty thousand dollars."

"That's not that much," she said. "Some houses even cost a hundred thousand dollars."

I spent the next week reporting this to anyone who would listen.

Grandma found a tiny, square house on Second Street near downtown Wichita, near both her childhood home and the Mexican American neighborhood where her lifelong best friend had grown up. Grandma's new place was just a five-minute drive from her job at the courthouse. She would stay at the house during the week and spend weekends at the farm with Grandpa, she said. He agreed to drive to Wichita on weeknights after his chores, unless the farm kept him tied up late into the evening.

Grandma bought the house for $25,000 through an owner-carry mortgage with balloon payments, a good trick in which the seller makes the monthly payments for the first couple years until the buyer's payments kick in and increase in amount over time. It's like being carried by Jesus on a sandy beach and paying him interest for every footprint.

The yellow-orange brick house was built around the time Betty was born and had a concrete porch and four rooms: a small bedroom and living room with wood floors, and an eat-in kitchen with a small bathroom connected to it. To turn the unfinished basement into more space, Dad and Grandpa Arnie swung sledgehammers at a wall, and Matt and I picked up the chalky pieces to put in a garbage bag. We jumped on a mattress covered in powdery plaster on the cool cement floor, until Dad started the circular saw to cut studs and the noise drove us outside.

Second Street was busy with cars, and I kept Matt at a safe distance. I held his hand as we wandered a few blocks toward the old, tiny brick general store with a 7Up sign that read GEORGE'S. It was one of the last family-run grocers in town, and Grandma had walked there as a kid herself. George, who was a thousand years old, gave us candy out of a jar on the counter above us.

After supper at the new house, Matt went back to the country with our parents. Grandpa Arnie went back to the farm so he'd be there for early-morning chores. I stayed in Wichita with Grandma Betty to help clean her new house.

We scrubbed the kitchen floor, the counters, the stove and refrigerator. Grandma couldn't believe how filthy somebody left the place. We scraped at the wallpaper, and Grandma couldn't believe how many sloppy layers of wallpaper somebody left on the walls. I pried staples and tacks and nails from the drywall, then dipped a trowel in a plastic cup full of wet plaster to smear across dents and holes.

We had a tiny black-and-white television going, and when the ten o'clock news came on, Grandma was ready to hang it up. We were hungry, but the new house was empty. For supper, we'd eaten bologna sandwiches and potato "shoestrings" from a greasy metal can. Grandma drove us to McDonald's and told me to get whatever I wanted. She often told me to get whatever I wanted when we went to fast-food restaurants, and I understood that her generosity was because of the hard life she had lived. She remembered what it felt like to be a kid who didn't get to order what she wanted. I ordered a hot fudge sundae.

Back at the new house, we dragged a mattress and sheets into the living room, and she moved the television to the corner next to us. She fiddled with the tall antenna until I saw Johnny Carson. It felt like a great adventure to eat ice cream on a bare mattress, on the hardwood floor of an empty, echoing house, while watching *The Tonight Show.*

Grandma Betty switched off the TV and the lights.

"You done good work today, Sarah Smurf," she said.

I had forgotten that darkness and quiet were not the same in Wichita as they were in the country. The cars seemed bright and loud, driving by just past the front door, which opened into the room where we lay. I thought and thought and thought like I did every night, until I wished my mind had a switch I could flip. I felt Grandma get up in the almost darkness.

She said she was going to go pee, and would I like a glass of water. She turned on the kitchen light and screamed.

"Oh, God. Sarah, get up."

Hundreds of cockroaches ran across the kitchen linoleum in a big, dark swarm.

Hit by sudden light, some of them ran to the bathroom. Others scurried around the bottom of the refrigerator. Some ran toward the dark dining room and our mattress.

I stood up on the mattress and took a step back. A line of roaches started up the side of the mattress. Grandma was searching for her sandals.

"Those filthy bastards," she said. "Get your stuff. We're blowin' this joint."

Then it was after midnight and we were rolling down the familiar strip of Highway 54 — stars, cattle, wheat fields that were wild prairie grass back when that same route west was called Cannonball Stage Coach Road. Grandma was cursing the cockroaches of the earth, wishing for spiders or June bugs but, by God, anything but a filthy cockroach because she hated those bastards.

Less than an hour later we were back in the country, climbing out of Grandma's car to the sound of locusts and the smell of the pigs and cows that lay sleeping somewhere in the darkness. Grandma quieted Sasha, the German shepherd, as we walked through the warm night to the front door of the farmhouse. She always got a big glass of water with lots of ice, and we went up the familiar creaky old wood steps covered in nubby blue carpet.

"Shhh. We'll scare Grandpa," Betty said when we were halfway up the steps.

She winked at me from the bedroom door and took a great leap onto the waterbed, and Grandpa's big belly went up with the jostling water mattress. He let out a startled yell, and Grandma and I laughed until our stomachs hurt.

"What in the hell are you doing here?"

Grandma lit a cigarette and used the big, boxy remote control to turn on the television, switching through four channels of late-night programming and picking, most likely, *The Twilight Zone* or the television series version of *Nightmare on Elm Street,* which gave me horrible dreams, though I never admitted it because I didn't want her to feel bad. As a treat, Grandma gave me half a piece of the Nicorette gum she kept on the headboard for nights when she tried to quit smoking.

Once she and Grandpa Arnie were both

asleep, I turned off the television and for hours it was the country air, Grandpa Arnie's snoring, a distant headlight on a highway across a field, black darkness, the smell of menthol ointment that Arnie used at night for muscle aches and that Betty put up her nose when her sinuses swelled.

Whenever it was time for Grandma Betty to take me back to my parents, the thought of my mom's mood filled me with dread. Grandma would cheer me up by being funny. "Time to hit it!" she'd say, and pinch me in the arm. "Let's scram! Let's blow this joint."

Then we were in her little car again, its ashtray full of butts, the cigarette lighter missing, the smell of smoke most powerful if it was summertime, a tiny dog in Grandma's lap with its paws on the driver's-side door and its tongue in the wind. In the glove box, a heap of napkins, ketchup packets, salt and pepper, moist towelettes, and plastic sporks left over from Wichita lunch-break trips to fast-food joints.

Grandma would yell "Goodbye!" to everything we passed. With her long, skinny left arm she waved madly out the window of her small car, her right hand managing both the steering wheel and a burning menthol cigarette.

"Goodbye, barn! Adios, garden! See you in the funny papers, mailbox!"

When we turned from the gravel driveway onto the dirt road, I tried not to laugh, wondering whether her performance was finished. She stayed quiet just long enough to worry me.

Silence.

Silence.

"GOODBYE, WHEAT FIELD! GOODBYE, CRAB APPLE TREES!"

She leaned from one side to the other as she yelled, yanking the steering wheel with her. The car veered so wildly toward the wheat on our left and the tree row on our right that it seemed we balanced on two tires. By this time, my face was red with laughter.

The farm shrank in a side-view mirror, dust rose behind the car, and Betty smiled in a swirl of cigarette smoke around her blond hair, which was lit by the country sun. She, my mom, and Grandma Teresa were all Wichita women who fell in love with farmers. But Betty was the only one of them who found her happiest home in the country, and in that way I was more like her than like any other woman who helped raise me.

I don't know where your heart would have been happiest. The country was your birthright, but the older I get, the less I think what side of a divide you're born on has much to do with who or what you are.

"City" and "country" is a dichotomy that predates the United States by centuries. What's particular about Americans is the way we move, along highways across big stretches of earth, to the place we think will do right by us, the place we hope we might belong.

Of all the forces that caused what social scientists call "rural flight," the most powerful one during my childhood was perhaps industrialized agriculture, in which big farming operations with massive machinery churn out products. Small farms like my family's, where the pigpen contained three sows and a litter of piglets, had no place in such an economy — one that was about more, bigger, faster.

In 1980, the year I was born, there were sixty-five thousand hog farmers in Iowa, working out to about two hundred hogs per farm; thirty-two years later, there were ten thousand hog operations with fourteen hundred animals each. Meanwhile, the grain industry consolidated, shutting down local co-ops. Rural jobs dwindled, people moved away, and the services and stores and schools that couldn't be sustained by a hundred people boarded up.

There's another sort of rural-urban imbalance, though: When so many people migrate to and populate cities that they experience overcrowdedness and high unemployment, sociologists call it "overurbanization." For working people, the fantasy of the city can shake out just as poorly as 160 free acres of hard silt. That only became more true as I was growing up. Incomes kept falling, and costs kept rising. Cities were gentrified and became unaffordable. It wasn't just the death of the family farm you would have been born into but the death of the working and even lower middle classes, regardless of their place.

When I was a kid, the death of a farm was often marked quite literally by the death of the old man who farmed it. So it was with my dad's roots when, in the spring of 1988, when I'd just finished second grade, Grandpa Chic died of prostate cancer at the age of seventy-nine.

During the funeral, I sat next to my parents at St. Rose, where by then I'd made my first confession and recently taken my first communion. Mom reached her fair, smooth hand with painted nails over to take my dad's darkened, calloused one with its bruised fingernails — an image I remember so specifically because they rarely touched, at least in front of other people. I couldn't think of a single time I'd seen them hold hands or kiss.

Dad was still struggling physically and mentally from the chemical poisoning at work just months prior. He was in a mental fog, maybe not just from the poisoning but from the trauma of it all. Now we folded our hands and prayed through a Mass, Grandpa Chic in an open casket before us. Dad cried knowing that, the last his father knew him, he was messed up in the head from getting poisoned on the job.

Grandma Teresa was somewhere nearby, probably the pew in front of us, looking at the man she'd spent every day with for the last fifty years. His body was about to go into the ground of the windswept Catholic cemetery behind the church, beyond the 1920s merry-go-round and the patchy grass where children had sat and eaten her pies on spring holidays. Grandpa's tombstone had a wheat-stalk design and bore her name next to his, awaiting the etching of her own end date.

Mom wouldn't wait for such a tombstone.

During the summer of 1989, while we were folding towels out of the dryer, she told me that she and Dad were divorcing. We would be moving to Wichita, she said. Matt and I would live with her but still see our dad. She wanted me to know it wasn't my fault, she told me, and I could hear in her voice that this was something that a magazine or friend advised that she say. I wondered to myself why in the world I would think it was my fault.

The house had already been for sale for more than a year, it turned out. I hadn't known since there'd been little interest during a down market and no would-be buyers streaming through. It took a long time to sell and didn't bring the price Dad wanted, especially for something he'd built with his own hands. Ten acres went with it. Grandpa Arnie always said never sell your land because they don't make any more of it. But Mom was ready to be done with it and move on.

I was ready to move on, too. The teacher who singled me out in first grade had switched to teaching third the same year I became a third grader, and I had been placed in her class. It didn't bother me one bit to leave Cheney and start at a different school.

I helped Mom pack and label boxes while

Matt, who was four, cried and smashed things.

Dad was quiet. He'd have to move into town to be close to us, and a newly single young man ought not live alone on the prairie, regardless. Living alone in the country is no good because there's always something that needs pushed or moved that requires more than one person. There are no cops on a sidewalk that doesn't exist when you need help, no city shovels coming by to scoop the snow off your road after a blizzard. To live alone in the country means isolation within isolation. It's the sort of thing that might turn a divorced man into a drunk, or more specifically into a drunk with a long drive home from the bars past state troopers itching to put a name on a citation. Plus, there was more work in Wichita than in the country.

Somewhere along the way of America, people moved from farms to cities until the nation was a more urban place than a rural one. My father's family had held out and held on for generations, though, preferring air to asphalt and lightning bugs to street-lamps. Or maybe they were just so far off the grid that they didn't know any other life for comparison. What took Dad out of the country wasn't a siren song enticing him with excitement, culture, and opportunity, but something more like a tornado siren saying that if you want to survive your ass had better move.

If I live to be an old woman and the trends of my early life continue, by the time I die half the Kansas population will live in only five of a hundred and five counties — people consolidated like seed companies. There's a strength in that, environmentalists and economists might suggest, but perhaps a greater weakness.

President Dwight Eisenhower, a native of rural Kansas, said, "Whatever America hopes to bring to pass in the world must first come to pass in the heart of America." The countryside is no more our nation's heart than are its cities, and rural people aren't more noble and dignified for their dirty work in fields. But to devalue, in our social investments, the people who tend crops and livestock, or to refer to their place as "flyover country," is to forget not just a country's foundation but its connection to the earth, to cycles of life scarcely witnessed and ill understood in concrete landscapes.

For Wendell Berry's vision of a sustainable world, one in balance both economically and environmentally, the American heart needs a strong, well-supported, well-respected chamber outside its metropoles. The life force that flows back into it will likely be from other places.

The meatpacking towns of western Kansas, for instance, have become some of the most ethnically diverse places in the country as immigrants stream in from Mexico, the Middle East, and Central America to take factory jobs amid industrial agriculture's boom. Statewide, according to the 2010 census, many rural counties had declined, and more than eight out of ten Kansans were white. But the Hispanic population had grown by 60 percent in the last ten years. That's a demographic shift not without tensions but one that has been embraced by some small-town whites, who knew their home must change to survive. As Europeans who moved west and built sod houses on the prairie learned, you either work together or starve alone.

Of all the gifts and challenges of rural life, one of its most wonderful paradoxes is that closeness born of our biggest spaces: a deep intimacy forced not by the proximity of rows of apartments but by having only one neighbor within three miles to help when you're sick, when your tractor's down and you need a ride, when the snow starts drifting so you check on the old woman with the mean dog, regardless of whether you like her.

When I was a teenager, in 1996, I went to New York City for the first time to compete in a national communications contest I'd qualified for from my tiny rural high school. We visited the Statue of Liberty, which I was excited to climb inside. As I neared the crown — ascending a narrow, winding staircase with hundreds of people packed in front of me and behind me — I suddenly had trouble breathing. I wasn't afraid of heights, but terror rose up in me as I looked around and realized I couldn't get out if I had to. I didn't know it, but I was having a panic attack — maybe not an altogether irrational one, but resulting from claustrophobia I'd never been anywhere crowded enough to know I had.

While the small space echoed with many voices, I closed my eyes and took deep breaths. I turned to the stranger behind me and looked him in the eyes, like we were the only two people on earth. He was from Boston, as I recall. I asked if he wanted to take a psychological quiz. Panic was coursing through me, making my lungs and muscles feel tight and clenched, but I must have hidden it well enough. My voice sounded steady. The man laughed and said okay.

I told him a long story, about him on a journey by foot through a forest and meadows. I paused to ask him questions: What animal is on the other side of the wall of vines? What's in the water when you kneel next to the pond and look down? The concept was something I'd heard somewhere, a person leading someone else through a kind of mental maze, but mostly I made it all up.

The crowd around us had gotten quiet to listen. He answered, and I told him what I thought his mind said about who he was. He and others nodded along in amazement or at least amusement. As for me, I had something to focus my mind on as we inched, one suspended metal step at a time, toward the crown of the Statue of Liberty.

I had harnessed an inner calm that can be found anywhere but that for me had been cultivated in rural lands under a state flag that bore a covered wagon and the Latin phrase *ad astra per aspera* — to the stars through difficulties. When we got to the top, I wasn't scared anymore. Someone took my picture: a relieved smile, a view of New York Harbor behind me through the little windows that at night glow as jewels in her crown.

That's how I'd come to resolve the tensions of my childhood, of my family members' lives, about country and city. I craved the opportunity that cities contained and I'd pursue it, but most essential to my well-being was the unobstructed freedom of a flat, wide horizon.

When I was well into adulthood, the United States developed the notion that a dividing line of class and geography separated two essentially different kinds of people. I knew that wasn't right, because both sides existed in me — where I was from and what I hoped to do in life, the place that best sustained me and the places I needed to go for the things I meant to do. Straddling that supposed line as I did, I knew it was about a difference of experience, not of humanity.

You would have been born on one side of that perceived divide, but that wouldn't have predicted anything about the core of you. Not your politics and most definitely not your character. It would have predicted the things you saw and did, to some extent, and one defining psychological tension guaranteed by your country's economy: Every day you would decide whether to stay, go, or try to go. And, if you went, no matter where you ended up, like every immigrant you'd still feel the invisible dirt of your motherland on the soles of your feet.

4

THE SHAME A COUNTRY
COULD ASSIGN

A couple days a week, after my parents'
divorce and our move to Wichita, Dad drove
us to school in the enormous white 1970s
Oldsmobile we'd grown up with. By then it
was dented and had a sagging muffler, and
you could hear its diesel engine from a
block away. Matt was in kindergarten and
would duck down on the maroon velour
seat so that the kids outside the school
wouldn't see him in such a jalopy. I was in
fourth grade, old enough to keep my head
up for Dad's sake, but sometimes I wanted
to hide, too.

Psychologists say shame developed as an
evolutionary function to curb bad individual
behavior that could harm the group. But
modern society has a way of shaming some
people for no crime other than being born.
Your original sin, the one I know well,
would have been being born in need of
economic help.

In the United States, the shaming of the poor is a unique form of bigotry in that it's not necessarily about who or what you are — your skin color, the gender you're attracted to, having a womb. Rather, it's about what your actions have failed to accomplish — financial success within capitalism — and the related implications about your worth in a supposed meritocracy.

Poor whiteness is a peculiar offense in that society imbues whiteness with power — not just by making it the racial norm next to which the rest are "others" but by using it as shorthand for economic stability. So while white people of all classes hate or fear people of color for their otherness, better-off whites hate poor whites because they are physically the same — a homeless white person uncomfortably close to a look in the mirror.

A higher percentage of people of color are poor. Meanwhile, population numbers being what they are, in the United States there are more white people in poverty than any other group. These two facts exist simultaneously and are not in competition, but the way our country talks about class and race would have you believe that only one of them can be true. For my family, the advantage of our race was embedded into our existence but hard for us to perceive amid daily economic struggle.

It was hard to see in the news and pop culture, too. The books I most identified with as a child were written in the nineteenth century. I saw many white girls on television, but I rarely recognized myself in their stories. When I did see my place or people, they were usually represented as caricatures.

To be made invisible as a class is an invalidation. With invalidation comes shame. A shame that deep — being poor in a place full of narratives about middle and upper classes — can make you feel like what you are is a failure.

No one around me articulated these things, let alone complained about them. The worker who feels her poor circumstances result from some personal failure is less likely to have a grievance with a boss, policy, or system and is less likely to protest, strike, or demand a raise. Further, the Midwestern Catholic ethos that surrounded me as a child defaulted to silence. Our sense that our struggles were our own fault, our acceptance of the way things were, helped keep American industry humming to the benefit of the wealthy.

But the source of the shame I felt was not

my own sin. It was our national disdain for anyone in financial need, which is spelled out in the laws of this country.

The clearest evidence for America's contempt toward the struggling might be in its approach to welfare programs, framed by public policy and commentary as something so detestable that my family refused to apply when they qualified.

When I was in middle school, Bill Clinton took office and helped usher in an era of "welfare reform" that emphasized personal responsibility. Federal legislation allowed states to require that recipients pee in a cup for drug tests; sign forms pledging that they wouldn't conceive children while receiving benefits; do volunteer work to "give back" to the society they were supposedly mooching off; have their personal information entered into databases accessed by cops; have their Social Security numbers checked against criminal records.

With that reform, discretion in dispersing funds was turned over to state governments. Some states chose to withhold monies from the poor to instead fund, say, marriage workshops attended by middle-class people, in the interest of promoting family values that were surely the cure for poverty.

In 1994, California created a costly electronic fingerprinting system for welfare recipients. It was unnecessary and would lose more money in surveillance than it gained in busting fraud, experts warned, but lawmakers were more interested in sending a message than in saving money.

The poor heard that message, loud and clear, across the country. For the next two decades, the number of people on welfare plummeted, even as need for assistance did not.

When I was an adult, the Kansas legislature passed a law forbidding using cash assistance to buy tickets for ocean cruises, as though poor people are notorious for spending weeks in the Bahamas on taxpayers' dimes. The same law limited the amount recipients could access as cash; regardless of their total monthly allotment, they could take out only $25 at a time via an ATM. It was a needless measure that benefited private banks contracting with the state, since every card swipe racked up a fee. Where once poverty was merely shamed, over the course of my life it was increasingly monetized to benefit the rich — interest, late fees, and court fines siphoned from the financially destitute into big bank coffers.

Meanwhile, Americans in the late twentieth century clung to the economic promise that reward would find those who worked hard. Society told us that someone in a bad financial situation must be a bad person — lazy, maybe, or lacking good judgment.

"Get a job," Grandma would say when we saw a homeless man with a cardboard sign at a Wichita intersection.

If your life was a mess, we thought, you brought it on yourself. You got what you had coming to you. We didn't buy excuses. Either you had your act together or you didn't.

My family didn't have its act together, of course, but then plenty of middle- and upper-class families didn't either. The difference was that we stood to pay more for our errors than did wealthier Americans who made the same mistakes.

If you work every day and still can't afford what you need, is it worse to steal a little from a big store owned by billionaires than to be a billionaire who underpays his employees? Is it worse to do business under the table with a couple hundred bucks than to keep millions of dollars in an offshore bank? Is a poor alcoholic worse than a rich one? Is a poor gambler worse than a rich one? Is a poor teenager who gets knocked up more irresponsible than a rich one?

On that last point, as a young girl I gleaned from cultural attitudes that the answer was yes. While it was locally accepted, to some extent, broader society hated the idea of a girl like me getting pregnant. Maybe it was because of the financial repercussions of having a child. But the shaming attitude about what my body might do sure felt personal.

For decades during the first half of the twentieth century, thousands of poor white girls were punitively sterilized by state eugenics programs that later targeted mostly black and Native American girls. Eugenicists said that genetic defects caused poverty and that sexual promiscuity among poor white females would sully the race.

America has an idea that people in poverty make sketchy decisions, but everyone does. The poor just have less room for their errors, which will be laid bare in public for need of help. The teenager's child will eat free school lunch on the taxpayer's dime; the drunk will beg on a sidewalk; the gambler will quickly go into debt and need bailing out.

When Grandma Betty confessed to me that she'd briefly gone on welfare half a century prior, she said it in the tone of a guilty convict.

■ ■ ■ ■

Throughout the 1960s, the decade in which Betty had her children, single mothers in poverty endured unannounced visits by caseworkers who tore through their closets, cabinets, trash cans, laundry baskets for evidence that a man had been there. Protecting the honorable taxpayer from the wily poor was the goal, and agents relished the chance to catch a man in a single mother's bed — essentially, in the government's view, catching a woman red-handed in the cookie jar of American wealth. If they found whiskers in the bathroom sink, the mother lost assistance for being deemed a scammer of the system. Surely the man was "head of the household" and hiding income support from the government, the thinking went.

Welfare rolls had grown quickly during the baby boom after World War II: from nine hundred thousand in 1945, the year my grandma Betty was born, to three million in 1960. Senator Robert Byrd of West Virginia did a highly publicized investigation of supposedly rampant welfare fraud in 1962 — the same year Betty became a sixteen-year-old mother.

With a newborn to feed, Betty saw no

other option. She had left Ray for beating her. Plus, he hadn't gone AWOL just from the Army; he had gone AWOL from fatherhood. Betty already had several years of experience waiting tables and turning frugality into an art form. But she couldn't wait tables and take care of infant Jeannie at the same time. She went on the dole.

"I'm ashamed to say it," she said when she confided in me about the welfare. I can recall only a handful of times she expressed a sense of shame about anything. Like most struggling families I knew, we presented ourselves as having an unassailable pride.

She was on cash assistance only for a few weeks until she had the strength to work again, she told me. She balanced her work schedule with her mom's so that they could trade off on baby duty.

Public condemnation of welfare was not just a poverty problem but a race problem. People of color and poor whites both faced stereotypes of indolence, but no one fared worse in those judgments than black women. During the 1960s, Louisiana passed a law excluding from cash benefits women in common-law marriages or those who had given birth out of wedlock in the last five years, in the process excluding 6,000 families with 22,500 kids. Ninety-five percent of these families were black. In 1965, New York politician Daniel Patrick Moynihan pushed a report attributing societal woes to the divorce rates and out-of-wedlock births among black families and, by extension, household leadership by black women.

Maybe due to the civil rights and women's movements, attitudes toward poor women improved some in the 1970s. Welfare raids on women's homes ended. Richard Nixon counted it as a point of pride that federal funds for food assistance tripled during his presidency.

By the time my mom was newly divorced in a small Wichita apartment with two little kids and no money, though, it was 1989, and President Reagan had just spent two terms demonizing the so-called welfare queens. This was code for the poor black women Moynihan had incriminated, and it suggested that mothers in poverty were to blame for wasteful government spending.

I didn't understand the racist component of the term when I was a kid, though. Sensing that it might apply to the women in my family, I absorbed the piece of the narrative that might someday apply to me: Unwed mothers were clever whores who deserved their poverty.

In 1979, Reagan had built his first presidential campaign around shaming poor, unwed teenage girls the same year that my poor, unwed teenage mother became pregnant with me. Maybe that's why she would be damned if she'd go on welfare even when she qualified those years after her and my dad's divorce. Society's contempt for the poor becomes the poor person's contempt for herself.

For this reason, in many cases, no one loathed the concept of "handouts" more than the people who needed them. In the years I would have had you, I can't think of anything I was worse at than asking for or receiving help.

Matt and I benefited from government programs after we moved to Wichita in 1989: free school lunches, our first-ever health insurance policies, after-school care for Matt — all paid for by the state. Meanwhile, Mom was working her ass off.

She had a string of retail jobs, for which she would leave early in the morning. Matt and I, then in kindergarten and fourth grade, would get ourselves ready for school. We walked north as cars tore along West Street to get there early for the free breakfast Matt got to eat in the cafeteria; I didn't get free breakfast because it was available only for kindergarteners, maybe. Then, the half of the day Matt wasn't in school like me, he'd spend in other poor-kid programs called Head Start or Latchkey.

It wasn't cash assistance, but these were government programs that kept us fed, kept us learning, kept us watched over while our parents worked. That they all centered on a 1920s brick building full of teachers, books, and a few early computers with green screens — the first I had ever seen — was a beautiful thing for a kid like me. What should have been a moment of psychological distress, following the divorce, the move, the change of school and environment, felt for me like entry into a safer and happier place.

The old building had no central air-conditioning. At the sweltering August start of the school year, we all got paper cups full of ice chips to keep cool. The place had been built when West Street was a dirt road and the surrounding area was farmland. Grandma had gone to the same school thirty years earlier. Almost half the students at my new elementary school were black and brown, whereas in Cheney they were almost all white.

The most crucial difference, for me, was that the teacher was nice and didn't seem to care who my parents were or weren't.

She was a funny old white woman named Mrs. Coykendall who didn't mind my hand shooting up for every question she asked.

In the afternoons, a handful of kids got up and left Mrs. Coykendall's classroom. They were going to the basement, which housed something mysterious called the "gifted program." I'd never heard of such a thing but had an idea about what it meant. Every day when they left, I longed to go with them. My whole life thus far had felt like my voice was in my throat about to explode, with no one to hear it, and I trained my sights on anything that had the ring of opportunity.

After school, Matt and I walked back to the apartment with the key Mom had given me. She would still be at work for a couple hours yet, which Matt and I spent watching cartoons on our small television with a tall silver antenna. We raked through cupboards for whatever snacks we could find, divvying up saltines and putting margarine on them to fatten them up. I'd climb onto the countertop to check all the top shelves. Once I found a can of SlimFast powder and made chocolate milk for Matt and me. That lasted until Mom found the can almost empty. SlimFast was expensive, she said, it wasn't for us. If I talked back about it she'd say, "Don't get lippy" or "Don't get cute."

That first Christmas season after the divorce, Mom took a second job as a UPS delivery driver. She put on the brown uniform, with its padded winter coat and work gloves, and threw her small frame against heavy boxes to get them in and out of the big truck she drove across Wichita early mornings and weekends. Her body was covered in bruises and ached in the morning. But it was good money, lots of overtime with all the holiday gifts to deliver. She'd be able to pay the bills and put Christmas presents on layaway.

Mom fixed dinner for Matt and me in her apartment, ate little herself, and sat on the balcony. Her cigarette was a small point of fire in the darkness while Carole King or Carly Simon sang from the tape player.

"It's too late, baby," Carole sang.

"This song perfectly describes your dad and me," Mom said between drags, so I tried to understand every word.

I considered the lyrics and told her it confirmed that I was living a "dysfunctional childhood," which was a term I'd recently picked up.

"You haven't the foggiest," Mom said.

"What do you mean?" I asked.

"You don't know the first thing about dysfunctional," she said, a variation on which I'd heard countless times from her side of my family. It maddened me with the implication that I was too young to understand, but I felt in their voices a truth: that their lives had been built on a foundation of chaos, violence, abuse, addiction, and wildness even more extreme than what I had witnessed.

Such was the progress of generations: Mom might slap me in the face and call me a bitch, say, but she wouldn't whip me with a switch. Like many children in bad situations, I often heard how good I had it. If you learn anything in an environment in which you're expected to be grateful someone fed you — as the poor are supposed to be humbled by their government's grand welfare gesture — it's that somewhere, someone has it worse, and you dare not complain.

I can't say the torment inside my mother was all to do with our economic struggle, because I know some better-off daughters endure it, too. But it heightened my awareness of whether I had a right to take up space, and that allowed me to notice when an entire society said I didn't for reasons that had everything to do with class. When

Mom used to say, "Stop breathing," it wasn't all that different from the words I read and heard directed at my people from time to time: "Stop breeding."

Ideas about the feeble-minded or dangerously primitive poor white found their way to me at the end of the twentieth century, whether it was things my friends' parents said or popular culture, like the movie *Deliverance*. I thus knew my existence to be resented on some level by both the young woman who gave birth to me and the society that was shaping me.

The resented existence is painful. It is dangerous, too, whether it's your sense of self-worth or your reproductive organs at stake. It took a lot of energy to defend myself on all those levels. It made every day feel like I was standing against something that I wouldn't abide.

All those wrong messages pierced and hurt me, but they didn't go to my core. If you had been born into this world, you would have felt that hurt, too. But as a spirit you were untroubled as the truth itself. I think that's the only way I survived like I did: having a voice inside me that I could trust to protect me, and that I could protect in kind. Class, like race and all the other ways we divide ourselves up to make life miserable, is what I'd later learn is a "social construct." That's what my family calls bullshit, and there are places in a person that bullshit can't touch.

Mom was forever getting pulled over for a busted taillight or expired tags she couldn't afford to replace. As the familiar red lights flashed in the mirrors and Mom went into business mode, Matt and I would sit frozen in the seats. Often, I traded promises with God: If I held my breath or held completely still, Mom wouldn't get a ticket, which I knew she couldn't pay. A few miles away, Dad was dodging citations pinned against the Kansas wind by windshield wipers of a busted car he'd left near an apartment dumpster, lacking money to pay for it to be towed to a scrap yard.

Increasingly, at that late-twentieth-century moment in America, counties and municipalities were turning to income from minor infractions to pay the bills that state or federal funding had covered before the severe government budget cuts that carved my childhood. My class was the prime source for those dollars, many of us ending up in county jails unable to pay mounting fines in veritable debtor prisons. This profit-driven criminalization of poverty disproportionately harmed people of color, whose very lives were endangered by brushes with law enforcement.

Just about every grown-up I knew had spent a night in jail at some point for a DUI and then worked extra hours to pay for a "diversion," the county's removal of the infraction from your record for a fee, which was often essential for keeping or getting a job, a loan, an apartment, or some other approval that hinged on a clean record. As I felt myself a burden to my family, my family must have felt itself a burden to society. When they did everything right, there was little reward, but one late utility payment and the bill collectors or patrol cars were on their ass.

"Everything I done was wrong," Grandma Betty recalled once about her father's abuse, and that's how being poor felt out on the streets where we intersected with society and its rules, the following of which often required money we didn't have.

We understood that all the ways we could mess up came with assured financial costs. "Don't act like a knothead or you'll end up in jail," people would say to drunk men leaving our family parties in an angry huff. The main concern wasn't killing themselves or someone else in an accident but posting bail and paying court fines, not to mention the hit on a criminal record that might cost you a job. "Don't be stupid or you'll end up pregnant," people told the teenage girls in my family. Beyond the moral shame I might have felt as an unmarried Catholic girl, my greater dread was the financial burden and hindrance to my own goals that you would have represented.

In that space where social mores and economic outcomes blurred together, we pointed out all that could go wrong and fixated on perceived failures. There wasn't much room left for pointing out the good in a person. A quiet pat on the shoulder from my grandpa after I helped move cattle from the pasture to the corral over a weekend was enough to make me turn red in the face, uncomfortable with positive attention.

Late one weekend night when I was at the farm with Grandma Betty and Grandpa Arnie, I sat in the living room waiting for Grandma to come out of the bathroom. We were going to some sort of country dance. Grandpa had on his good boots, scratchy dark jeans, a bolo tie, and a gray felt cowboy hat with a little feather in it. The smell of his cologne and his whiskey and Coke filled the room.

We were watching *Hee Haw* reruns, which

I never found funny. But everyone said Grandpa Arnie and his sideburns looked like Roy Clark, and it was fun to watch him crack up at a guy with a banjo who looked just like him. He'd squint his eyes, and his round, bald head would turn red when he let out the deep, sincere laugh that Betty had loved the night they met.

While we waited for Grandma, I don't remember why or how it came up, but Grandpa said to me, "You're pretty dang smart."

"I am?" I asked.

"Why, you're smarter than most thirty-year-olds I know," Grandpa replied, looking straight ahead at *Hee Haw* because the only thing more unthinkable than praising someone was looking at them while you did it. He nodded gravely as if to confirm what he had just said, and I felt a deep pleasure.

It felt something like my first Catholic confession, at St. Rose on the prairie, when I was six years old. I messed up by saying "Forgive me, Lord, for I have sinned," rather than "Forgive me, Father" — telling in that it was always God I talked to, and I would end up leaving that religion over its claims that I needed a man in a robe as a conduit to heaven. But the Church's teachings hung heavily enough on me that, when

I left St. Rose that spring day, I skipped down the steps. I looked across the two-lane road at the open field and felt a lightness I can't remember feeling since — such freedom, such absolution, true ecstasy.

Beneath the frame of mind where badness was an assumed default by way of cultural, political, and domestic cues, somehow I maintained a layer of psychological, maybe spiritual strata that insisted I was good, even that I deserved to be seen and heard in a manner no person I knew had ever been. I was a little girl on a warpath of accomplishment, public school the battleground. When a teacher, a television show, my mother, and anyone else said something to diminish me, I knew they were wrong.

But a knowing does little to improve your life if no one else shares it. Grandpa Arnie saying I was intelligent both validated and absolved me, suggesting I was less of a burden to the world and perhaps even had something to give it.

After I had been at my new school for a month or two, Mrs. Coykendall said she'd noticed how well I did in the classroom. The school psychologist would be doing some tests with me, she said. I was used to Grandma Betty telling me about interrogations of suspects on the witness stand at the courthouse. It had never occurred to me that a person might be examined for the purpose of measuring their strengths.

A few days later, someone gave me a report in a folder to take home to Mom. I pulled it out to read it for myself first. It listed results, numbers, percentiles, qualitative assessments in the psychologist's own words. She described me as something excellent. I read it over and over and cried. The next time a handful of children stood up to leave homeroom class for the gifted program, I stood up and went with them.

The basement of OK Elementary was a strange, amazing world. There were two rooms with cement floors: a snug classroom of ten or twelve desks and a large open space. It held artwork, a reading loft with a wooden ladder the teacher had hammered together himself and filled with books and beanbags, a small stage, shuffleboard numbers painted on the floor, and a piano.

The man behind it all, Mr. Cheatham, had red cheeks and a graying walrus mustache. He taught math at the chalkboard with palpable joy. He tested our knowledge of constellations by poking holes into a sheet and shining a flashlight through them. He wrote plays for us to perform on public television, and guided us through production of a "magazine" — our original stories, puns, and artwork, printed from green-screen Apple computers and held together by brass binder clips. He submitted a story I wrote to a national children's magazine and, when they published it as an illustrated spread, he bought me a copy of the issue. He thought I was funny. Soon the other kids did, too. It was the first time that creative side of me had been deeply acknowledged, and I felt a surge of energy from it that I now know to call joy.

Grandma Betty, who had hated school and distrusted the institution in general, was less sure about this turn of events. At the farm over Christmas break, when I told some family members visiting from Denver that I'd been placed in the gifted program, she uncharacteristically snapped at me.

"Sarah, don't *brag*," she said, and my face went hot and red.

We were in a world, I see now, where going on welfare as a teenage mom or receiving accolades for your academic work had the same outcome: admonishment to keep you in your place. One was an offense to taxpayers who were supposedly pulling your weight; the other, an offense to grandmothers who had left school in tenth grade and were averse to anyone thinking herself too good for where she came from.

Grandma was right: I did think I was too good for the environment I'd been born into. But I thought she was, too. I thought everyone was. So my intention was to get as much attention as possible. Not because I reveled in it — I was a quiet loner, most often — but because I knew that was the only way I'd ever receive the chances I wanted.

Sensing that mission was up to me alone, as the American Dream will tell a poor child, my ability to do the right thing rather than the wrong one hung on my shoulders. On the cusp of adolescence, amid a family of people who had been marginalized as "troublemakers" at schools, jobs, and dirt-road beer parties broken up by county sheriffs, I would need to take extra care to show that I was a good kid.

From where I sit now, I can and must look at those years as a time that fortified and defined me in ways for which I am grateful. But I thank God you never had to fight such a battle — a child required to prove her worth to the richest economy in the world.

In the mornings when Grandpa Arnie went to the shed wearing stained jeans and plaid shirts, Grandma Betty went to Wichita wearing baggy pantsuits from Kmart clearance racks and earrings that turned her earlobes black from the cheap metal in the posts. I tagged along with her at the downtown Sedgwick County courthouse many summer days. My parents were working, babysitters were expensive, and the courthouse was so big I could scram without getting Grandma into trouble.

I followed her through the doors of the severe eleven-story 1970s building, to my Kansas eyes a skyscraper. I hurried to keep up with her fast step, feeling proud as her high heels clacked on the marble floor of the lobby. Attorneys, who were usually white, gave her waves. Security guards, who were usually black, gave her high fives.

"Let's take the stairs," she'd say, "for the exercise." We'd huff up the echoing stairwell to her office. When she was running late, we'd take the elevator. If it was empty, she'd get in a few Jane Fonda–style stretches and I'd copy, touching my toes, then my shoulders, then the sky. People couldn't believe how much energy Grandma had. She was in her forties and vivacious — an uncommon feat among people like us with lives that could age you quickly.

Sometimes we shared the elevator with

men in handcuffs on their way to trial or back to jail. Other times it stopped and with a ding the doors parted to reveal the new district attorney, Nola Foulston — the first woman ever to hold that job — dazzling in shoulder pads and big earrings.

"She's full of herself," Grandma would say. "Only wants to be on camera." In that place and time, even strong women like Grandma Betty absorbed a culture in which ambitious women were suspect.

That's one bit of trouble I don't think I would have passed on to you, perhaps simply because my generation got better messages about women than Grandma's did. The district attorney didn't seem full of herself to me. She seemed like a hero who, like Grandma Betty, had devoted her life to helping society. She did end up on TV a lot. In decades to come, she'd prosecute a Wichita serial killer and the man who murdered abortion provider George Tiller.

But, while Foulston's job was to prosecute, Betty's job was to rehabilitate the newly freed. She did it by drawing on what she knew from her own life about the difference between a reason and an excuse.

"I had them tell me that they came from this dysfunctional family — I couldn't understand none of it, because I'd had it easy," Betty remembered years later. She was unimpressed when probationers blamed their rapes, cocaine deals, and first-degree murders on their childhoods while assuming someone like her came from an easier place.

"I just told 'em, hey, don't give me any bullshit about 'dysfunctional family,' honey — our family invented it," she told me. "I'd have people come back later that had got off probation, or I'd run into somebody in the store. They'd say, 'Thanks for being such a tough bitch.' 'My pleasure,' I'd tell 'em."

From the same source of that tough love arose an ability to see a so-called criminal's humanity, though, to not be afraid of the people society most villainizes. All those years, our home address was public record. I asked Betty why, years later. She said it never occurred to her that one of her probationers would try to hurt her.

If she had carried that sort of fear, she would have had to be afraid of her own flesh and blood. Most grown-ups I knew had at least a misdemeanor on their records, but my criminal lineage ran even deeper than that. Mom's biological father, Ray, had been a hired criminal for much of his life, according to family talk — beating and threatening people, burglarizing, even bombing a local business. Betty had spent her youth helping protect him from the law, refusing to talk to the police. His last words to my mom, just before they were estranged when she was fourteen: "Stay out of the pen."

Those summer days when school was out and I went to work with Grandma, we'd pass the barred entrance to the county jail in a basement hallway near the elevator shaft.

"Be good," she'd say. "You don't want to end up in there."

Was I a good kid or a bad kid? The answer to that question, I knew from both Catholicism and capitalism, would decide my fate. Heaven or hell. Wealth or poverty. Freedom or prison.

In Grandma's office, there was a chair for visiting probationers and a big window looking out over windy downtown with its short skyline, a mix of nineteenth-century warehouses and midcentury angles. On the wall hung a framed certificate from a small local business college, which she had attended with a federal grant when she was in her thirties, along with little wooden plaques of cute drawings and goofy phrases: "Quiet, genius at work!" A file cabinet was topped with nickel items I had picked out for her when she gave me a quarter to spend at the garage sales she liked to hit over her lunch break: ceramic kittens, plastic birds hovering atop wires soldered to a metal base. On her desk, a typewriter that, over the years, became a clunky word processor and, then, a green-screen computer with access to criminal files throughout the county and beyond.

Sometimes Grandma would leave me in her office when she had business elsewhere in the building. To keep me busy, she'd suggest I pore over her paper caseload files. I was seven, eight, nine years old paging through grisly police reports about homicides and bestiality.

I look back on that formative experience with some gratitude — I knew a lot about the world at a young age, and I have a feeling that helped me more than it hurt — but that's the sort of thing I would have shielded you from where my family didn't shield me. It's funny how often we would protect something precious in a different way than we would protect ourselves.

When Grandma was out of her office, attorneys stopped by, and I took down notes like a miniature secretary. Sometimes, she sent me around the building like a messenger, running up and down the halls with files to be delivered to stern women who looked down at me from the other side of their counters and raised their eyebrows. I got to be famous around the place. At the courthouse, I was "Betty's granddaughter" the way I was "Nick Smarsh's girl" when I worked the wheat harvest in the country.

Judge Watson's chambers could be reached through Betty's office. Smoking recently had been banned in the building, but cigar smoke wafted from beneath his door. "Judge," as Grandma and his court reporter in the next office over called him, was the first African American to sit on the Sedgwick County bench. He was an ancient man who had been a judge for a thousand years and whose grandmother, he said, had been a slave in the South. He would smoke a cigar if he damn well pleased.

That meant that Betty got to sneak a smoke, too. When big-shot, white male attorneys charged through the office, Betty and Judge would exchange looks. After the white men had left, Grandma would flick cigarettes over Judge Watson's ashtray of cigar butts while he threw back his head and laughed through the tobacco phlegm in his chest, his long, wet, black curls falling past his collar.

"You can come listen, Lou," Grandma would say before a hearing. "This ought to be a good one."

I'd set down a probationer's cocaine-possession file I was reading, leave Grandma's office, and enter the courtroom through the public entrance. From a bench like the polished-oak pews of churches, I'd watch the court stenographer and Grandma, her blond bob and frosted lipstick shining in fluorescent light, walk in through the bench entrance, followed by Judge Watson in his black robe. Grandma would wink at me from her raised seat next to Judge while I wrote down my observations of the defendant and arguments. The courtroom reminded me of *Night Court,* a TV show that Grandma watched before bedtime. Sometimes television news crews showed up.

Judge had a reputation as a hard one who handed down merciless sentences. This had earned him an unfortunate nickname from defendants: "Hang 'em High Watson." If a lawyer or defendant got lippy with him, he'd say something witty in return to shut him up. Grandma would lower her head to cover a smile. Later I'd sit at her office typewriter and type up my "report" on district court letterhead and present it for her review.

I had to leave Grandma Betty's office

when probationers showed up for their mandatory check-ins. While I waited in the lobby outside the frosted privacy glass, convicted murderers, drug dealers, and sex offenders walked past me, their shoulders slumped and their feet dragging, into Grandma's office to tell her why they hadn't shown up for addiction treatment or behavioral counseling. Her office was a triage unit of sorts for the government's "war on drugs," the racist implementation of which arrested, convicted, and imprisoned black people at wildly disproportionate rates.

Sometimes while she counseled probationers, I'd take the elevator to the top floor and, with markers shoved in my pockets, climb a ladder in the empty stairwell to the roof hatch high above Wichita. I'd dangle from the top of the ladder and cover the walls of the building's highest ceiling with the logos of my favorite sports teams. But other times I'd eavesdrop through the frosted glass.

Grandma Betty wasn't well-read on policies or politics. Unlike Mom, who read the news, Grandma only took the paper for the Wednesday grocery ads and the Sunday classifieds telling us where the garage sales were. But, as with so many people in our community, she knew more about the system she worked in than a criminal justice professor at Harvard might.

She claimed to take the hard-punishment stance that both political parties were pushing then. But, as often happens when you're of a class that isn't groomed and formally educated to be a political creature, her behavior revealed a different perspective than her words. Through the frosted glass, I'd hear the men talk about their struggles. Then I'd hear Grandma's voice — firm but tender, for all her big talk. I'd hear the men laugh and cry. When they walked out, they stood a little straighter, as though someone had treated them like human beings.

Betty's empathy had been earned with a lifetime of sorry situations over which she had no control. Violent offenders didn't impress a woman with her past, which reached across years of violent husbands to a violent dad. Her eyes went distant when she told me how, when she was five, Aaron and Dorothy were hammering together the little house where Betty spent most of her childhood. He told her to pick up nails in the yard.

"I don't want to see a single nail when I come back out here," he told her. When he scanned the yard, he said she missed one.

"I got my ass reamed," she told me. "Aaron would just snatch hold of you. Mom would try to stop him, but then she'd get it herself." He used a switch or a strap on the kids and his fists on Dorothy.

That sort of upbringing can send you in different directions, depending on your disposition. Betty's older brother Carl became quiet and shy to avoid conflict. Betty turned into a fighter, even as a child. She liked to tell stories about how, as a kid, she took on someone who deserved it. When the neighbor children pinned a litter of kittens to a clothesline, for instance, she beat every one of them senseless until their mom came to the door threatening to call the cops.

"I was ready to whoop on her, too," Grandma told me.

When a rich girl made fun of her new poodle skirt for being too long, she knocked her down the school steps with her clipboard and was suspended for three days. For getting thrown out of school, she got her first beating with fists to the face from Aaron. The punishment was just an excuse for his anger, Grandma told me. Her dad couldn't have cared less about school. Betty didn't care that she'd been kicked out, either.

"Best three days of my life," Grandma told me.

One of her proudest confrontations involved Dorothy's third husband, Joe, a Boeing worker she married after sixteen violent years with Aaron and a brief marriage to a line cook named Paul, who never hit her. ("He was a pussy," Dorothy would later say.)

Betty was a teenager when her mom married Joe, and she loathed him.

"He was the kind of person who would eat right in front of you and not offer a bite of it," Betty said, like nothing could irk her more.

One night Joe called Dorothy a goddamned pig, which he did most nights, and Betty came out of her bedroom and told him to leave. When he didn't, she picked up a cast-iron skillet on the stove, still full of grease from dinner.

"I slung that son of a bitch as hard as I could, and it knocked his ass down," Grandma Betty told me. "I bet he seen stars."

Joe was lying on the kitchen floor with his head bleeding. Grease had splattered across the fresh wallpaper that Dorothy had just hung, which Betty remembered like it was the main regret.

At first Dorothy thought Betty had killed Joe, but he managed to stumble out the back door and collapse again. Betty picked up a broom leaning against the doorframe and beat him with the handle for good measure.

"Mom was screaming, 'Let him go, let him go, you're gonna kill him!' " Betty said. "I told her, 'That's what he deserves.' "

Violence like that is passed down from parent to child just like poverty and so many things. The current that moved through Betty when she beat her drunk stepdad could have been passed to you. But you might have received a sad gift along with it. What she and so many poor Americans lost in safety, lawfulness, and peace, some of us gained in compassion.

"Get a job," Grandma would murmur about homeless people holding signs at Wichita stoplights under highway on-ramps. Then she would start cranking her window down.

"Lou, find Grandma's purse, please," she'd say. "Hand me my wallet."

I didn't know it, but I was the only female in my family who didn't have a violent or absent father. I'd like to think you wouldn't have had one, either, because having a kind dad let me expect kindness in a man. Not so for the women around me: Grandma Betty and Aunt Pud had vicious, drunken Aaron. Their little sister, my aunt Polly, had vicious, drunken Joe, the one Betty beat with a skillet. My mom had Ray, a man who by several accounts had killed people. My cousin Candy: a Colorado man she didn't know. My cousin Shelly: a quiet Navy man who fled the responsibility of a child.

My dad had more than a few moments with the bottle. But usually when he was gone, it was to work a job, and his love was almost always apparent. Once, before their divorce, Mom was tired of him being the nice guy and told him he had to spank me. He did it so softly it didn't hurt, yet he felt so bad about it he cried anyway.

But those years after the divorce and his chemical poisoning on the job, circumstances took their toll on Dad mentally. He wasn't himself.

The summer we sold our place in the country, the house he'd built and planned to live in for life, he decided to take Matt and me north across Kansas and Nebraska to the Black Hills of South Dakota. We'd had few family trips to speak of. As a baby, I'd gone with my parents and grandparents on the long drive to a horse-racing track in

New Mexico. When Matt was a toddler, Mom and Dad had driven us three hours north to an amusement park in Kansas City. This was the closest thing we'd ever had to a vacation, though.

Dad cleared out some tools and covered the metal floor of his work van with a large rug. Matt and I wrestled and rolled on it while he drove along highways that made straight lines through expanses of Nebraska corn. We stopped at midcentury roadside attractions such as a jungle gym made of painted concrete dinosaurs. Dad took pictures with a 110mm camera of Matt and me dangling from them in neon shorts and dirty canvas shoes.

He seemed like he was doing something to try to make us all happy. He did not have a happy feeling about him, though. The man into whose arms I used to jump when he got back from the fields, when we all lived in the country together, was more distant in those years after such a string of hard times: the total loss of his work barn and machinery, a harrowing roofing job at a factory, near-fatal poisoning on another job, his father's death, divorce, sale of the house he'd built — all in less than two years.

As we curved along the sides of South Dakota's small mountains, the highest place

I'd ever been, Dad was even quieter than usual, staring past the cliffs in a way that frightened me. I looked over the edge of the road down into the deep ravines and held my breath. I told God that if he would please keep us from falling off the mountain, I would hold my breath until it was painful, over and over until we got home, which I did.

After we shivered, underdressed, at windy Mount Rushmore, Matt and I waited in the van while Dad gambled at a casino in Rapid City. He said he'd just be a minute, but the sun went down. Stars came out. We shivered again and I stared at the casino door, filled with worry and rage.

That night we had a hard time finding a room in the touristy area. Finally, we saw a place with the VACANCY sign lit up. Inside, the man at the desk said they had a room.

"Thank God," I said with a sigh. "We're desperate."

The price he quoted was too high, Dad said, and the man at the desk wouldn't budge. When we got back to the van, Dad told me to keep my mouth shut from now on. He couldn't bargain a lower price if someone knew we were hard up for a room.

The next day, in some little town in the Badlands, Dad sprang for ice-cream cones.

My scoop fell off the cone onto the sidewalk, and I cried at the loss of it and at having wasted Dad's money. Dad said to stop crying and brought his closed fist down on the top of my head. I fell against the van holding my head. My skull ached.

Worse than the bump swelling up on my head was the betrayal I felt in my heart. My whole life, Dad had been the parent who was never mean. He had found a way to not put his anger on his children almost every moment of their lives. How could he have done what he did that chilly day in South Dakota?

The responsibility for our actions is ours and ours alone, I had been taught. But I see now that my dad changed under the pressure of his situation. I would watch his spirit flicker over the years as his economic situation fluctuated.

Not long after we moved to Wichita, a friendly, nervous woman with big, teased blond hair appeared at Dad's apartment. I sized her up to determine the nature of their relationship.

"I found a G-string in Dad's bed," I told her, lying.

"Oh my God, I am so sorry!" she said, covering her mouth.

Chris had recently been in a bad car wreck that messed up her back. She'd been prescribed painkillers but still had a lot of pain. She took them every day. In fact, she had been addicted to opioids since a Wichita doctor prescribed them for menstrual cramps when she was nineteen.

I didn't know it back then, of course. She was highly functional — maintaining an immaculate home, making and crossing off to-do lists, always helping a friend. She laughed a lot and had generous compliments for everyone, including me. Like Mom, she smoked a lot of Marlboros, but hers were reds, not lights. Unlike Mom, she drank a lot of beer on the weekends. She liked that red, too, mixed with Clamato and a shot of vodka.

Dad and Chris got married at the courthouse in the spring of 1991, when I was ten, and moved into a ranch house on a modest but well-kept street on the west side of Wichita. During the week, Chris operated a children's daycare service out of the house while Dad worked construction. On weekends, when Matt and I were there, Chris obsessively cleaned and organized the house while Dad fixed door hinges or spread bills across the kitchen table and dialed customer service numbers.

It was a warm, happy enough place. But Dad and Chris, like the rest of the adults in my family, couldn't get through a weekend without getting plowed. Usually, it was easy enough to steer clear of their house parties and loud, drunk friends. During a rare trip out of town, though, when they drove Matt and me east into the Ozarks to the tourist town of Branson, Missouri, I couldn't escape on my bicycle.

One night during our stay, Chris, drunk next to our motel's outdoor pool, snuck up behind me while I was fully clothed, looking at the sky and thinking. She pushed me into the pool with a hard shove. Something about the shove didn't seem playful to me. Out of instinct, I grabbed her head and pulled her in with me.

I had never been one to hit anybody. I was generally devastated by the thought of hurting someone's feelings, let alone their bodies. But, when Chris and I came up for air from the glowing water that smelled of chlorine, our summer clothes clinging to our skin, I clubbed her in the face with my fist.

I climbed out of the pool and took Matt, who was crying, back to the motel room. As go all such stories that are worth telling where I'm from, she never pushed me again.

Meanwhile, the time Matt and I waited for Dad outside a Rapid City casino turned out to be part of a bigger problem. Dad now had a regular gambling habit. When he was done with his weekend chores and repairs around his and Chris's house, he drove Matt and me in his work van to the Wichita Greyhound Park between fields on a highway at the northern outskirts of town. Dad would park at the back of the big parking lot, even if there were plenty of open spots near the entrance, so that it would cause less of a scene if the engine didn't start back up and the van needed to be towed. He would become focused, like Great-Grandma Dorothy did at a bingo parlor — like he needed to pay close attention and pray in order to get what he'd come for.

He directed me and Matt on how to sneak into the dog track, not only to avoid paying our admission but because children weren't allowed inside after certain hours. He'd distract the ticket lady while we ran ahead. We needed little instruction, already experienced in sneaking into movie theaters any summer afternoon we pleased. Sometimes he told us to wait in the car while he collected earnings from a recent win, which were always less than recent losses. He'd end up placing a few more bets, and then a few more. Grandma Betty, who often bailed her mother out of gambling-related debt, said it was silly to hand someone your hard-earned money like that. I agreed.

Matt and I spent hours outside the track racing each other to yellow lines on the black asphalt, or tossing a baseball back and forth over tall pickup trucks with the mitts we kept in the back of Dad's van among piles of tools and his hard hat marked Key Construction. When we tired of playing, I'd seethe and rant about Dad's forgetting us, and six-year-old Matt would start to cry.

As for my own bad habits, I had developed a taste for swiping small items from stores. I was only nine, ten, eleven years old but spent afternoons roaming neighborhoods alone. I walked or skateboarded along Central Avenue, four busy lanes that intersected Dad's street, past a big drugstore and the discount grocery called Food 4 Less where we shopped, which we liked to call Food 4 Losers. Sometimes I took Matt along. Wearing a black White Sox baseball hat and a Bart Simpson T-shirt from a garage sale, I'd dangle off busy street bridges over stormwater ditches to make Matt shriek and beg me to stop. I often had with me a pocket full of markers for tagging public walls and fences.

In the eyes of grown-ups, I was a well-behaved, straight-A student at school. I felt so much at stake in my life, in my actions, that even a rebellion — in some young lives an unconscious plea for attention — had to be kept a secret. My bad behavior amounted to taking the things I wanted but couldn't have.

They were small things. I was a sports lover who got dolls as birthday gifts. So, at the drugstore, I slid entire cardboard boxes of baseball cards beneath my jacket. In a short time, I amassed hundreds, maybe thousands, of Donruss and Topps cards. Down the road was a small sports memorabilia store that I lurked in for hours, poring over and stealing whatever small item interested me: a Detroit Lions pennant with Wichita hero Barry Sanders, a Michael Jordan sticker, a George Brett commemorative coin. The person behind the counter barely looked up as I walked out the door. If I had a particularly large haul, I would pay for one thing — say, a bundle of plastic card protectors — to alleviate any suspicions, though a small white girl elicited few in an old man's sports store.

One night, sleeping on the couch at Dad's, while Matt and Dad slept in the bedroom, I was praying as I did every night. It occurred to me that I could not go on talking with God while building a collection of stolen baseball cards. I remembered the time when I was little, before I started school, when I took a gold ring with a purple stone from a display at the mall. Back in Mom's parked car in the parking lot, I presented it to her as a gift. She was mad, and I felt confused. There was the pretty ring, and I wanted Mom to have it, and now I was in trouble.

Now I knew full well what I was doing, but the feeling was no less confusing. On Dad's couch, I promised God that I would stop. I kept on anyway, though.

At the cusp of adolescence, an angry indignation was swelling inside me. I felt compelled to take, to gather things into my arms and claim them as my own. Stealing was wrong, I'd been taught in church and everywhere else, but I had a feeling that the money system was wrong, too. I didn't think the world owed me anything, but it also seemed the world wouldn't give me anything that I didn't reach out and grab for myself. To do so, though, was both a mark of moral failure and something that could ruin my life, if I got caught.

Those are the moments, the struggles, the decisions when I relied on you the most — the vague sense that someone else depended on me, and if I couldn't do right by myself then at least I ought to do right by you.

The first time I heard my voice ring through an auditorium, the first time I felt seen and heard in a big way, involved a contest about drug abuse.

In early 1991, when I was in fifth grade, Mom moved in with her longtime boyfriend, a newspaper humor columnist named Bob, on the far east side of Wichita. Matt and I had to change schools, to my dismay. At OK Elementary, I had friends. I had Mr. Cheatham's fun classroom in the basement. My new school, Minneha, was a harder adjustment. I spent most recesses alone on the playground swing set. Things felt harder at home, too.

Mom was selling residential real estate, which was a good way to make a living without a college degree. There was enough money to buy necessities now, but she didn't notice when I outgrew my clothes. One day, I wore pajama pants to my new school, feeling humiliated because they were sheer enough to see my underwear through them. When I needed a training bra, she bought me only one, which meant I had to wear the same one every day. It was made completely out of lace that irritated my skin and was discolored with playground dirt by the time Mom laundered it once a week.

Bob had a higher income than she did and lived a middle-class life, but to my knowledge she didn't ask him to foot many bills for us kids. I benefited from my nearness to Bob's belongings, and he paid the check when we went out to eat. But, in many ways, having a poor mom who dated a middle-class guy was like living next to a pile of things you need but can't access — which is what it's like to be poor in America.

As I'd done before when life got especially difficult, I did two things: talk to you and work hard in school. I managed to find a couple of girls to eat lunch with, but whereas many of my friends at OK Elementary had also eaten school lunches, it seemed all the kids at Minneha Elementary came with cool lunch boxes full of name-brand, prepackaged food. I was suddenly ashamed to get my free lunch, for which Matt and I still qualified through the state since Mom and Bob weren't married and she filed her taxes separately from his. Most days I didn't go through the line and instead sat hungry at the cafeteria tables, watching as other children opened sandwich bags and packaged snacks. Teachers somehow didn't notice. One boy did and took to giving me bits of his lunch out of a plastic box.

Minneha, a midcentury building with a colder feeling than my last school, had a gifted program, too. The teacher, Ms. Dunn, was a no-nonsense woman who wore a short, curly wig. She had cancer and the treatment made her hair fall out, she explained. One day she took the wig off to show us her scalp. She didn't care what anybody thought, she said, which sparked my admiration. I threw myself into her assignments for the joy of it and for her approval, which was harder won than Mr. Cheatham's.

As the school year wound down, Ms. Dunn announced that it was time to nominate someone for the annual public speaking contest.

It had to be me, I felt, burning for the chance. It had to be me who stood onstage and had her voice heard. The thought of it being someone else felt all wrong, though I'd never given a speech in my life.

This year's theme, Ms. Dunn said, was illegal drugs. As a child of Reagan's "War on Drugs" era, from a family rife with addiction, I took the matter seriously. I had red ribbons in my bedroom from DARE school assemblies funded by the Department of

Justice and the Drug Enforcement Association.

Ms. Dunn shared the name of the event's top judge. It was a name I knew: District Attorney Nola Foulston, the shoulder-padded powerhouse at whom I gazed when I went to work with Grandma Betty. This information fanned my ambition into a four-alarm fire.

I spent the next weekend in the country, at Grandma Teresa's house. Getting there required passing the country home where my immediate family had lived together in one place not so long ago. Just a couple years prior, the parents of one of my Cheney classmates had bought the place, and it annoyed me to think of her in my old bedroom.

Grandma Teresa's house was quieter than ever. Since Grandpa Chic was dead, there was no one smoking while watching the console television in a nubby recliner, making Grandma howl about ashes dropped on the marble carpet. I settled into his old chair to read the latest *Reader's Digest,* among the scant reading material in the house besides a set of 1960s encyclopedias. One feature story, it turned out, was about drugs. It was called "The Devil Within." This struck me as a great phrase, one I understood. I'd watched my family members disappear into their addictions — alcohol, gambling, painkillers, a man's approval — things that felt to me apart from who they were, like an infection.

Inspired, I got out a pencil and notebook and wrote an ominous warning of a speech about the hard drugs described in the magazine story and newspaper articles I'd read. Cocaine, heroin, crack — they were harder drugs than the ones I knew up-close, but I applied to them what I believed about every other vice, which was that they might take you over if you give them an inch. With my speech, I laid the responsibility for avoiding drug addiction squarely where I'd been taught it belonged: yourself.

On a cold, spring morning in 1991, I went over my speech about willpower. I'd been chosen to compete in the contest.

I put on my best outfit, a forest green cotton skirt and a short-sleeved shirt with green and tan stripes. I'd been in school plays but had never had an auditorium of people stare at me alone on a stage. I had recently lost one of my top incisor teeth and was worried about how I looked. I practiced smiling with my lips shut. My chin was still scarred from a sledding accident at the farm the previous winter, when I got tangled in rope and dragged behind a tractor. I put a pair of dangly earrings in my pierced ears and ran over the memorized speech in my head.

The auditorium's foldout metal chairs were filled with families from across the city. Mom, Bob, Dad, Chris, Matt, Grandma Betty, and Grandpa Arnie all showed up, somehow, which made me more nervous than the whole rest of the crowd. They had fought to get off work, which was how I knew this was a big deal.

The other contestants and I had numbers pinned to our shirts. We sat on chairs at the back of the stage facing the audience and were called to the microphone to give our short speeches, one by one. As the other competitors took turns at the microphone, I paid little attention to their speeches, instead going over mine in my head while I looked at the huge crowd. My body shook.

"Sarah Smarsh," the teacher said into the microphone.

I walked to the center of the stage and heard my own voice, deep and grave for my age, through the speakers. The audience applauded. I smiled on my way back to my seat.

After all the speeches were done, while D.A. Foulston huddled with a handful of other judges, I found my family in the audience. They were looking at me, their faces shining with nervous smiles, from a row of chairs toward the back. They never felt comfortable sitting in the front anywhere, especially since they might need to sneak out for a smoke.

Finally, the winners were read.

"And first place goes to —"

I prayed that it would be me. It was.

D.A. Foulston walked onstage to shake my hand. She gave me a certificate and a scientific calculator that, I was told, I'd need next year in middle school. This was a lucky break in a family that would have balked at a $20 school supply. Far more valuable, though, was feeling the whole place clapping for me. I was so happy I forgot about my missing tooth and let a big, unabashed smile cross my face.

I saw my family cheering in the crowd. I'd written a speech with tidy ideas about right and wrong, but no one knew better than they did that those judgments get complicated when the cards are stacked against you. The probationers I watched stream in and out of Grandma Betty's office were overwhelmingly poor and disproportionately people of color. The violence men and sometimes women erupted with was usually

247

born of stress and fear, or of their own parents' violence. Dad's booze and gambling, Mom and Grandma's incessant smoking, and Chris's pills were just as much the result as they were the cause of difficult situations.

As for me, I never got caught stealing or vandalizing. If that hadn't been the case, I might have been branded a "bad kid" and seen the trajectory of my life change. Instead, public school teachers had noticed I was smart — the defining intervention of my life.

Many children from similar places weren't so fortunate, due to the color of their skin or other disadvantages. But a speech about individual triumph and personal willpower beating out massive societal pressures — not unlike the ones that had me fighting against your would-be existence in my arms — is what had won me first place.

I left the stage and walked straight to my family. Matt, who was six years old, was yelling and jumping up and down. Mom had a big smile on her face. Dad and Grandpa's clothes didn't have dirt on them. They all hugged me, laughed, and took pictures. I had no choice but to understand that people can demean and hit you and in their better moments love you, at once be a mess themselves and carry a deep pride in your strange togetherness.

They suffered from weaknesses of character, yes — just like every other person, in every other income bracket. What really put the shame on us wasn't our moral deficit. It was our money deficit.

Chris's addictions got worse over the years, and even as an adult I found myself judging her as a "bad person" for it. A combination of prescription opioids, aspirin, and alcohol eventually burned such a hole through her insides that she had surgery to remove most of her stomach. Having been extremely thin to begin with, her inability to eat almost withered her to death. For years, her behavior was erratic and sometimes put all of our safety at risk. She went on spending sprees, shoplifted, passed out in her parked car. Cops brought her to my dad's door.

I was mad at Chris for what I saw as failing my dad, who was her caretaker and enabler in those years. But something was going on in America that was bigger than Chris, her willpower, or her goodness. Opioid addiction was a national health epidemic on the rise, most deadly and financially devastating within poor populations. It was hard for me to see it that way when it was my aging father's finite energy and hard-earned wages taking care of the problem.

If Chris had failed, what about the systems that failed her? The criminal justice system that, rather than finding her help for a health problem, put her in handcuffs and collected bail. The job market in which her high school diploma diminished in value just as she was acquiring it in the early 1980s, such that her wages couldn't keep up with living costs. The for-profit health-care industry pushing opioid prescriptions that made them rich, like the small-town doctor who prescribed Chris's drugs for years and eventually went to prison.

I sometimes felt ashamed about my proximity to the situation. I used to imagine taking a friend to my dad's house. How would I explain Chris's wild behavior and scrambled language? Could I do it without feeling embarrassed? I hoped the answer was yes. But I'd learned that most people had no idea what to say or do and felt uncomfortable when presented with stories about my family's troubles.

Dad refused to vilify Chris, long before unscrupulous pharmaceutical companies were revealed in the news. Chris had early-onset dementia and brain atrophy, he told me doctors had said. But those likely were symptoms of the problem he wouldn't name. For a man raised as a Catholic farm boy, to call his own wife an "addict" was too much, I guess, even as her substance use disorder and related legal and financial troubles hurt them both. He had made a promise to Chris to stand by her as her husband and he would keep it, he told me. He couldn't leave her like that, he said, when people told him to save himself. He never once complained or said a bad word about her, which is more than I can say for myself or this country that views addiction and so many other systemic problems as personal failures.

After more than twenty-five years of struggle with opioids, Chris got a prescription for methadone, which numbs the addiction. It also rots your teeth — a side effect that surely harmed Chris in the court of public opinion. But, for seven years, she dutifully went to the clinic every morning for her dose — her mind clearing and focusing along the way as she rebuilt her health and her will to live.

In the years after that, by then wearing dentures that were superglued together due to a crack she couldn't afford to fix, Chris maintained her recovery by helping others who struggled as she had. She let broken and addicted people — penniless, jobless, just out of jail — into the house, sometimes at her and my dad's peril. She gave selflessly whatever she could: her time, her encouragement, her understanding. She drove them to work at McDonald's at dawn when their drivers' licenses had been revoked, their cars busted or repossessed. She never judged what they had or hadn't done with their lives.

When I was still a kid, though, Chris was not yet a debilitated addict or a recovered Samaritan. She was a fun, sweet young woman whose economic vulnerabilities were setting her on the hard path that so many Americans would follow into the twenty-first century: too much trouble and not enough help. Along the way, she lost not just money and health but lifelong friends. They were embarrassed by her behavior, angry about what they said she had done to herself.

It was around the time that I first met Chris, those couple post-divorce years when I lived in Wichita in fourth, fifth, sixth grade — my last moment as an unnoticed girl before puberty — that my concept of you came into view.

I would guess that's because those were such pivotal, defining years for me and my trajectory. My life contained a tension between what people think of as two different kinds of life paths. I was old enough to roam the streets unsupervised, at least in my family's eyes, and in those moments I found release by doing things that sent kids in my neighborhood to juvenile detention hall: stealing, vandalizing. I was coming to understand, too, the deep well of violence, substance abuse, and brushes with the law — the generational markers of poverty — within my family and their implications for my own life. Where my earlier childhood years had been lonely and frustrating, my new reality was chaotic and confusing.

I'd gone to three different schools in the span of a year and a half. Both my parents were newly partnered with people who, in some ways, didn't have much business caring for children. My cousin Shelly, who was four years older than I was and who had been forced by the transience of poverty to attend fifteen schools by the time she was in high school, was running around with tough teenage characters. A girl my age was abducted while walking alone in a poor neighborhood not far from where I lived. Her body, raped and strangled, was found in a field.

Life increasingly felt like the courthouse where Grandma worked — dangerous people and innocent victims, with poor people like my family filling both roles. The only thing I did harder than study and read was pray.

I sometimes prayed alone on my knees until they hurt as a sort of sacrifice to a God I'd been taught dealt in trade. My prayers were for my family but also for me in my quest for a better life. That quest, I thought, was threatened by a B on a test at school. "I promise that I will stop stealing baseball cards," I'd pray out loud, "if you will let my report card be all A's."

The American narrative of a poor kid working hard, doing the right thing, and finding success for it is so deep in me, my life story so tempting as potential evidence for that narrative's validity, that I probably sometimes err on the side of conveying a story in which I'm an individual beating the odds with her own determination. There's some truth in that story. But my life is a litany of blessings somehow sewn into my existence rather than accomplishments to my own credit. My awareness of you is one of those.

When deciding my actions, in late childhood, I vaguely felt a new question.

What would I want my daughter to do? Or sometimes it was, *What would I tell my daughter?* Or, *What would I do for my daughter?*

When I heard those questions inside me, I felt an immediate calm and clarity. It felt like when I was small and stumbled onto the trick with the mirror, looking into my own eyes until I felt a little shift behind my forehead and knew myself as a presence beyond that little girl.

But now the child I intended to protect wasn't just myself. Now the child I intended to protect was you.

It was a handy way of reframing my life on the cusp of American adolescence and the angry urges toward self-destruction that can come with it. In certain moments, I could and would fail myself in the struggles ahead. But in those precarious years, even as I was still a child myself, I'd think of you as my responsibility. For some reason, I could be impeccable with that assignment.

You were like the baby farm animals I hovered near at dusk when the coyotes came out, earning Grandpa Arnie's farmer respect as someone who would crouch in the cold to help keep a fragile thing alive. But they had their own mothers, which in some important ways I did not. That void is where

I found you.

Unlike with the piglets, calves, and chicks, no one could take you to auction or grind your flesh in the butchering shed. You were above the markets that defined the lives of farmers and farm animals, beyond the shame a country or a church could assign. You were more real than the girl I saw in my own bedroom mirror — quieter than my uncertain world and somehow holier for being invisible.

5
A House that Needs Shingles

You probably would have lived in a strong, old house, purchased at its most broken moment and fixed with my hands. That's because I learned renovation skills from my own parents, whom I now think of as a sort of god and goddess of houses: Dad was a carpenter who could see the ghost of the people who died in old homes. Mom had an eye for transforming interior spaces and got paid to find a house's next inhabitants.

A construction worker and a poor-neighborhood real estate agent aren't what people think of as artists, but that's what Nick and Jeannie were. Dad could draw a home addition on the side of an envelope with a carpenter's pencil and then make it real with materials salvaged from commercial job sites where he made his hourly wage. Mom could go into an estate sale with a $50 bill and come out with antique light fixtures and hardware to refit an entire neglected home, her effort the difference between the property sitting on the market for six months and selling in two weeks.

I doubt either of them would have worked in that industry if given many other options. Dad didn't read books but had a habit of secretly jotting original poems onto lumber scraps; Mom used the language and humor of an intellectual. Theirs was not a world where natural gifts and interests decide your profession. Dad inherited his craft from his father. Mom was a saleswoman for whom charm was a professional asset and a house was the biggest possible commission. But they both had talents about houses that school can't teach and money can't improve, as well as an appreciation for homes that had been deepened by deprivation.

Like me, over the years they had no choice but to move into and out of the places people see when they picture poverty: trailers with dents in the metal skirting over the wheels, bad apartments with unlit stairwells, houses full of outdated finishes and broken appliances. Sometimes, though, they were able to make a decent and even beautiful home out of something bought or rented cheap, given up on by people with less vision and fewer skills. They taught me everything they could, if only because I was free help.

From Dad: The actual dimensions of a two-by-four (about 1.5 by 3.5 inches). How to angle a hammer to pry a crooked nail without denting the wood. The engineering process that keeps parking lots from flooding when it rains, the relationship between contractors and subcontractors, the politics and corporate influence behind safety standards. The economics of labor unions. The tradesmen who price-gouged (electricians) and the ones who earned every penny (plumbers). How to get all the subcontractors on the same page with a cut-the-bullshit group meeting of hard hats. How far down to bedrock. How to lay a concrete foundation, how to lay brick. How to run every kind of saw, which saws really called for safety goggles and which really did not. How to put up sheetrock, how to mud and sand its seams. How to not inhale or absorb through your hands the tiny, painful particles of fiberglass. How water flows through houses; the hell of a septic tank, of a crawl space. How to stay a foundation, shifting with the silty Kansas soil, with beams against a basement wall. How to make anything level with a shim.

From Mom: How to drive a FOR SALE

sign's metal legs into hard, dry summer earth while wearing high heels. The reliable financial return, via word-of-mouth recommendations, on a $50 house-closing gift for the client. How to make a crappy house look less crappy for a showing. How to deal with idiots. How to operate a mortgage calculator (the handheld sort, before the internet). The terms: mortgage, broker, seller, commission, owner carry, buyer, prequalification, refi, showing, open house, contract pending, under contract, sold, kickbacks, inspections, loan approval, HUD, 30-year conventional. The sort of advertising that was cost-effective (business cards with one's pretty headshot, to be handed out personally) and not (expensive space on bus-stop benches or billboards). How to affect a Business Voice. The names of the three credit-reporting bureaus and the ways they were and were not full of shit about what actually affects one's credit score. Rent was money down the drain. Real estate is the best investment because you have to live somewhere regardless, and there was a federal tax deduction for mortgage interest, to boot. How everything happens for a reason, however mysterious, because inevitably if some poor young couple had their hearts broken when a contract fell through, they'd find a better house the following week. Remember, if something goes sour after the contract has been signed, legally you can make a seller sell, but you can't make a buyer buy. Above all else: In negotiating a purchase price, he who cares the least, wins.

I'm not as good as they were at building, fixing, beautifying, negotiating, designing, drawing up contracts, intimidating bank appraisers. But I've done all those things. There is a good chance you would have been poor in a house that didn't look it.

That mattered to my parents and me because we were sensitive people who thought a house was more than shelter — an expression of yourself, an environment whose colors could affect you almost as much as the weather outside the walls. When my parents were still together and Dad had just finished building our house, Mom painted one wall in the family room a deep, rusty maroon; like a director or a painter with a visual signature, she painted one wall that exact color in every place she lived from then on, even if it was a rental and she wasn't supposed to.

My grandparents were different sorts of people. Chic and Arnie were farmers who appreciated smart, efficient construction but for whom a house was mostly the bathroom, where the straps of overalls were unsnapped to shower after evening chores, and the bedroom, where they slept until dawn at the latest. Betty and Teresa were both rigid, pragmatic women who wanted things clean and functional but didn't have an eye for beauty. I don't know where Nick and Jeannie came from sometimes. But what you inherited about houses would have been mostly because of them.

Their sensitivity wasn't just about spaces but about what a space holds. When they were dating, Dad slept on the couch at Betty and Arnie's farmhouse and left in the middle of the night because of something he saw in the doorway to the dining room, which he never would talk about. In the houses she listed for working-class Wichitans, Mom just had a feeling when the would-be buyers walked through the door. I don't necessarily believe in ghosts or psychic abilities, but I do believe in a person's honest, sometimes unexplainable experience of the world. Like my parents, I've seen too much to ignore those sort of mysteries.

For them, a current of time and meaning ran through every house. Time was marked by different people moving in and out, but the meaning stayed the same: security, safety, stability, structure, home. All the things they valued more for having lacked. All the things they were never quite able to give me.

Once, when she first got her real estate license in the early 1980s, Mom helped push through a loan for a big family of Vietnamese immigrants trying to buy a little house on the south side of Wichita. They were so grateful that they insisted that she and her family come to a celebratory dinner in their new place. They didn't speak fluent English, and my parents definitely didn't speak Vietnamese, but the honor of their invitation was understood at the table. The bit of the American Dream they had obtained involved a bank, where someone whose name they'd never know wore a tie at some desk. But their human connection to the deal was a young woman in high heels walking up their driveway with a talkative blond toddler and a nervous husband wearing snakeskin cowboy boots. The market turns housing into an abstract measure. But there is nothing more personal than a house.

My parents had seen houses the way a doctor has seen a body — reduced to its parts, stripped to its studs, condemned or repaired, cosmetically rearranged, a list of costs someone writes a check for. That might sound like a detached and cold relationship to homes, and for many people in that industry it must be. For us it was the opposite. Dad's blood was inside a wall somewhere, on the beam that he'd cut by running a board through a table saw that nicked his hand. Across town, in another house, probably near train tracks, Mom's heart was in the closing-gift bouquet she gave the young couple who bought the place with a down payment they'd saved by working overtime for five years.

On weekends, I swept up Dad's sawdust and lit candles in strangers' kitchens before Mom's open houses. I understood the construction and the sale. But I absorbed from Nick and Jeannie that houses were less important as economic investments than they were as containers for souls.

In America, meanwhile, the house is the ultimate status symbol, and ownership is a source of economic pride.

That pride is by design. After the American industrial revolution and World War I made the United States a wealthy world power, the government that once enticed people west with false promises of an agricultural paradise would entice people away from the vertical, communal living space of city centers to the "single-family unit" of suburbia.

"The man who owns his own home has a happy sense of security," future president Herbert Hoover said as secretary of commerce during the 1920s. "No man ever worked for or fought for a boardinghouse." That was the thinking behind a national push for homeownership in that money-fattened, postwar moment: The hard work that maintains an orderly country is tied up with ownership of an orderly block. In this way, the American homeowner was envisioned as both a linchpin of the national economy and a steward of civil obedience.

Hoover's campaign tapped local contractors, furnishers, and even Girl Scouts to put on information fairs in thousands of communities across the country, pushing suburban homeownership — a pursuit the government hoped would disperse foreign-born immigrants in congested urban dwellings teeming with potentially subversive ideas.

The federal initiative went bust with the great stock market crash of 1929. The newly unemployed and homeless were forced to live in shantytowns across the country called Hoovervilles. But today, thanks in large part to the private industries that benefit from it, the notion of homeownership in America remains romanticized in culture and encouraged by policy.

While she took many other jobs over the years to make ends meet, Mom maintained the real estate license she had studied for in the 1980s. Her career would track with the national housing boom in the 1990s and early 2000s. She specialized in finding affordable homes and negotiating mortgage tricks for low-income Wichitans with low credit scores. "Real estate" is an idea that connotes wealth in some places, but what Mom sold was a step from poverty toward the middle class.

In the '90s, that was an honorable enough mission. Home values weren't so inflated, and banks approved loans they knew borrowers could repay, if barely. Mom loved to hand house keys to young families moving out of crappy apartments. During the holidays, she led donation collections at her real estate agency and carefully chose gifts for a family referred by a local women's shelter. I helped her wrap and deliver them out of the trunk of her car, which needed new brake pads she couldn't afford.

She never talked about it, and I'd wager she didn't even think about it, but the satisfaction Mom derived from putting people in houses had its origins in her own wildly unstable upbringing. Seeing what she'd seen, if she'd lived in the 1920s, she would have rolled her eyes at Hoover's propaganda about security and homeownership.

About a home, Jeannie was surprisingly sentimental. She saved all manner of keepsakes in tubs for me and you both, without ever telling me she hoped that one day you would exist. About the housing market, though, she was the most cynical of realists. When she had to move for some reason or another — money, divorce, money again — she painted another wall maroon and never looked back.

Transience was my mother's family's way by necessity — in part because of poverty, and in part because of mental illness that went untreated, also a function of poverty. The two decades before I was born were the wildest years.

My great-grandmother's clinically diagnosed schizophrenia flowered around the same time my mom was born, in the early '60s. Dorothy had recently kicked out Joe, the factory worker Betty had beaten with a skillet. She was forty-one and pregnant with his child in her house that had now seen three husbands come and go.

"That was the downfall that pushed her over the edge," Aunt Pud told me about this period, when her mother's third divorce and midlife pregnancy collided. It was around then that Dorothy started getting distant looks in her yellow-green eyes and relocating impulsively with her kids in tow.

Dorothy was pregnant, restless, newly single, and ready to say to hell with the house and Wichita altogether. She had recently visited a distant cousin in rural Oklahoma and decided she liked it there. She would sell the house, where she'd raised her kids for over a decade, which Aaron had long ago signed over to her. She would open a restaurant in Oklahoma with the money.

After the house sold, while Dorothy was busy buying restaurant equipment, she and Betty, Pud, and baby Jeannie stayed down the street with Dorothy's parents, Ed and Irene, whose house would be a landing place for years to come. In December, Dorothy gave birth to a baby girl, Polly. Then she had an explosive fight with her parents and, as planned, headed south for Oklahoma with the growing clan of females — Betty, eighteen; Pud, ten; Jeannie, one; Polly, an infant.

"That's when the caravan started," Pud told me.

In coming years, the tight group would bounce around the center of the country more times than any of them could count. As a young adult piecing it together, I had to dig up yellowed, postmarked letters and court records and make charts on walls just to map the dates and places — let alone what happened when and where, let alone why it might matter to me or to you.

First there was Pond Creek, Oklahoma, just south of the Kansas line. In the winter of 1963, Dorothy rented a building on the highway and opened a truck stop. Dorothy cooked, Betty waitressed, and Pud babysat the little ones whenever their shifts overlapped. At some point, Joe came down from Wichita and started strangling Dorothy — a memory relayed to me in the same nonchalant voice as mundane details about industrial kitchen equipment. To get free, Dorothy grabbed a butcher knife and stabbed Joe in the arm. It ended up being an unfortunate move altogether. The truck-stop restaurant failed, and Dorothy lost all the money from the house sale.

They all went back to Kansas to stay with Ed and Irene again. By the next spring, though, they'd left Wichita again, this time going past Oklahoma to Irving, Texas. They stayed with Carl, Betty's brainy older brother, who had made good as an accountant after he got out of the military. Betty worked as a hostess at Kip's Big Boy hamburger restaurant. Pud was in fifth grade and wanted to play the flute. Dorothy rented one for her, but after two lessons they were on the road again.

They must have had money troubles, because the whole brood left Texas within a few months and returned to Wichita to stay with Ed and Irene yet again. Pud was enrolled at the same elementary school for the third time in a single school year. She was embarrassed, she recalled. She couldn't keep up with the schoolwork because she had missed so much of what the rest of the kids had studied.

Joe still came around hoping to win Dorothy back, but she was having none of it, having sworn off men altogether for being lousy sons of bitches. She said she would never date again, and she didn't. Meanwhile, her paranoia was getting worse.

"She'd go off her trolley," is how Betty would describe it.

Betty was the main target of Dorothy's paranoid accusations. She was going behind her back about this or that, stealing money out of her purse, Dorothy said. In truth, Betty was the one who was trying to help her. She finally committed her mom to the state mental hospital in Larned, Kansas, a little town in the middle of the state.

When Dorothy got out, she decided to stay there to be near her doctors. She must have been stable enough to be released but not so stable that she felt comfortable losing proximity to health-care professionals she trusted, for the moment. She got an apartment near the hospital with Pud and Polly.

That was early 1965. Betty and Jeannie lived near downtown Wichita. Betty was still legally married to Ray but fell for a guy named Johnny, who was also separated from a spouse. Betty told him she was pregnant, even though she wasn't. He left for California to find work and a great life to offer her, he claimed. He wrote love letters nearly every day for two weeks on pulled-apart used envelopes since he couldn't afford to buy paper, let alone a bus ticket for Betty and Jeannie. Betty wrote to her mom and little sisters in the state hospital town:

I don't know where your living but will send this as soon as I get your address. I am still working. Jeannie's Baby Sitter lives across the Street. Thank you Pud for the necklace & the 1.00 & 25 cents for Jean-

271

nie. I like the necklace real well, it's real pretty. I wear it everyday to work. We love & miss you all very much. Johnny is still in Calif. & I called him last night, he'll be coming home Fri, I think. How are you getting along. Any prospects for jobs yet? I will try & get up to see you before I leave, if I can get a way up. John is working in a clothing store & he likes it pretty well. They say you can make a lot in Calif. I'm gona try & save as much as possible for my divorsee, I hope I can swing it.

That spring, Dorothy quit the hospital outpatient treatment in Larned and took Pud and Polly south again. They went back down to the red dirt, to Medford, Oklahoma. No one remembers why. That didn't last long, of course. They rolled back into Wichita just as Betty was itching to roll out.

Johnny had gone back to his wife, and Betty wanted a change of scenery. So the whole bunch of females got in two cars and left town on a whim. Betty drove a Mercury that Dorothy had bought her with money earned at a restaurant in Texas.

"It was the coolest car," Betty told me.

They stopped at a highway intersection.

"I don't know if it was Mom or me, but one of us said, 'Let's go west,' " Betty said.

The Mercury broke down somewhere near Syracuse, Kansas. Betty hoofed it to a mechanic. The repairs would be boo-coo bucks. What were they gonna do with the goddamn Mercury?

"We just left it," Betty said and laughed. She threw her stuff into Dorothy's car and climbed in holding three-year-old Jeannie.

Dorothy's car was running hot when they got to Limon, Colorado, about ninety miles past the state line. They caught a break for a change — it was a minor issue. But Dorothy wanted to stay. She liked the looks of the small highway town where truckers and tourists stopped on their way to the mountains.

"It looked like a ghost town to me," Betty told me.

Betty got a job waiting tables at the Corner Café. Dorothy got a job at the Dairy King on the other end of town. They moved into the Silver Spur Motel while they saved enough for an apartment. The motel was dirty with bugs in the walls and tired truckers in the parking lot.

"It wasn't like what you'd wanna take your friend to," Betty said. "They's scabby. But it was a place to sleep."

That's a feeling I understood sometimes, growing up — that something was good enough for me but would be too embarrassing to share with someone else. Sometimes I didn't even realize there was anything to be embarrassed about.

I'd looked at our farmhouse so long that I didn't even notice the details a visitor saw: the crumbling chimney, the chain-link fence, pans of food on the ground with a dozen cats around them, our well water gurgling yellow from the faucet for a moment before it ran clear. Over the years, many friends had been startled by where I lived — perhaps because I didn't look, act, or speak like their stereotype of poverty.

Like a lot of the women in my family, Betty lived in run-down places but was admired for her appearance — a funny juxtaposition in that America associates poverty with ugliness, or at least uncleanliness, and a well-put-together woman will receive attention opposite that toward her rental with a sagging porch, stained carpet, and brown leak spots in the ceiling. Betty looked quite a bit like Tammy Wynette, with long blond hair in a headband and a beehive, a long, thin face with puffy eyes and frosted lipstick. Men went to the Corner Café hoping she would be their waitress.

"I don't know, I suppose that's where I met Dipshit," she told me.

By "dipshit" she meant the skinny blond guy named Bob who came into the diner and asked her out. Before long, she was pregnant.

She didn't love Bob, but marriage was what you did if you got pregnant, and practically speaking, she'd need help raising the kid. Bob had a steady job as a typesetter for the *Limon Leader.*

But when she neared the chapel on their wedding day, she couldn't bring herself to stop. She kept driving and left him at the altar.

They tried again, and that second time it took. Betty wrote a letter to Dorothy, but it wasn't about a honeymoon. It was about money and addresses. One side effect of poverty is that it's hard to keep addresses and phone numbers straight. As an adult, I used to get frustrated with my dad when his cellphone number changed every few months, since one would get shut off when he couldn't pay the bill and then he'd manage to get another through a new employer or some prepaid deal at Walmart for people with bad credit. Logistics were even harder in the 1960s.

I called Anita, but couldn't get ahold of her so will try later. Bob is working late tonight.

He should be home anytime now. What did you find out at the Dr's office? Anything? Has Joe been giving you a bad time? How is Pud doing in school? How is Polly feeling now? Better I hope. I am trying to write this & watch Badge 714. Did Grandma get the phone Bill yet? If so how much do I owe? Tell her I will pay it just as soon as I get my tax refund. The one for Kansas I had mailed to her address. Because I thought I'd be there. The Colo. One will be mailed here. So when-ever you get the bill let me know. Well I cant think of any more to write about so will close for now. Tell Grandma & Gramp I said hi & to write. Well will see you all later. Love Sis. P.S. Got a letter from Drug Store. They found the check, so will pick it up tomorrow. If there is anymore checks, you'll have to mail some more money Because I've spent the 10.00. Sis.

What letters like that left out was that Bob physically and verbally abused Betty. He was what Jeannie later remembered as "a belt-snapper." Other than Arnie, he was the only one she'd call Dad out of the seven step-fathers she'd eventually have to choose from. Bob never wanted a stepdaughter, though. Once he beat her all the way home with his belt for playing in a sandbox with the neighborhood kids. Betty was used to getting hit herself, but no one had ever hit her kid.

"After a few months of it, I thought, this ain't gonna get it," she told me. "What the deal was, he could accept me but he couldn't accept the kid. And my motto is, you take one, you take both. In my eighth month of pregnancy, I'd had about enough shit from him."

So in the spring of 1966, pregnant and broke, Betty took Jeannie back to Wichita. She got on at a factory called Southwest Grease and Oil. She stood next to a conveyer belt and filled little caps with oil, one after another, that got sent overseas to U.S. soldiers, maybe in Vietnam, who used them to oil their guns.

Soon Dorothy was back in Wichita, too, renting a house on Emporia Street, and Betty and Jeannie moved in to save money. Betty worked right up to the April day she delivered her son. A week later, she was on the factory floor again.

Bob heard about the baby's birth and drove out from Colorado. He managed to get the boy named after him. Betty refused to go back with him, but he persisted, and she finally gave in.

"I can remember goin' home and just fallin' down on the couch absolutely exhausted," Betty said. "Mom cookin' and cleanin' and I laid on my ass, but I think it was mainly because I just had a kid and I just was so wore out. And that's mainly the reason I went back to that fuckin' Bob."

They loaded into Bob's car with four-year-old Jeannie and baby Robert, whom they called Bo, for the long day's drive to Colorado. Once they were on the road, Bob told Betty that the only reason he came to get her was because he wanted his son. Her heart sank to hear the cutting, cruel tone back in his voice now that he had his way.

The next spring, Dorothy sent Pud and Polly from Kansas to stay with Betty and Bob in Limon while she went back to the hospital in Larned.

"For her nerves," Betty said.

Pud was thirteen and hated living under Bob's roof.

"He was an asshole," Aunt Pud said. "Never saw him crack a smile. Everything out of his mouth was hateful." She hated his whole family, especially his mother. She didn't like how Betty acted around them, trying to be proper. Pud went to school with one of Bob's younger brothers and saw the way his family was admired.

"Shit, you would've thought they founded the town, the way they carried on," Pud said.

Betty took a job waiting tables at the Blue Star Grill in the Blue Star motel, which sat next to the highway that would soon become Interstate 70. Sweaty truckers, frying oil, coffee, and good money off mountain-bound tourists. On a smoking break, she wrote her mom at the state mental hospital in Kansas.

Well we moved over the weekend. Sure is nice over there and 1000 times more room. Polly & Jeannie share a room. Pud has one fixed up in the basement. It was quite a job. I've got about 150 loads of wash. Ha Well the kids are all doing fine. I went up and talked to the school board and got Pud back in school. She starts tomorrow. We drove by Nall's Motor Co. & Polly said "That's where my mommie got her car fixed." Polly tells me every day, my mommie is coming out here & get me when she gets out of the hospital. But she is real well ajusted now. Pud is working out here from 5 to 9. She's doing dishes, but business hasn't been to good so she isn't working too hard.

Jeannie dictated a few lines to her great-grandparents Ed and Irene in Wichita. "I like Kansas better than Colorado," she said, and Betty wrote it.

When Dorothy got out of the state hospital, Pud and Polly switched households yet again, leaving Colorado to move back in with her in Kansas. Then, within a few months, Dorothy had another whim and they moved back to Limon.

"It was like living in the circus," Pud told me. "Without the fun."

For the women in my family and their daughters, the constant moving was about staying safe from violent men and finding new ways to pay the bills. Leaving sad places behind, they seized on the promise of new ones. But they knew well enough that tomorrow's promise would end up yesterday's sadness. Unlike women in so many sad stories, they always found a way to leave. But in matters of house and home, they often had nowhere to go, and the same cycles would begin again.

Moving in with her serious, much older boyfriend just over a year after her divorce from my dad presented some challenges for Mom, who was used to running the show around the house. Unlike other men we knew, newspaper columnist Bob had ideas about how things should look. Mom liked things to be elegant and feminine with rich colors. Bob liked things to have hard edges and wild designs in black and white. His house was full of evidence that their life histories didn't match.

He had a collection of subprofessional tennis trophies and a shelf full of art books, biographies of writers, collections of Beat poetry. I'd stare up at the spines, a list of names my sporadic, largely rural education had not introduced to me, and pull them down one by one. He filled the refrigerator with foods labeled "low fat," preposterous in our family of laborers who needed hearty food to get through the day. He kept a weight bench in the basement, unnecessary for the men I knew who lifted things for a living. He had a subscription to something called the *New Yorker,* which Mom liked to tell him he kept on the coffee table just for show. He earned a newspaperman's modest salary, but that stretched pretty far in Wichita.

Bob was well into his forties, eighteen years older than Mom. He had a grown son and teenage twin daughters whose closets contained sweatshirts that read BANANA RE-PUBLIC. They had cool, round wire eyeglasses and curly brown hair. Their mom was Jewish, they told me. I had never before met a Jewish person, that I knew of. My new stepsisters loved to read, write, and draw. They were like me and Mom, I felt, where in our own family we were strange for our creative and intellectual passions. Mom acted fun and patient around the twins, which drove me mad with jealousy.

Bob wanted to spend every weekend staying in and watching rented VHS tapes of Woody Allen movies and French documentaries. He liked things to be just so. Loud noises made him grit his teeth. He listened to public radio, which I'd never heard aside from commodities reports on AM radio. The dull crackle of it made me want to drive knives into my ears in the backseat of his sports car. Mom, who preferred to drive but didn't get to in Bob's car, sat in the passenger seat and made witty comments that delighted Bob. He'd never met a woman like her, he said. She was charming even when she was acting foolish, he said. Mom would roll her eyes and tell him to go read the *New Yorker.*

Bob didn't criticize where we were from directly, but he made his distaste for our side of town one of the running jokes of his column that ran three times a week in the

Wichita Eagle. He liked to razz the west side as backward country bumpkins and trumpet the east side, where he lived, as the only civilized part of town. The town's first Gap had recently opened there. There were nice restaurants, ivied old brick neighborhoods. The west side was highway diners, discount shops, and bingo halls.

Bob did offer plenty of direct criticism on other points, including our behavior. Mom scrunched her eyebrows too often, which would cause wrinkles, he said. Matt and I laughed too loud, he said, at things that weren't even funny. He fretted over stuff I'd never seen a man fret over, like where to hang a picture on a wall. He also praised my artwork, bought cool toys for Matt, and took us to a tennis court, where he patiently taught us both how to serve. For my birthday, he gave me a Paula Abdul cassette tape I'd longed for. Sometimes he was interested in hearing what I had to say. It was hard not to like the guy.

Still, I was distraught living in their house on the east side of town. Matt and I couldn't escape the tension in Bob's house the way Mom could. At her real estate agency, she had made a new best friend — a smart, funny, pretty woman about her age who had survived a hard upbringing and volunteered at the hospital holding rape victims' hands. So far as Mom was concerned, she was one of the few people she ever worked with who knew anything about real life. They started partying together, hard, a rebellion against her second husband. When she was still with Dad, she began to get a taste of the nightlife she'd never had, having married and had babies so young in a remote country place. Now, Bob resented her wild nights on the town. The more he frowned at her partying, the shorter her skirts got.

I knew she was failing me in the process, and I told anyone who would listen. While we were still in the apartment, before we moved in with Bob, two agents from Social Rehabilitative Services knocked on our apartment door to ask Mom questions and look around. They said they were there because the school psychologist asked me about my home life, and I told her my mom was mean to me. Mom had sent them packing and lit into me with rage. Now, as I finished fifth grade, things hadn't improved much.

At the start of that summer of 1991, Grandma Betty and I sat in her little Toyota, parked in the driveway of the tiny house she'd fixed up on Second Street. I'd been telling her how much I hated where I lived.

She listened seriously, like someone who had been miserable as a child and promised herself that when she grew up she'd always believe children who said they were miserable.

"Would you want to stay with me?" she asked.

She meant for good, or as far as "for good" ever counted. The moment recalled when Mom and I visited a ritzy private school, where teachers and staff showed me around. Mom asked whether I wanted to enroll there. The answer inside me was yes, but I said no, and she was relieved; I now know that the cost of tuition was probably more than half of her annual salary. This time, though, again faced with a question whose importance I understood amid the anguish of guilt, I said exactly what I felt: yes.

I don't know why Mom agreed. Maybe it was about money. Maybe it was stress, or a boyfriend who often seemed put upon that she came with two children. Maybe, being so young herself, she deferred to her own mother's suggestion. Dad wasn't consulted and, I imagine, didn't expect to be. In our family, women made the decisions and no one pretended otherwise. In this case, the decision felt to me like it was mine, though

I was just shy of eleven years old.

Being broke has a way of separating families: Unaffordable children put on trains and sent west as farm labor. Divorced dads without gas money stuck across town from their kids. Children driven north to live with an aunt after a hurricane floods a low-lying ward the city didn't tend to.

I didn't know that at the time. I only knew my interpretation of a feeling: My own mother didn't want me.

And I was right, to an extent, in those years. Parents with less money than my mom have made sacrifices to hold on to their children that she wasn't willing to make. What separated her and me was far more than money troubles. It was a wall that a hard life had built in her. But then that hard life had a lot to do with money. She too had been split from her mother as a result of poverty.

The separation that came between you and me was of a quite different sort, but it had to do with our economic class, and in that way I couldn't escape repeating a family cycle even as I broke it.

The incessant relocating that Betty began in the early 1960s wouldn't slow down for a long time, and the worst of it coincided with

Jeannie's grade-school years. She went to four different kindergartens. Her first one was in Limon in the fall of 1967.

Dorothy and Betty had pooled their money from the Blue Star Grill to open their own place, the Frontier, at a major all-night truck stop on the northern edge of town.

All the family letters back and forth across the plains from those years are about money and where people are going to live. In one, written during a 4 a.m. work break at the Frontier, Dorothy wrote to her parents in Kansas after the first snow of the season. It was five degrees outside and cold inside the restaurant kitchen, where she sat down before the breakfast rush.

Guess Betty called you today. Bob told me she did. I ain't talked to her yet since she called. I just ain't got around to call yet. I got up & got Pud & Polly & drove around to find a house to rent. I found 3 but I will probably rent the one I looked at first. It's nice & clean, newly decorated & bigger. Only 10.00 month more than the others. Well there ain't much news around here. We are doing O.K. with our place. Guess we'll keep it another month & see how it goes. Last week our gross sales were

1494.94. They will be about 200.00 less this week counting tomorrow. We only had a little over 300.00 worth of stock when we opened & a lot of our profit first month went back into stock so our profits should show up better this month as we've got about 3 times as much stock as we started with when we opened. I'd like to save enough to come back there & buy another house before too long. But won't know how we'll do for a while yet.

Their truck-stop diner would turn out to be a big success. "A helluva good business," Grandma Betty told me years later. Home life, however, was getting worse.

When Bob hit Betty, it was officially a crime, but there wasn't any use in calling the cops. Domestic violence wasn't taken seriously, and Bob knew everybody in their small Colorado burg on the plains, from the police station to the grocery store. Betty, meanwhile, was a twenty-three-year-old outsider from Wichita, a social challenge likely not helped by her unapologetic wearing of miniskirts and go-go boots.

Betty had left Bob twice before. First, when her gut told her to keep driving past a Colorado wedding chapel. Then, when she drove to Wichita late during her pregnancy with their son. But she finally decided to leave him for good — especially for Jeannie, whom Bob still treated hatefully.

"If it had been just me, I probably could've handled it for a while," Betty told me. "I couldn't even tell you what he would say to her, but I can remember — everything she done was wrong."

Betty left, taking both of the kids with her. She got her own place in Limon and filed for divorce. She was awarded custody of Bo, and Bob got visitation rights.

Before too long, Betty hooked up with a new guy named Johnny, this one tall and broad-shouldered with a crew cut.

"He was kind of back-asswards," Betty remembered.

But he was good to the kids and could help pay the bills, help her get away from Bob and Limon and its gossip. Soon Betty, Johnny, Jeannie, and Bo moved west toward the Rockies. Jeannie started her second kindergarten, in Denver.

Betty's divorce from Bob was final on Valentine's Day. She married Johnny right away. They moved into a house on a hill above a sidewalk in Alameda, a small town outside Denver, which everyone said was haunted. Jeannie had bad dreams there. Noises came out of the basement. Johnny stood at the top of the stairs with a flashlight, peering down the steps, Jeannie remembered.

Back in Limon, Dorothy's mental health was getting bad again. Teenage Pud couldn't stand her mother being off her rocker, so she moved back in with Betty. That was good for Betty since Pud could babysit Jeannie while she and Johnny worked, and Betty never turned down an unhappy family member who wanted to move in, regardless.

Within months, they moved again, up into the mountains. Maybe it was for a job. No one remembers. Jeannie started her third kindergarten, in Colorado Springs.

Next, maybe a couple months later, they moved right back out of the Rockies into a trailer park in Aurora. Jeannie started her fourth kindergarten there in the spring of 1968.

Betty took a factory job. She updated her Wichita grandparents, Ed and Irene, with a letter I later found that was, like all the rest, about money. Funny enough, here I am writing you a letter, of sorts, about the same thing.

When I was a kid, it was Betty who told me that if I had trouble saying something to someone, sit down and put it in a letter. Back then the letters were for another reason — she couldn't afford a phone call. I had some moments like that, too. But Betty was the only person other than me in our family who wanted to plainly say what the hell was going on in the most practical terms.

> Here is a check for the two phone calls I called collect, when I talked to mom, it should pay for it. If it isn't enough let me know & I will send more. I am working now doing factory work, parts for missles (dont know how to spell it).

Johnny had decided he didn't like her working, though, so a week later she was off that job and writing another update to her family.

> Jeannie had her party yesterday & had all her friends over, they all had a big time, was glad to get it over, Bo is growing up too, he gets into everything he can reach. He is really a pill. Johnny is at work. He works everyday of the week. We are trying to get all our bills paid off. But I dont like to see him work everyday. But I guess when we get a couple bills paid off, then we can afford for him to take a day or two off each week. As for me, I was working at

a factory, But I quit, Johnny wanted me to, he said, I should stay home with the kids. But I feel bad about not helping out with the bills. Well I guess everyone is in debt through, so guess I shouldnt feel bad about it. Johnny needs to go to the hospital & have his teeth fixed. They are all real bad, I guess he will go sometime in Dec. & have them all pulled & get dentures. I dont know when I will have my done, I need to do it though. Well I should get busy. It's 10:15 now, Johnny will be home about 4. So better get started on this house & cook dinner, so better close till later.

A week later, Betty was working again, this time because they needed money to move their trailer back to Limon. She waited tables at the Isle-o-Pines Lodge and Motel by the Stream, wedged against a mountain-side on Highway 6.

Mom is still working at the same place, Pud quit school & is going to go to work I guess. Polly is okay. Jeannie get's out of school the 6th of June. Her teacher said she is very smart, she has a real high I.Q. She (the teacher) said she was in the top ten of her class. So that made me pretty happy. Bo is growing real tall & still as blond as ever, He is partly potty trained now. As for me & Johnny, were both okay. We are moving back to Limon for sure. I guess it will be okay once we get there, It's just getting there that's going to hurt, It will cost 125.50 to move the trailer. But I guess were going to buy a lot or acre from his folks, so after we pay for it, we wont have any parking trailer Rent. So guess we'll be better off money wise anyway.

P.S. If you see Aaron, tell him to send Mom some Child Support money for Pud. If I was Mom, I'd have his ass in jail for about 15 yrs back child support!

They wouldn't ever buy an acre from Johnny's parents to park their trailer. Johnny was good to her kids, and he was a hard worker. But one day he punched Betty in the face and broke her jaw.

Her mouth was wired shut when he came to beg her to take him back. She said no. My mom remembered talking to him as he left for the last time.

"I went downstairs and he was sitting in the car and had all his shit in there," Mom said. "He was crying."

Meanwhile, Bob had court-ordered visits with Bo every six weeks. He was still in Limon, involved in a new relationship of his own.

"I think he was running around with her, actually, before we ever split up," Betty said. "At the time, I thought it was her friend that he was jackin' around with. But it turned out it was her. At least, it turned out he married her."

With a new wife, Bob had a complete household to show the courts. Betty was served with papers charging that she was an unfit mother. Bob was suing for custody of Bo. He said that, if she didn't cooperate, he'd not only take Bo, he'd have Jeannie taken away from her, too.

A court-appointed attorney told Betty it wouldn't help her defense that she was gearing up for her third divorce and umpteenth place of residence. She needed to prove to the judge that she could provide a stable home.

So many interactions with society require a permanent address: Car licensing and registration. Insurance applications. A public library card. Voting. The transience of the poor suggests instability, but what it really represents is poverty itself.

Betty's long list of residences wasn't for poor decision making but something like the opposite. She was somehow finding a way to get out every time a situation became too dangerous for her and her children, yet she was all but condemned by circumstance to another dangerous situation.

In court, Bob's attorneys used both her gender and her poverty against her. They shamed her for being single with three ex-husbands in her early twenties and said her numerous past addresses suggested an unstable environment. So the judge awarded custody to a violent man with small-town community standing rather than to a divorced waitress with pro bono counsel.

Betty worried that Jeannie would be taken away, as Bob had threatened. She called her brother, Carl, who had left Texas and was living with his young family in Detroit. He had met his hardworking, no-nonsense wife, Pat, when they were teenagers in Wichita in the 1950s. Pat's childhood home had been even worse off, moneywise. Now they had three kids and a nice little house on a decent street in the Motor City. He was an Army veteran and a clean-cut professional accountant. If Jeannie went there, Betty thought, she'd have a stable home that the courts couldn't argue with.

"I knew that if I signed her over to Carl, I couldn't lose her," Betty told me.

Dorothy raised hell at this idea. She said

she would take Jeannie herself before she let her be sent off to Michigan. But Betty wouldn't have it, knowing how her mom was prone to going off her rocker.

Adoption papers were drawn up in Detroit. Carl didn't finalize the process but had the paperwork in case he needed it. In August 1968, Betty put her six-year-old daughter on a plane. Maybe Carl paid for the ticket. Jeannie took a yellow plastic coin bank shaped like a cat on the flight. She told the nice stewardess its name was Banana. The stewardess took her to the cockpit, where she showed Banana to the pilot. She was buckled into a seat near the front of the plane. It was her first time flying.

In the fall of 1968, Jeannie started first grade in Detroit — her fifth school in five towns in one year.

Like my mother, I came to know firsthand the relationship between place of residence and place of schooling. Attending eight schools by ninth grade taught me that, if you can hold to your center without going crazy, you're the same person wherever you go, even as the scenery changes. That scenery is shaped, in part, by money and class.

If you live in a house that needs shingles,

you will attend a school that needs books, and while sitting in that school's desk you'll struggle to focus because your tooth needs a dentist or your stomach needs food. Teachers, for such children, become mothers; schools become houses; and cafeterias become hearths. It can be brutal, then, to exit a school for what an adult has informed you will be the last time, when that school has been the steadiest place you've ever known.

I remember being at a middle-school teachers' meeting once when I was an adult reporting a news story about public education, and one of the teachers let the others know that a student had been kicked out of her house and was ostensibly homeless.

"So have a little extra compassion today," she said.

I was fortunate to always have a roof over me and at least a couch to sleep on, but cycling through schools as I did, I learned young that friendships, clubs, and activities would go on without me, would forget me, just as a year prior they'd never known I existed. In our obsession with home as a material thing, we forget that primal needs can be met even as the human spirit is hurt. Belonging is, on a psychological level, a primal need, too. It is often denied to the poor.

As a divorced young woman in poverty, Betty never belonged in small-town Colorado, and they let her know it. While Jeannie was trying to belong in her new school in Detroit, Betty was back in Aurora fighting the Arapahoe County courthouse. That's where a judge had given Bob custody of their son. She would fight the decision with an appeal.

Betty got nervous standing in places like that with people in business clothes, truth be told, but she acted confident and insisted on seeing the judge.

"Some attorney was standing there," Betty recalled. "The gal told me I couldn't see him, couldn't see the judge, and this attorney offered to help for next to nothing in pay."

With a new lawyer lined up to appeal the custody ruling, Bo legally assigned to live with his dad in Limon, and Jeannie safe in Detroit, Betty moved back to Kansas. Her divorce from Johnny had come through, and she wouldn't be safe returning to east Colorado.

"Because, I mean, two ex-husbands in one town the size of Limon, it was time to get the hell out of town," she told me.

When court proceedings rolled around, though, after she'd begged for time off work, saved up gas money, and made the long drive from Wichita to Colorado, Bob's attorneys would reschedule dates and times at the last minute. He let her visit the house but tormented her when she was there and told Bo lies about her when she wasn't. It was an unwinnable battle, she came to realize. Somewhere along the way she had what they called a nervous breakdown.

"That was when I went overboard — when I lost him," she remembered. "Because I tried every damn thing that I knew. Ya know, you had to be married, provide a good home and all that crap. He married a schoolteacher. It was his town, he grew up there. So, hell, he had it in the bag. And no matter what I'd have done, I didn't have a rat's ass chance. I flipped my lid. They put me on drugs. Kept me in the nut ward for a couple weeks. And they did counseling."

"Did it help?" I asked.

"Not particularly," she said.

In Michigan, Jeannie was miserable in her new house. Uncle Carl was at work and rarely around; Aunt Pat was a meticulous, perfectionist tyrant, in her eyes; and their three kids acted mean, presumably because they suddenly shared toys and competed for attention with a sibling they never asked for. She lost a baby tooth for the first time there, in the bathroom, wiggling it from her bleeding gum while the other kids yelled, "Pull it, pull it!" She got kicked out of ballet class. She felt like everything and everyone was against her. It wasn't her home.

She was playing on the swing set in the yard when one of her cousins noticed someone had trampled her perfectionist mother's flower bed.

"Look, you broke the flowers," she said to Jeannie. Jeannie didn't know what she was talking about. She ran into the house, afraid she would be in trouble. She hugged Banana, her yellow plastic cat-shaped coin bank. She fed it peanut butter through its little coin slot to comfort it. Then one of the boys had Banana in the yard. He was spraying it with the garden hose, blasting it across the grass. Jeannie cried for him to stop.

"I'd pray every night," Mom told me later, " 'Please God, please, let me go home.' "

In Wichita, Jeannie's father, Ray, had been filled in on the situation. Betty still hooked up with Ray sometimes. She didn't want a relationship with him, but she'd never gotten over him. He offered to kill Bob.

"I thought about it," she admitted, her

loathing for Bob a growl in her voice even after decades had passed. "I could've had him bumped off. But I knew I might end up in prison, and I didn't want to go to hell."

Betty's prayers to get her son back weren't answered, not for a long time. But Jeannie's prayers to get her mom back were.

The day before the holiday break for Michigan public schools, her teacher told everyone that it was Jeannie's last day. All the children lined up by the door to say goodbye. Jeannie walked past them, crying because everyone was looking at her.

When she got off the plane in Wichita, her mother and father were at the airport to pick her up in Ray's convertible. She was overjoyed to be home. Her parents were messed up, but they were hers — and at least her mother's love was clearly felt. Any crummy place with them in Wichita was better than a nice little middle-class house without them in Detroit.

My relief about home came in the opposite direction, moving away from my parents into the house where I was reliably loved and never alone — my grandparents' farm — rather than the ones in which my parents were drunk or absent, cruel, or partnered with someone being cruel. The child

I used to be had a lot of sense in that way, I think, even though the separation from my mom, in particular, tore at my emotions. That self-preservation makes me think that maybe I would have done right by you, somehow. Even in poverty. Even as a teenager in that farmhouse with the tilted chimney.

The economic inequality that took a bad turn the year I was born finally snapped the American economy, and it was the housing market that did it.

By the early 2000s, the mortgage industry was swelling with predatory loans to people who banks knew damn well couldn't repay them. Little mortgage shops proliferated across the country. Mom worked with them as a real estate agent and later worked directly for one or two title companies, the kind that for a few years popped up quickly in generic business spaces and would close just as abruptly. Without understanding who would get hurt — thinking herself a friend to poor people who could finally get a house — she helped process the big banks' loans with gusto.

Like much of the country, her own life at that time was built on debt. Christmas gifts were bought with credit cards, houses were double-mortgaged. Mom would sacrifice true ownership and financial footing before she would sacrifice standard of living. Better to be in over your head with the bills in a house than own a trailer outright, she reasoned. It was all a game anyway, she said. The people making the rules were screwing around with debt bigger than she ever could. I can't say that I completely disagree.

Dad was a harder sell. You couldn't be raised by an old man who farmed wheat through the Great Depression and not see that — in an economy where people didn't have any equity in their own homes — the banks were the real winners.

The finance industry had left people like my family outside of homeownership for decades. From the late '80s into the 2000s, Dad found himself a carpenter working on other people's homes while he himself couldn't save the down payment to purchase one, or even afford the materials to build one again himself.

So he paid $375 a month in rent for a three-bedroom, one-bathroom ranch in a decent neighborhood for sixteen years.

During that time he earned most of his living doing commercial construction rather than the country craftsmanship he'd been raised for. With his brothers and father, he had built homes in Wichita and the sur-rounding countryside with old tools and old ways. There was little demand for that sort of work in the cookie-cutter suburban development market of the 1980s and '90s, though. The integrity of housing in the United States was degrading in so many ways at once, from affordability to owner equity to quality of construction.

When I was grown, Dad told me a story he'd heard that really got him.

"This carpenter works for this bad dude," Dad said. "He builds houses for him, one after another. He's a really good carpenter, does his best on every job and shit like 'at. But he gets to feeling like, damn, this employer doesn't value my skills. He's underpaid and can barely get by. Well, his boss gives him his next job building a house, and the carpenter finally thinks, well, fuck this, I don't get paid enough to keep giving it my all. So he does a poor job on that house, first time he ever did that. When he's done, the boss comes up and says, 'Hey, I got something to tell you. I been watching how hard you work, and I wanted to finally reward you. Here's the keys to that house you just finished. It's yours.' "

Dad paused.

"See, you can't stop working hard, not

even for a second," he said, wiping tears from his eyes, "because that's the second you'll be given a chance, and you'll miss it."

There weren't many chances going around, even for a man who almost never missed a day of work. Once subprime, zero-down mortgages came on to the market, he finally qualified for a loan but resisted the urge — sensing that something unsustainable was afoot.

In 2007, though, the rent on his place had gone up so much that he could pay less each month for a mortgaged house than for his longtime rental. So he finally took out a mortgage, his first bid at "ownership" since his and Mom's divorce in the late '80s.

The bank said he and Chris qualified for $150,000, but he knew they couldn't afford that properly. They bought a $125,000 house, a 1970s trilevel near a grocery store. It was the same year I bought my first house, a tiny brick cottage in a different town, for about the same price.

I drove south to help move Dad and Chris into their house on a tree-lined street. That was around the time that Chris's opioid addiction was at its worst. Dad and I moved boxes from our vehicles while Chris buzzed around inside with her cigarettes and tried to remember where she had set something.

About a year later, the housing bubble finally burst. Big banks, it turned out, had been fleecing homeowners. While a sketchy, shadowy finance system profited from historic national levels of mortgage debt, millions of buyers lost their houses and — when the broader economy tanked — they lost their savings and incomes, too. In 2006, there were about 717,000 foreclosures throughout the country; in 2008, that number was 2,330,000. The foreclosure count peaked in 2010 at almost 2.9 million and wouldn't return to pre-crisis levels until almost a decade after the bubble burst. In the meantime, taxpayers picked up the tab in a massive bailout of the banking industry.

A crash of the housing market meant a lending freeze for buyers and builders alike, which meant construction work dried up. Dad was laid off along with other older, higher-paid construction workers at his company a couple months into the 2008 crisis.

By that time, I had a good, secure job as a professor. I kept making my mortgage payments. When I sold the place a few years later, I even made a small profit thanks to its high-demand location. Dad wouldn't fare so well. His house was foreclosed on.

I helped him and Chris move into a lot at

the edge of a Wichita trailer park. He planted a garden to make it his own. Once he and Chris took cover in the community tornado shelter while the wind peeled the vinyl siding off. Dad never complained.

You might have lived in a house that didn't look poor, but trailers would have been closeby.

In coming years, the deregulated banking industry would remain largely unchecked by the government. In a speech touting a supposedly rebounded housing market, President Barack Obama would reflect on what the defining economic event of several generations had meant to our country: "This housing crisis struck right at the heart of what it means to be middle class in America: our homes," Obama said. "The place where we invest our nest egg. The place where we raise our family. The place where we plant roots in a community. The place where we build memories."

What we lost in stability, by way of our economic lot, we gained in adaptability, in hard clarity about what does and doesn't last. During the Great Recession in 2008, both my parents lost their jobs and entered one of the hardest stretches of their lives. But, while some members of the middle class saw their assets dwindle for the first time, people like my family had known economic trauma before.

Perhaps for that reason, my parents had no illusion that banks or markets were a safe investment. Mom didn't purchase more house than she could afford with the idea that she'd live there forever. She did so precisely because she didn't believe in security and figured life is short so you might as well have a big bathtub when you can get it. Like Dad, she knew all about a "mobile home" — an oxymoron, seemingly, but encoded with a deep truth: No house is truly secure. The body is the only permanent home, and even that one comes with an eviction notice.

Most of the people I grew up with lived in a trailer at some point. In the 1970s, Betty and my mom lived next door to Dorothy, Pud, Polly, and Pud's little girl Candy at the Lakeside Mobile Home Park on the southwest side of Wichita. Three generations of women parked on two little lots, tied to the Kansas earth by nothing but wheels. The trailer court was around the corner from a drive-in movie theater near railroad tracks and a sandpit filled with water — hence, "lakeside." Then, when I was a toddler, Mom, Dad, and I lived in a trailer on prairie dirt a few miles from the farm where Dad was raised. And, over the years at Betty and Arnie's, a trailer sat next to the farmhouse for whatever family member or friend needed it for a few months or years.

Another thing we all grew up with, there where Rocky Mountain air clashes with the Gulf Stream on the flat plains, is something that goes hand in hand with trailer parks in the public imagination: tornadoes. They are, according to atmospheric scientists, the most violent of all storms. Tornadoes are more common to the Great Plains than anywhere on earth, and Kansas is one of the most frequently struck states. The weather shaped our lives: state-mandated tornado drills at school, springtime trips to the tornado shelter beneath workplaces, tornado sirens, hard sheets of rain turning into hail the size of golf balls or worse.

During the spring of 1990, when I was nine and Matt was five, Grandma and Grandpa drove us a few miles west of the farm to see much of the small town of Hesston leveled after a massive tornado. "Like toothpicks," people would say about the bits of houses left behind.

But even after having seen that, tornado warnings remained less scary than mundane. While emergency alerts crawled across the bottom of the little TV screen on the kitchen counter, Grandma kept smoking and stirring the gravy, or Mom pulled out a file folder to look up the amount of the deductible on the roof insurance.

A couple months before I moved out of Mom's house, on a single day in April 1991, twenty-one tornadoes dropped in Kansas, most of them in our south-central region. Mom and Bob watched the most hellish of them, an F5 on the National Weather Service's old rating scale, tear up the Air Force base on which Mom had been born. An hour's drive south of us in Red Rock, Oklahoma, storm chasers clocked a tornado at 268 mph — at the time, the fastest wind speed ever measured on earth. Another whipped a trailer park east of Wichita into twisted shreds; thirteen people died there, more than half the tornado outbreak's fatalities across six Midwestern states.

That tragedy was covered by national media, perhaps contributing to a question I've heard people ask many times: Why do tornadoes always hit trailers?

In fact, they hit other places just as often. But a home without a foundation, a small rectangular box of metal and plastic, is less likely than a well-constructed house to survive high winds. A lightweight structure is more apt to blow away, and people without basements are more apt to die. That level of devastation makes the nightly news.

When it does, somebody who survived is on the TV screen with what society considers her bad grammar, maybe bad teeth, bad clothes, bad hair, and viewers' suspicions are confirmed: Shabby dwellings contain shabby people who perhaps got the house they deserved. It's a joke in America, the trailer park and the tornado. We weighed in on the joke, too.

"God, can they talk to someone who doesn't sound like a moron?" Mom would say, shaking her head over the ten o'clock news segment.

For us, as viewers, more important than the post-tornado interviews was the pre-tornado warning.

"Get to the basement right now, Kingman County," broadcast meteorologists would say. "There is a tornado on the ground. I repeat, there is a tornado on the ground. If you do not have a basement, stay away from windows. They may explode. Get to the bathtub and pull a mattress over you in case the roof falls."

We got the warnings, but what we were able to do with them depended on where we lived.

To hear the Kansas wind beating against the side of your trailer, while a meteorologist says to run to the basement you don't have, is to know that the structure you live in can be wiped away as easily as sand.

Not long after the big tornado outbreak of 1991, after living for less than a year in the cold house at the eastern reaches of Wichita, Mom and Bob moved closer to the center of town. The place was an old, weathered two-story house with squirrels in the attic. It stood at the edge of a nice neighborhood of beautiful old trees and houses called College Hill.

Mom told me that buying the worst house on a block was always the smartest investment, because its market value would be buoyed by proximity to nicer homes. She and Bob were just renting, as I recall. The house had wood floors, charming window sashes, and a pretty, old staircase, but it butted against Highway 54, which is how we could afford to live in one of Wichita's most desirable neighborhoods. Matt and I sometimes stood at the edge of the yard for the fun of having oily, dark rainwater puddled in the highway splashed onto us by honking semis.

Then, just before school started, I packed

my things and moved into Grandma Betty's one-bedroom house in Poorville.

I took the one proper bedroom in the house, a tiny upstairs room whose south window was just a few feet from a busy street. Grandma and Grandpa slept in the finished basement with a low ceiling and old cement steps that they'd somehow gotten a bed down. The one bathroom was entered through the small kitchen, which Grandma had decorated with a black-and-white checkered vinyl floor and cows to remind us of the farm. There was a good-size backyard for digging in the dirt and several old corner stores to skateboard to. I didn't realize it then, but it was a hard neighborhood — the kind where some people might lock the car doors when they drove through.

I spent a lot of afternoons playing catch with a baseball in the middle of a side street with Trevor, a white boy with shaggy black hair who lived next door. His dad was a Boeing factory worker who was on disability after hurting himself on the job. One day, Trevor's dad shot himself.

Trevor's mom couldn't afford a professional crime-scene-cleaning service. So Grandma and one of her neighbor friends, a former hippie who worked at an airplane factory and rode a motorcycle with her husband, who also worked at an airplane factory, went next door and wiped blood off the curtains and carpet. They did the whole cleanup job.

A few years later, Trevor's teenage sister would be murdered. As with the child abduction case in my part of town when I lived with Mom, her body was found in a field.

Mom and Matt lived with Bob in a nicer, safer part of town but visited our place sometimes, and I often stayed with them on weekends. We were by no means estranged. Matt and I would resume playing together like no time had passed, but I'd begun to idolize my mom the way a little girl might idolize her cool, pretty older sister. I was mad at her, too; she treated the fact that I lived with Grandma like it was no big deal and as if I had orchestrated it, like some manipulative feat she had decided to permit. When I saw her, my stomach clamped into a confused knot.

I was reminded every day that kids are supposed to live with their moms. School permission slips asked for her signature above a line that read "parent." Teachers told me to tell my parents about the fund-raiser when I got home. Kids asked why I lived with my grandparents. Every family image on TV was of children in their parents' house, or at least their mother's. It was a sorry situation indeed, I gathered, if you weren't even living with your mom.

My family acted like there wasn't any problem with the arrangement. Mom wasn't a crack addict living on the streets. She was a smart, employed woman who charmed everyone she met and had enough for basic survival — just enough, painfully, sparely, with credit-card balances mounting, but enough.

The problem was more about her past than our present. That past was a list of addresses, a depth of poverty that left her with no security in the years she needed it most. During the 1960s and '70s, Betty had moved more than sixty times — up, down, and across the center of the country — with Jeannie at her side.

Aunt Pud had described those years as a sad circus, and I grew up in the circular patches of dirt that circus left behind. Before I finished high school, I would move twenty-one times within two Kansas counties.

Houses were foremost economic units, which people rightly treasured — none more so than I did, as I'd grow up to

renovate and decorate houses with the deepest creative joy. But I'd moved so many
times I knew the difference between shelter
and security. One eventually blows away,
and the other exists only as a formless thing.

I would have tried to give you both, of
course. But the first home you needed was
one I made sure you wouldn't enter. A
mother is the first residence, and I kept the
porch light turned off.

6
A WORKING-CLASS WOMAN

In some ways, where I grew up there was less of a line drawn between men and women than I've found in more privileged places. The women who raised me cooked in cafeterias, drove tractors, waited tables, baled hay, worked assembly lines, cared for the elderly overnight as nursing assistants in small-town hospitals, moved boxes in the stock rooms of discount stores. The concept of "a lady" was laughable and almost non-existent. My family never told me to act like one, maybe because a lady doesn't get much done. You, too, would have had dirt under your fingernails, not for being unclean but for the way you worked.

The men I grew up around didn't scoff at a woman's capability. They were from families whose females had been holding their own for centuries. When the women I knew spent money, they asked for no one's permission. That didn't mean they made enough money to get by, of course. A working-class woman is reliably more underpaid than a working-class man. In my households, though, there was at least as much ownership of finances and decision-making among women as among men.

Grandma Teresa was nine years old when the Equal Rights Amendment, prohibiting discrimination based on sex, was introduced in Congress in 1923. On my maternal line, Great-Grandma Dorothy was one year old. The proposed amendment to the U.S. Constitution made unsuccessful rounds in Congress throughout their lives, throughout Betty's life, and then my mother's early life, finally failing ratification for the last time in the early '80s, when I was a toddler.

Kansas, however, had been the sixth state to ratify the amendment, the day after my mom's tenth birthday, in 1972. Our state had deep progressive roots on the matter of women's rights, reaching back to the so-called pioneer days. When you have twelve European immigrants with a wagon, some tools, and a bag of seeds trying to turn a windswept grassland into a point of commerce, and seven of those people are women with mud on their boots, circumstances have a way of leveling the opportunity for work. Often, women carried power in a small, nascent community and had the economic leverage to demand that they be able to own land, to divorce a drunk, and to vote.

My female Kansas forebears were political trailblazers, in fact. The journalist and activist Clarina Nichols lobbied men drafting the state constitution to cut the word "male" from the suffrage clause. Thanks to her and other women's hell-raising, Kansas was the first state in the nation to hold a statewide popular referendum on women's suffrage, in 1867.

The American Equal Rights Association campaigned furiously in Kansas for this and another measure for black suffrage. New York suffragists Elizabeth Cady Stanton and Susan B. Anthony joined the fight leading up to the vote. Both measures received sizable support but failed to pass. Stanton later wrote, "There never was a more hopeful interest concentrated on the legislation of any single State, than when Kansas submitted the two propositions to her people to take the words 'white' and 'male' from her Constitution."

A few years prior to that battle, Kansas women had secured voting rights in school-district elections, laying the groundwork for the historically excellent state public school system that I would benefit from. The University of Kansas, founded in 1865, was one of the earliest to "receive both men and women on an equal basis," at least in theory. The first black student admitted, in 1876, was a woman.

During the Progressive Era in 1912, eight years before the women's suffrage amendment to the U.S. Constitution, Kansas became the eighth state and the first in its region to give women the right to vote in all elections. Along the way, Kansas women had secured the right to obtain and own property and to have legal custody of children equal to that of the father's — rights that were largely unheard of at the time throughout the rest of the country.

These state-level triumphs disproportionately benefited white women in the wake of slavery and the decimation of indigenous tribes. They occurred while racial segregation, violence, and economic disenfranchisement harmed women as the law of the land. But within that awful context, Kansas was ahead of the national curve on gender.

In decades to come, women's battles would intersect with the labor movement and leftist populist uprisings among immigrants across the country. In 1921, a pack of Kansas immigrants made national news for halting business at their husbands' coal mines. The miners were on strike after two hundred of them had been hurt or killed that year in two southeastern Kansas counties, and the women who loved them and depended on their wages were livid. While the company bosses and scabs they had hired tried to get past, the women blocked their way. They held babies, rifles, and American flags, and sang songs in their native tongues — German, French, Slovene, Italian. They successfully shut down the mine, with support from the Kansas Coal Miners' Union, until the National Guard was called in and forty-nine of the women went to jail.

No one in my family was a political activist or even engaged in civic action beyond voting for president every four years. No one used the word "feminism," and no one knew much about state history. But a spirit as strong as the female prairie populism that shaped Kansas's early years doesn't leave a place. It reverberates through culture, through generations, whether people a hundred years later consciously perceive it or not. It would have been in you, deeper than modern-day politics and as strong as blood.

When I was a young adult, Kansas state

politics would take a hard turn against women's reproductive rights, specifically. But as a child, for all the strains of conservatism in my state, I almost never saw a woman's capability — to work, to think, to drive a wheat truck or run a business — called into question.

Class and its implications for literacy and access decide what feminism looks like in action. For those of us who would have been holding rifles at the mine entrance rather than lobbying lawmakers in Topeka, one result of that legacy was that we were often the "breadwinners" of our households well before middle-class women flooded the workforce in the 1960s, '70s, '80s. There was in our family, therefore, no semblance of the notion that a woman should or might be "taken care of." There never had been, back to my great-great-grandmother Irene on the Boeing factory line and beyond. For the women I knew, work wasn't a liberation from the home or a revelation of self. It was a way of life — familiar, essential, and unsung for generations.

Yet men were the poster image for our class, clanking against pipes with wrenches or descending into mines with headlamps in the popular imagination. Dolly Parton challenged this notion with a song called

"He's a Go Getter," in which a lazy husband's contribution to the household was to "go get 'er" when his wife got off work.

"He never turned a tap," Grandma Betty would say with disdain about some man she knew who didn't earn his keep or fulfill his responsibility to his family. Like her dad.

Aaron had rarely paid any court-ordered child support after Dorothy divorced him in the 1950s. She was struggling as a single woman with three kids to feed when she heard through friends that Aaron was living as a regular wino in downtown Denver. She meant to wring some money out of the son of a bitch.

Dorothy had recently ended a short marriage to her second husband, Paul, a tall, swarthy man who flipped hamburgers at the Takhoma Burger, a tiny dive offering hamburgers, chips, and a pinball machine. Working as the manager, Dorothy was closing alone one night when a stranger entered the place and raped her. One of her sisters had committed suicide, and another had been institutionalized to receive electroconvulsive therapy. It had been a very hard year. Dorothy needed money, and if the state wouldn't enforce Aaron's child-support requirement, she was angry and desperate enough to try to enforce it herself.

She drove all the way to Denver, across a three-hundred-mile stretch of flat Kansas, to a street where dirty men in sweaty shirts sat on steps amid broken bottles. She got out of the car with the kids and knocked on a door. A dark man opened it.

"Some big Indian dude," Betty later remembered.

They stepped into a small, clean apartment with a couple twin beds, a small bath, and a kitchen. Aaron was there without a shirt on.

"He looked about as big as a turd," Betty told me.

Dorothy told him that the courts had ordered him to pay $25 a week for the kids — so where in the hell was it? But he didn't have any money to give them if he had wanted to. Dorothy and the kids got in the car and drove three hundred miles back home.

During those same years, Betty fell in love, at age eleven, with someone even more dangerous than her dad. She first saw him playing pinball at the Takhoma Burger, where she helped her mom after school. He was sixteen and had black hair. He carried her on his shoulders once, and she knew that someday he would be her guy. By the time she was a teenager, she was right.

Ray was never faithful, but they always got back together — dragging Douglas Avenue through downtown Wichita with their gang of friends, hanging out at drive-ins, partying.

"We had this one chick friend with some sort of pharmacy connection," Betty told me. "We called her Vitamin Vic 'cause she could find all kinds of drugs."

Betty and her friends wore miniskirts before they were considered acceptable in society. Their boyfriends didn't like it.

"My best friend had this one dress that every time she wore it she got her ass whooped," Betty said with a shrug.

By then, Ray was a legal adult, five years older than Betty. He no longer got sent to boys' reformatories for petty crimes. He had gone to the state penitentiary for burglary in the late 1950s when he was eighteen or nineteen.

"He always ran with gangster-type kids," Betty said. "They just went from kids to adults. He got sent to the joint. He met a lot of people up there."

Ray joined the Army to get his act together. He was stationed in Nebraska. It wasn't clear how long he'd be there. It was the summer of 1961; Berlin was building a wall between east and west, and President Kennedy was putting National Guardsmen on active duty.

In jerky script with dramatic loops, Ray wrote to Betty as Aaron had written to Dorothy from his barracks sixteen years earlier. He was "in some little hick town making our pad on the baseball field," Ray wrote. He won a little money playing poker, he said, and his division might get sent to Germany. He signed it, "loving you always," and added a postscript: "P.S. Do me wrong and I'll break your head."

Betty was back in Kansas missing her period.

"That was the surefire kicker," she told me, meaning that getting pregnant was the moment that bound her to Ray forever. She was sixteen.

Ray never went to Germany. He made it only as far as Camp Ripley in Minnesota. When he got back to Kansas, they married at the county courthouse with Dorothy as their witness. There was no romance to it, no honeymoon, and no celebration. Just a baby in Betty's belly and a plan to live the life of a military family.

Betty moved in with Ray in a family housing unit on a military base in Junction City, Kansas, a bleak dot surrounded by prairie in the middle of the state. Everyone called it Junk Town. It was her first time living outside of Wichita away from her family and friends. The Army base was too small and boring for her taste. Ray did more drugs than ever and gave Betty her "first real beating." He knocked her to the floor when she was eight and a half months pregnant.

When I was in my twenties, I would work as a grant writer for a legal-aid organization that served the whole state of Kansas. The majority of cases our pro bono attorneys represented involved abused women who needed to file restraining orders but couldn't afford a lawyer. Their plight was as much about economic disparity as gender disparity. The grant funds I helped manage reached those women through state programs funded by the federal Violence Against Women Act — passed more than thirty years after Betty got together with Ray. Back then, Betty had neither money nor public policy on her side. She had only her willingness to try to escape.

Betty left Junk Town and moved back to Wichita, back in with Dorothy, her stepdad Joe, and her sister Pud. But, like her mother on that tear to Denver just a few years prior, Betty found herself dependent on an unreliable man for money. Once, after Ray had abandoned his military post and found a bartending job in Wichita, she stopped by during his day shift to get cash for baby formula. She found him kissing one of her friends. Betty took the woman into the restroom and held her head in the toilet until someone ripped the lock off the door and pulled her away.

Meanwhile, Ray wanted say over whom Betty could and couldn't date. After Betty hung out with one of Ray's friends, someone showed up at his house, threw gasoline on his face, and lit a match, Betty told me. He needed reconstructive surgery.

"People didn't want to be on Ray's bad side," Betty said.

The people Ray had met in prison, she thought, found him work as a gun-for-hire for bosses in Chicago and Oklahoma City. He got a job driving a rig, hauling timber from the Rocky Mountains to Kansas for Eagle Pass Lumber Company; he would work as a trucker for decades to come. Betty suspected he used the truck to move drugs and guns. Ray didn't talk about his unofficial job, but he wore it through the expensive clothes and jewelry his family couldn't afford.

Ray and Aaron were the sort of men I wouldn't have let anywhere near you. But the ways in which women before you had no choice but to rely on them — and be vulnerable to them — would have been part of your life, to some extent. It is perhaps the aspect of your life I feel most triumphant about having prevented.

In 1969, when Betty was twenty-four and back from her years in Colorado — where she'd married twice more, given birth to a son, and lost custody of him — Ray still came around now and then. She tried to avoid him, but sometimes they'd end up in the rack. One day he sat in her living room smoking a cigarette and dangling a .22-caliber handgun from one finger. The gun was Betty's. She kept it to protect herself and Jeannie, who was in the front yard playing on the gas meter.

"I think I'll just shoot you," Ray said.

"If you do it, do it good," Betty said.

From a few feet away, he pointed the gun at her and pulled the trigger. The bullet hit Betty's left upper arm, not far from her heart.

"Did it hurt?" I asked when, at age twelve or so, I finally uncovered the story behind the splotchy white scar on her arm that I'd touched many times.

"Hell yes, it hurt!" she said.

Blood pumped out of her left bicep while Ray's sister drove her to the emergency room, where someone called the police. Betty told a cop the gun had gone off by accident while she was handling it.

In theory, women were being liberated during those years, but the poorest of them had the least agency for independence in real life. In some cases, dependence on men was deadly. Domestic violence occurs at all socioeconomic levels, of course, but the woman who can't afford to leave will have more chances to be killed.

Not long after his relationship with Betty, Ray moved in with a woman who soon died. Rumor was that she fell out of Ray's semi while he was driving.

"Fell out," my mom would say with a skeptical look the handful of times I heard the family story. "Right."

Meanwhile, Betty, who had been abused by three out of three husbands — Ray in Wichita, and Bob and Johnny in Colorado — was repeatedly told she had to have a spouse to win back custody of Bo. She needed to show a "stable household," male lawyers told her, as if any man she'd ever been with had been a force of stability, economic or otherwise. It was true that she had little chance of establishing one herself then as a single, poor female so often transient by necessity. Based on that legal advice — never having truly given up on getting her son back — she went on what she would later call her "marrying kick."

In early 1971, when she was twenty-five, she made a deal with a Mexican immigrant named Miguel who barely spoke English. He had light, pinkish skin, blue eyes, and black hair. He said he was of Spanish descent and had a sister with blond hair. He went by Mike. They married so that he could get his green card and Betty could show the courts a husband in her fight to get her son. Before they parted ways, Mike got his visa, but Betty didn't get her son.

Betty moved to Belle Plaine, a small town south of Wichita, to work in a diner in a highway motel. She and Jeannie lived in a room there, while Dorothy and Polly lived in the main employee quarters. Pud had gotten pregnant by a biker when she was fifteen and they were all still in Colorado. She lived on her own now with her little girl, Candy. Dorothy managed the restaurant and helped run the whole motel. They ate all their meals for free in the motel restaurant, which wasn't a bad deal.

Waiting tables in that little farming town, Betty met a Vietnam vet named Galen who worked at the Case tractor dealer the next town over. She was twenty-six when he became her fifth husband.

On the Fourth of July, Galen freaked out when the fireworks went off. He hadn't been back from Vietnam for long and was too messed up to live with. Betty divorced him the next year.

She and Jeannie got their own apartment back in Wichita. Then she fell in love, for real, with the only man she ever loved but didn't marry. Herb worked at a salvage lot near her place and asked her out when she was there for a car part. He was small, rugged, and Jewish, which in that area was a rare thing to be. He was going through a divorce, he said, which was another way of saying he was still married.

"He thought he was good-lookin'," Betty said. "And he really wasn't."

Herb had a camper, a motorcycle, and several cars he'd fixed up. He took Betty and Jeannie camping at Cheney Lake. He bought Betty a necklace, a jade stone on a silver chain, such a rare gift that she never forgot its details. He came over to their apartment, and when Betty cooked him dinner, he always said thank you.

Herb encouraged her to get a government education grant, probably federal funds for women by way of recently passed Title IX legislation. Not having been in a classroom for well over a decade, since she left school during tenth grade, Betty attended a small business college in Wichita, where she learned to type, write business letters, and do general office work.

She worked for the next couple years as a teacher's aide at a private school and then as a secretary for a chiropractor. In 1975, Betty and Jeannie moved into a trailer park on the southwest side of Wichita. As had happened so many times before, Dorothy and Polly moved to be close to Betty and Jeannie. They took a mobile home in the same court.

Betty had been with Herb for a couple years, far longer than some of her marriages combined. She told me Herb might have become her sixth husband had she not said to herself, *That's all I've ever done, my whole life, is be married to somebody. I don't need to get married. Seems like every time I do, it ends in disaster.* It was a good decision. Herb ended up getting another woman pregnant and marrying her, Betty told me.

I look back on that story with something close to fondness. That time, Betty had her heart broken for perfectly pedestrian reasons that have nothing to do with class. Infidelity

— a common and perfectly survivable trouble. I sometimes feel that way about my own life now, when something feels like the end of the world. I calm down realizing that it's the sort of problem everybody has, whereas the problems I was born into really could kill a person. Your problems as a working-class girl would have included true peril.

By then, Jeannie was a teenager getting busted by her mom for smoking and drinking. Since she and Betty were going rounds, she decided to go live with her dad in Oklahoma City. There, quiet men followed her around like they had been assigned to protect her. She waited in the car while Ray had meetings in bars. She saw the men come out into the parking lot. They laughed at everything her dad said while he smirked.

Jeannie made long-distance calls from Ray's house, where his rig was parked out front, and he complained that she was costing him money. He took her to the mall and stole a diamond ring to impress her, but what she felt was shame. She only lasted a few months there before she returned to her mom in Kansas. She never saw her dad again.

By then, Betty had managed to steer clear of violent men like Ray and most of her other husbands and end up with guys who had more tolerable problems, like philandering Herb.

One was Dean, a short, religious guy who owned a construction company. He had a clean new home on the northeast side of town where the "rich people" lived, in Betty's eyes. He was lower middle class but stunned Betty by taking her shopping at Sears and telling her to pick out three or four outfits, which she had a hard time doing without feeling wasteful, because who bought more than one outfit at once?

The other man Betty met soon after her breakup with Herb was Arnie. He asked her to two-step at a dance hall on the highway. He didn't appear to have much to offer — a divorced farmer in a gray felt cowboy hat with grown children and little money, thirteen years older than Betty was. She thought he was fun, though. When he called and asked her to go to the Ice Capades, Betty said yes. But then she decided she didn't want to date a farmer who lived way out in the country. At the last minute, she changed her mind and came up with an excuse to cancel.

Dean asked her to marry him. She said yes, but it wasn't for love.

"He had money up the ass," she explained.

She'd get even with Herb for marrying another woman, and she and Jeannie could live comfortably with Dean's income.

They moved into Dean's house. Life with enough money for a shopping spree at Sears turned out to be a hard trade, however. Dean had a high, squeaky voice. He whined and complained about every damn thing, Betty and Jeannie agreed.

That sixth marriage lasted a matter of months, as most of her marriages had. It was pretty clear by then that bad reasons could make Betty marry someone but couldn't make her stay.

In 1977, Betty landed a position that would change the trajectory of her life, financially and therefore personally — working for the state as a secretary at the county courthouse in downtown Wichita.

She earned $800 a month to work in a comfortable office, which struck her as a joke after years of making far less for grueling labor in restaurants and factories. She and Jeannie had moved out of Dean's home and back to the trailer park across town, where Dorothy still lived with Polly, now a curly-haired teenager. After a long string of wild moves, marriages, and divorces, the group of single moms and their daughters was together again. They had traveled thousands of miles and changed dozens of addresses together, all to return to the same place.

But things were different now. When Betty went to work, she put on high heels and clicked across the lobby of the courthouse that employed important, powerful people.

For all the blessings of the job, she found secretarial work boring, typing and filing documents while male coworkers came and went. So when she heard the county sub-poena officer for the juvenile court was leaving, she asked for the job.

"That's no job for a woman," Betty remembered the judge she worked under telling her. A few years prior, though, the Civil Rights Act had been expanded to prohibit employer discrimination against women in state agencies.

"Check the law on that," Betty told him. She got the job.

As a subpoena officer for the juvenile courts in Sedgwick County, Betty drove through Wichita's rough neighborhoods to walk up crumbling sidewalks and deliver bad news. She told parents they had to show up in court for their children's crimes, or that they were on the verge of losing custody of their kids. Sometimes they got irate. A drunk man with a gun said he would blow her away. A woman pulled a knife on her in a stairwell. Betty calmly talked her way out of those situations — a lifetime of survival skills put to good use.

Emboldened by her success as a subpoena officer, Betty signed up for the Wichita Police Reserve. The Equal Employment Opportunity Act of 1972 had opened doors for female officers, previously barred in many places from, say, arresting adult offenders or riding patrol after dark. It was the late 1970s, and they didn't even have to wear high heels anymore. There was just one other woman in the mix when Betty joined the reserves, but she didn't give it much thought. She enlisted to do a job, not to make a point.

Around the same time that I started thinking about you — asking myself what I would do, what I would want, for my own daughter — I found notes Betty had taken during training classes. The spiral notebook was evidence of a courageous moment when Grandma sat in a room full of men. She had written down the chain of command, types of traffic accidents, how to identify pot, when to discharge a gun, the meaning of a "29." What type of evidence goes to the lab? When can you enter a house without knocking? What is the difference between "aggravated battery" and plain "battery"? What do you do when the person you've arrested is intoxicated?

After long days serving subpoenas, Betty put on a blue uniform, got in a patrol car with a male partner who was a full police officer, and went out into the night. Mostly they put drunks in the tank, which she found satisfying. One night, though, she opened her car door outside a robbery in progress and heard the zip of a bullet. She and her partner ducked behind their car doors before they gave chase through a nearby graveyard. Betty's heart pounded as she ran with her heavy holster. The man escaped.

"Was it at all a relief that he got away?" I asked her, since she'd admitted she was scared.

"No," she told me. "I wanted to catch the bastard."

In just a couple years she'd gone from being a woman who married men out of economic necessity to a woman who was financially stable on her own. Along the way, she'd been mailing birthday and Valentine's Day cards to her son, which Bob probably didn't give him. Now she could finally do what she'd been working toward. She renewed her custody fight with gusto.

It had been a decade since she lost custody during those worst of years in small-town Colorado in the 1960s. Bob said she was wasting everyone's time.

"I told him forget it," she remembered. "I would never give up."

She was served papers stating that the court had again sided with Bob, maintaining his full custody of Bo. She sent a letter refusing to relinquish rights to see and raise her son. The next month, she got a letter from her attorney saying he couldn't represent her and was withdrawing from the case.

"The bastard took him, and I never got him back," Betty said. "And it wasn't because I didn't fight for him."

It was because she was a woman in poverty, beholden to so many men over the years — to provide money for baby formula, to hire her for a job that would allow her to feed her family, to decide whether she got to keep her children. Economic power is social power. In the end, for all her hard work and tenacity, the poor woman lacks both.

Around the time I moved in with Grandma Betty in Wichita, Aunt Pud and Uncle Larry moved into an old house across the alley from our place. I was excited to live so close to my cousin Shelly, by then an eighth grader who was old enough to be a high school sophomore. She'd been held back in elementary school for struggling to keep up amid so many changes of school, curriculum, teachers — a common plight for kids with impermanent addresses.

Aunt Pud had made a living cooking for restaurants since she was a teenage apprentice to Dorothy. Uncle Larry worked at the Boeing airplane factory that seemed to employ half the men and women of our neighborhood of small postwar houses and spotty grass lawns. Pud took a job in the kitchen of a Catholic school not far from us in the Mexican American enclave. It was close to North High, where Grandma had dropped out of tenth grade in 1960.

Since Aunt Pud prepped school lunches at the private Catholic school, Shelly got to go there for free. Pud somehow finagled a discounted fee for me too and offered to drive me to and from school when she went to work. It was in an impoverished neighborhood — private for being run by a church, not for its prestige.

Mom sewed my uniform skirt, as she had sewn many of my clothes growing up, from a navy, white, and yellow plaid fabric. She took me to the mall and bought me the two pairs of shoes I most coveted: black Adidas sneakers and brown leather Eastland loafers. Grandma took me to the Dollar General store for the rest: navy slacks, white imitation Polo shirts, navy cardigans.

I rode to school with Shelly in her mom's long, maroon 1970s car with cigarette burns in the seats. We left before dawn so that Aunt Pud could start prep work in the kitchen for school lunch. While Shelly hung out with eighth graders dropped off early for their own reasons, I spent the hours before the first bell roaming the halls. I slunk in and out of storage rooms, stealing whatever I pleased. An American flag folded into a thick, precious triangle was my favorite score.

Most of the kids at my new school had brown skin and black hair and spoke in half Spanish. My first and only friend, Dawn, was from an interracial family; she had light green eyes and a huge mass of long hair that was at once blond and frizzy. We didn't have much in common. She'd already hit puberty, and eighth-grade boys liked to look at her large chest. I could have easily passed for a boy with my hair tucked in my baseball cap. Dawn liked New Kids on the Block and *Beverly Hills, 90210,* and I liked rap music and cop shows. But she doubled over laughing on her bed when I prank-called boys from her bedroom telephone.

A lot of people talk about how much they hated middle school. I remember it as the happiest years of my life — a brief window in which I was old enough to leave the house on truly independent adventures but was not yet viewed by the world as a woman. My family didn't put anything on me about being a girl, either. Maybe in some families I would have been "protected" and discouraged from roving the streets, especially poor ones like ours, more so than a boy would have been. But what I felt in those years, when I could walk down a sidewalk without male attention and nobody cared where I was or what I did, was true freedom.

We worked on the farm every weekend, and that's where I felt most at home. I was happy when, less than three years after I'd left that countryside, Grandma said we were moving out to the farm for good.

She had decided to rent out the little Wichita house. She'd have a long drive to work again, but Grandpa wouldn't have to drive his truck to Wichita after a long day of chores and fieldwork.

For the remainder of sixth grade, a small school bus picked me up and took me south to the tiny post of Murdock, population 275, where the dirt was red and almost everyone was poor. There was a white, two-room schoolhouse that had been there since the horse-and-wagon days. The entire school, kindergarten through eighth grade, contained thirty-two students. I made thirty-three.

My grade consisted of three other girls and me. Each day we were handed an ancient textbook and instructed to work out various assignments, which I completed for all four of us. Then the teacher let us go outside to climb in the dusty playground or roam down the dirt road to Main Street's remaining wisp of a general store with a wooden walkway under its awning. Since there were so few students, lunch was a homemade meal cooked by a handful of old women with German last names.

Like everyone else at Murdock, I joined the track team and rode buses across the area to compete against other farm kids, our white tennis shoes stained the color of rust from the red clay dirt of our dying hamlet that other towns called "Mud Rock." Though I was short, I was good at jumping and ran hurdles against Amish girls who wore bike shorts underneath their home-sewn skirts.

The Amish girls almost always won every event, which the rest of us small-town teams attributed to their farm work being even harder — and thus their bodies being tougher — than ours. They didn't have the help of modern machinery, and if you took the two-lane blacktop north from our farm you'd see the women in bonnets working behind a plow.

The Amish boys never took home as many track meet medals, as I recall. I can't say why. I do know what you would have learned, being the daughter of laborers: Doing "men's work" as a female can develop an inner defiance that, channeled to your legs, will win a race. Even if you're running in a skirt.

Betty's parents were turning elderly just as I moved in with her, so Betty soon was taking care of them and me at the same time. Great-Grandpa Aaron had returned to Kansas from Colorado decades prior. He and Great-Grandma Dorothy lived in different parts of Wichita, but both had cupboards holding little more than tubs of government-issued peanut butter and fake cheese from a county food pantry. They didn't have any crackers or bread to put it on, so Grandma and I would make grocery runs for them at a run-down store in the area. To make sure the peanut butter and cheese didn't go to waste, we'd take a full tub for our own cabinet.

Aaron's small apartment in a poor neighborhood was clean, thanks to his wife, but he gave me the creeps and his eyes were always cloudy-looking. He had opened a can of beer first thing in the morning for so many decades that doctors warned him not to stop.

In Dorothy's apartment, the blinds were drawn. She was worried the man in the television was talking to her. She was obese by then and had type 2 diabetes. "Diabeetus," Grandma called it.

Dorothy was always saying, "That can't be." If she didn't believe what you were telling her, or if she didn't believe the nightly news, or whatever else, it was always, "Well, that can't be." Even her stare said it. She had a way of looking at you, an animal distance in her eyes, one eyebrow pointed toward her dry hairline, dark and graying. Her eyes were yellowish green like Betty's and mine, but schizophrenia made them see things we didn't.

Dorothy carried with her the mysterious aura of her apartment, which smelled like Vicks VapoRub. On tables lay her day-of-the-week pillboxes full of medicine she pretended to take, along with astrology magazines, little ceramic figures of cats and clowns, bowls of sugar-free candy, Publishers Clearing House mailings opened with hope. An old television flashed images with too much red tint. On one wall hung an awkwardly placed portrait of Jesus Christ, his brow drawn and imploring.

She moved in with us for a while at the farm. I had started seventh grade ten miles west in Kingman, a town of more than three thousand people, after telling Grandma Betty that I wasn't learning enough in Murdock. After the long bus ride home, I'd find Great-Grandma Dorothy sitting quietly at the kitchen table. But soon she moved back to Wichita.

When I was a little older I'd come to wonder whether my mom and grandma's vagabond ways amounted to behavioral training from a mentally ill matriarch. I'd come to wonder, too, how so many women ended up feeling crazy. It seemed to have something to do with kitchens, and most of the recipes of my childhood could be traced back to Dorothy.

The last time I saw her, Thanksgiving of 1993, she was seventy-one years old, sitting in the farmhouse living room and painting her long, brittle nails, ridged and yellow beneath a pinkish-orange lacquer. I was thirteen, an eighth grader newly uncomfortable around her and most adults. She wore a bright rayon muumuu and sat with her legs parted to make way for an abundant middle. She breathed with an oxygen tank and smoked cigarettes anyway. Dangly moles dotted her fleshy upper arms, and her mostly gray hair was curled with an at-home perm. She smiled and hugged her grandchildren and fed them her macaroni-and-cheese casserole or her cranberry salad, which had more walnuts in it than any salad has a right to. She scowled at the men because she thought they were good-for-nothing.

A week before Christmas, Dorothy had a stroke alone in her apartment. She pushed the Help button her children had ordered, but help took too long to arrive. At the hospital, her grown children agreed to take her off life support.

Grandma Betty was quiet in the front seat on the way to the funeral. We got to the mortuary chapel, and I saw Mom. It was only the third time I had seen her cry. She was hurting because she had lost her grandma, who decades earlier had been a mother to her. I knew that when Mom was a baby, and teenage Betty went to work or out on the town, it was Dorothy who fed her a bottle.

At the gravesite, the casket wasn't situated correctly and nearly slid off the metal lowering device. Dorothy's body shifted to one side with a thud, and the casket's buckles came partly undone, allowing the lid to pop open slightly. The corpse's face pressed against the opening. Aunt Pud turned away quickly, closing her eyes and putting a tissue to her mouth. Betty stared right into her mother's gray face with a pained but steady look.

As Betty lost her mom, I looked at mine and realized how much I missed her. Her strange poise made her even less a mother in my eyes and more a beautiful, funny, smart woman whose locked-up love I wanted. By then, I was old enough to glimpse an understanding of her — the cracked foundation of her life that I overheard in hushed family conversations about the past.

Mom was even less inclined to talk about that past than Grandma was. At the farm, I dug through photos and documents hidden in drawers to piece together her own childhood. I saw there a black-haired, dark-skinned father and a blond baby no one had ever told me about.

Living in the same corner bedroom that Mom had inhabited as a teenager, I cried when I found a little trunk of her teenage keepsakes deep in the narrow old closet beneath our collapsing brick chimney. I'd been living with Grandma for over two years, and I'd never been as happy as I was living at the farm and going to school in Kingman. But I'd never stopped worrying about living so far from my parents and brother. I knew I was happier that way, but I felt like I was failing my responsibility to my immediate family — to protect and teach Matt, to discourage my parents' bad habits, to simply be present. And I needed them, too, in the way any kid needs her closest relatives or at least feels like she does.

I've done so many things different from and apart from my family that it's a surprising part of who I am, maybe — a deep allegiance to the same environment I increasingly wanted to leave. Considering that and my strange maternal relationship to you, I think, if born into a different environment I might have thrived in a mostly domestic life, maybe even been a very happy mother. That pull inside me was always there. I decided I should move back in with my mom.

I moved my things from the farm to Mom

and Bob's house in Wichita and started ninth grade at a big high school on the northeast side of town. Mom and Bob, who had recently been married in their home by Judge Watson, were getting along well. Matt was ten years old and happy to have me back; we played catch and cut tiny cardboard "Marlboro miles" from Mom's cigarette packs to buy a poker set to share.

Now that I was a teenager, people often thought that Mom and I were sisters, the consensus being that we looked just alike except for hair and eye color and a few years. We quietly read the newspaper together in the mornings, wore each other's clothes, watched the news together in the evening, and talked about astrology late at night while she and Bob drank their wine.

Mom was thirty-two and starting to drink more. Her reserved demeanor disintegrated into bawdy troublemaking when she was with her friends, and I would raise my eyebrows in disapproval. I hated my new school and felt like moving had been a mistake.

Mom didn't try to stop me from leaving again — like maybe she thought, deep down, that she didn't know any better than I did. So, in the tradition of my maternal line changing addresses in a matter of months, at age fourteen I moved, yet again, back to the farm. It was about two months after the school year started — an awkward moment to arrive at my new small-town high school. It was the eighth school I'd attended, and I'd just begun ninth grade.

The horror of being financially reliant upon a man who hits you, blows town, cheats on you, disrespects you, and generally works less than you do was so deep in the women I knew that I understood it by proximity. The men who helped raise me were good ones. But I carried such doubt of the economic institution of marriage that it never even crossed my mind that someday a man's income might help me survive. I had trouble asking my own family for money, often pretending I wasn't hungry when my friends bought food with their allowance. I grew into a command of my own finances as early as I could.

To pay for gas to and from school and outings with friends, in high school I worked two jobs, as a waitress at a Pizza Hut on Highway 54 and as a secretary at the county parks and recreation commission. I would hold two or three jobs at a time for years to come, by necessity. I remember high school and college — the peak of physical energy, in theory — as the most tired years of my life.

I looked at my family then and felt I had two choices: be a relentless worker with a chance at building my own financial foundation or live the carefree way so many of my friends did. The latter, by my estimation, almost assured my becoming a young mother and an underpaid worker, too. It was an easy choice.

The maternal cycle I was born to felt so hostile to my mission in the world — my amorphous intention to do something "big" in places those women had never gone — that I perceived it as a threat rather than a fate. It wasn't you that was the threat, of course. You were an orb in my aura like a zygote in a uterine wall, helping me answer questions about how to live my life: *What would I want for my daughter?* It was the demanding earthly life you might have had that worried me. For both of us.

I pictured myself marrying and having kids one day, but there were a lot of things I wanted to do more. I wouldn't have thought of it in those terms when I was a teenager in a small town, but it's plain to see from what I've prioritized in life.

I was never one of those girls who want to hold every baby they see. Some of them struck me as a little too eager, to be honest. There's often a big performance to the whole thing. That's true everywhere. But being a Catholic girl in rural Kansas gave me endless opportunities to see it. There, the baby shower invitations from friends began in high school. A lot of those young moms were just repeating what their own mothers had done. It's not much different from a girl going to the same elite school her mother attended, having the same liberal politics as her mother, and starting to think about raising a family in her thirties just as her mother did.

I had a feeling my mom had given up her life for me, and not without regrets. That's what I never wanted you to feel. My being a poor teenager's baby, then, is why you and I had the sort of connection we did. I knew deep in my cells what it felt like to grow inside a girl who couldn't afford or even love me because of some mix of financial and emotional poverties that I had no choice but to inherit.

I guess a person could say that a girl with that depth of awareness would have done okay as a poor mother. Jeannie and I had a lot of interests in common but different natures. Babies fell asleep when I held them.

"Her moon is in Cancer," Mom would

explain to other people in the room. "Nurturing and protective."

I'm not so sure that means I would have done right by you, though. The mother I would have been then was doing well on the outside but was deep in pain alone at night. Like it did for my own mother, I think, that pain would have taken over when you cried or tried my patience. I would have slapped you or screamed at you to shut up or, worst of all, beamed the same quiet hatred in your direction that I once felt.

I therefore rarely talked about having kids one day, and no one inquired about it. Oh, people gave me dolls galore when I was little, told me I was a good mommy for how I held the doll. But once I got to a certain age — ten, maybe — that all stopped. No one asked me whom I was going to marry or how many kids I wanted, that I recall. No one in my family, especially. They must have known I was on a different path. That was apparent to them, I guess, in my fervent devotion to school, my vocal views on alcohol and drugs as a trouble I didn't have time for, the crushing schedule of extracurricular activities I organized myself if only to list them on a college scholarship application.

When I moved out of my mom's house

again and returned to Kingman, I quickly got back into that almost mindless achievement frenzy. I was too late to try out for the football cheerleading squad. Moving always came with missed opportunities like that — art contest deadlines just past, school play auditions too soon for preparing a monologue. But I threw myself into everything else — basketball, theater, track, student organizations — and by the next fall I was holding pom-poms again on the squad that in a small town comprises the same girls who lead student council.

My friends had changed quickly while I was in Wichita, I found. We had been a chaste pack of middle schoolers, but now they smoked, drank, and had sex with older boys on the hoods of cars on dirt roads. I myself had made my mind up about what I was in high school to do: wring it for everything it might be worth on a résumé and, above all, not get pregnant. I went to road parties but didn't drink, instead getting my puking friends home safely along dark dirt roads in their cars that I didn't yet have a license to drive. I had boyfriends but kept my jeans zipped.

My first big party was in a barn miles outside of Kingman. A senior girl's parents were out of town, and about a hundred teenagers stumbled up and down the ladder to the enormous loft, where they sat on hay bales with beer cans in koozies and danced to country and grunge rock on a boom box. Boots stomping on the boards kicked up hay dust, lit by buzzing lights in the autumn night. I had fun but felt like I was on the outside of something — careful not to drink, not to let anyone touch me.

Striving to always do the right thing was at once the ultimate rebellion against my family and a boost toward my goals in life. The exalted virginity of my Catholicism, the prized work ethic of my class, the competitive ambition of my country's economic order — I took them all seriously and saw no room for error, knowing that high school was the moment that would make or break my dreams.

Grandma noticed my straight A's but couldn't offer much about the path that lay ahead, except for the most important advice of all for women like us.

"Be careful," she'd say. "You don't want to get tied down."

Like her and Mom, I had been a poor girl's baby, and I knew exactly what she meant.

For many poor women, there is a violence

to merely existing: the pregnancies without health care, the unchecked harassment while waiting tables, the repetitive physical jobs that cause back and foot pain. Then there are the men — whose violence I'm not convinced is any worse than a middle- or upper-class man's, but whom a woman without economic means will have a harder time escaping.

I had dreams in which I killed men who were coming after me. I sometimes imagined such moments in real life, figuring out the ways I would fight. But my greatest strength was not showing any fear.

When I was a freshman, a senior boy who was angry that I didn't want to be his girlfriend drove me to a dirt road late at night and pulled out a handgun. I sat in the passenger seat, scared but refusing to let him know it, and told him to take me home until he did.

If it wasn't pregnancy tying poor girls down, it was dangerous men.

Maybe that's why the person I fell in love with when I was sixteen was a passive, peaceful boy who had no interest in having sex with me. My family assumed I was doing what they'd done, what most teenagers do — sex, cigarettes, alcohol, drugs. But they were wrong, and it had far less to do with "morals" or Catholicism than it did with my intention to graduate and get a full ride to college with no baby or addiction or controlling partner.

This was such a foreign turn in our family that they looked at me with a deep suspicion. With my involvement in clubs and sports teams, I often didn't get home until late at night. Grandpa Arnie had quit school after sixth grade in the late 1930s and couldn't fathom the schedule of a modern-day student. He analyzed my tire tracks in the dirt. If my car had weaved on the loose gravel, he accused me of driving drunk. In truth, I just had a habit of driving too fast. When I was nominated for Future Farmers of America "sweetheart" at my high school, I won the nail-driving contest, and a boy made me a plaque with a horseshoe and the engraved words HELL ON WHEELS. Grandpa Arnie thought a teenage girl that bold must be causing trouble.

"I wasn't born yesterday, by God," he would say.

I would roll my eyes and fasten the bathroom door's old hook lock.

"You're not too old for me to spank your ass!" he would bellow. Grandma Betty would get out of bed and come downstairs, yelling, "What the hell is going on?"

Great-Grandpa Aaron and his longtime wife had moved into the trailer that was parked next to the farmhouse. His wife's cooking and caring had slowed down with age, so Betty cooked almost all their meals. Maybe it was out of a sense of duty that she would have felt as a middle-class woman, too, but she didn't have the option of paying for someone else to care for him.

I hated being around Aaron. When he wandered over for Betty to feed him, I'd rush out of the house, hoping to avoid talking to him. He started drinking Natural Light first thing in the morning, so there wasn't much to say.

I'd hang buckets of feed on the three-wheeler handles and, after stopping at the bumpy pasture to take care of the cattle, ride for miles until the sun went down. My thumb would be numb from pressing the accelerator — past Old Lady Miller's house, where I sped up because her dog always chased me, past the potato patch where Grandpa Arnie had found a young woman's body after her boyfriend killed her and dumped her there in the 1970s, past the abandoned farmhouse where I took my friends to scare them and throw rocks at the glass, over the bridge where I dangled my legs as semis passed underneath and honked. When I got home, I made my dinner plate and slunk away as quickly as I could.

Aaron detected my disdain and didn't like the looks of it, there being no worse crime than thinking yourself "too good." When his shy wife let me keep a collection of swing-music CDs she had loaned me, that was the final straw for Aaron.

"She's up to something," he'd tell Grandma Betty. "Keep an eye on her."

Mom didn't trust me, either. She was still a thirty-something going out with her girlfriends, changing from pants to skirts when she left Bob at home, and drinking until she passed out. Our rebellions were simultaneous, opposite in purpose, and reversed by generation. It was an explosive mix.

Once, staying with her during summer months, we had an argument, and she said something so awful and inaccurate that I refused to speak a word in her presence for two weeks.

Finally, one night, I was lying in bed trying to fall asleep. Mom appeared in my doorway. With the hallway light behind her she was a tiny, dark silhouette. She stepped slowly to the side of my bed. She smelled strongly like herself, workday perfume and cinnamon gum and wine. She sat down next to where I lay. I sat up.

"I'm sorry," she said.

She leaned toward me and slumped her pale, soft arms onto my shoulders. I put my arms around her. Her slight weight hung on me like a flower on a fence. I held her while she cried. Her brown hair was curled and full of smoke, and her face was wet and soft. I couldn't remember her saying sorry to me ever, once, in my entire life.

"It's okay," I said. You couldn't be her child and not feel the difference between how much love she had inside her and how little she was able to let out or in.

I think that gulf was because of the violence she endured — the childhood in poverty, the abuse and neglect, the frustration of being a brilliant woman with little opportunity, the early pregnancies. For some reason, I could always feel the love inside me and other people — even ones like you, who didn't exist.

The women I knew were always talking about how their nerves were shot or they were at their wit's end or the end of their rope. The men who apparently played a role in putting them there were faces marked out or torn away in buried photo albums I exhumed from the farmhouse's wooden drawers — unnamed feminism revealed, maybe, by women refusing to throw away perfectly good photos of themselves in which unkind men could simply be erased.

Back when Betty was dating Herb, the guy who ran the salvage yard, he, Betty, and Pud used to meet for beers at a bar called the Calendar Girl across the street from his auto shop. Pud liked Herb because he had a sense of humor and a beautiful Thunderbird. It was good to get out and blow off some steam with a few beers at the Calendar Girl. She always remembered the old woman who ran the joint. She was seventy years old and would dance under black lights on the dark floor.

"She had a good body but an old face," Pud told me. I knew that woman, I thought. There was a particular look about females of my class who survived that long and ran their own business — a dive bar, a tax-preparation service out of their trailer, a junkyard inherited from a father. They wore thrift-store jeans originally sold in the juniors section at shopping malls and held cigarettes like they were permanent extensions of their wrinkled hands. They were usually blissfully single by choice and had too many pets. They felt to me like warriors back from battle, full of love but capable of being provoked back into fighting mode. That was Grandma Betty in her later years. It's a part of your lineage that I'm proud of.

Once we were walking out of Walmart, the summer heat on the asphalt parking lot making me nauseous and my sweaty hand sticking to a plastic bag. I looked over at Betty to see how she was holding up. We approached her car, which was parked legally in a spot with a handicapped sign. She'd recently had a botched surgery on a foot deformed by decades of wearing high heels that had ended up making the pain worse.

As we put the Walmart bags into the trunk, a woman with permed hair walked behind us toward the store. We were climbing into the car when she spoke.

"You don't look very handicapped to *me*," she said to Grandma.

Betty's cheeks suddenly seemed to sag. She drew a long breath through her nose. Something changed somewhere behind her green eyes, and there she was — the Betty of the past that was rarely discussed but always felt.

Betty grabbed the roof of the car with her left hand and jerked herself out to point at her bad foot.

"Look here, you dumb broad, I had surgery on this foot."

The woman stopped, and her mouth fell open.

"I've got a tag right here," Betty yelled, yanking the blue permit from the rearview mirror and waving it around.

Tears were coming.

"I know one damn thing, I can still kick your fat ass with this foot!"

Her voice shook. Tears ran down her face, but she didn't sob.

The woman turned and hurried off with an indignant frown. Betty climbed back into the hot car. She wiped at her face, shaking and smearing gray eyeliner across her cheeks.

"Are you okay?" I asked.

We drove down Highway 54 from Wichita to the farm in silence. By the time we passed the Cheney exit I knew she was thinking about something else, maybe what she would make for dinner.

"Here, Lou," she said. "Look at this receipt and make sure she rung up all the coupons."

Grandma qualified for disability benefits and took an early retirement not long after that. She'd worked nearly nonstop since her first job at a soda fountain in the 1950s.

She'd spent almost twenty years counseling men in the criminal justice system, doing twice the work of her male colleagues, she said, for less pay. Her mom had been dead less than a year, and now her career had passed away, too.

Once she quit her job, it was the first time an adult had ever been home when I got back from school. I'd walk from the bus, past the garden and the dogs on the porch, through the screen door, and up the sagging wooden stairs beneath ceiling tiles collapsing with water damage. I'd hear *People's Court* on the heavy, square television that sat on top of the dresser in Betty's bedroom. She'd be asleep there; she and Arnie slept in separate rooms, partly because of his snoring. There would be a *Redbook* magazine lying next to her, open to the recipes in the back. On her nightstand, a pack of menthol cigarettes and an ashtray that made the air in the room burn my nose.

Half wrapped in a cheap, faded comforter of white and blue, Betty would be sprawled across her full-size mattress, twisted and bent into an anguished position. Sometimes I walked in to pet the tiny dog that slept next to her, guarding her, and I'd see that even in sleep Betty's light eyebrows were furrowed and there was a frown on her mouth, which had finally begun to wrinkle as a smoker's lips will do. She smelled of ash and mint — the cigarettes, her candy Red Hots that she kept in a Mason jar, the chalky pink candies from the dollar store that tasted like Pepto-Bismol, the strong odor of Icy Hot menthol ointment spread across her shoulders to distract her from the pain she felt there.

Betty had been diagnosed with chronic fatigue syndrome, which some doctors said was all in her head and others said was real. Chronic fatigue, or whatever it was, came with another problem, called fibromyalgia, also dubious if one believed medical texts. That caused the tissue in Betty's shoulders to swell painfully.

It made sense to me that she would develop something called "chronic fatigue." I had a sense of how much living she had done. I remembered, too, how infinite her energy once had seemed. There had been a time when, if she couldn't sleep at 4 a.m., she'd say to hell with it and go downstairs to organize the kitchen cabinets. All that restlessness, all that living, to my mind were tied up with the exhaustion that now left her sleeping in the afternoon sun.

The room was completely silent, *country* silent, and the sun came through the windows, making the flimsy white curtains transparent and revealing a cat sleeping in the windowsill. The bedroom walls were reddish-brown sheets of wood chips held together with glue. On one wall hung a cheap crucifix from when she had converted to the Church nearly twenty years prior. A "palm," as we called the dry, yellowed palm leaves used in Palm Sunday ritual, was wedged into the doorframe, just like in my bedroom and in Arnie's. Her dark wood bureau, a real bargain at a farm sale years ago, was covered with family photos, most of which were of me and Matt over the years, in cheap frames made of aluminum and sold for $1.99.

On the hardwood floor lay small rugs covered in cat hair and dog-poop stains. Betty was a voracious housekeeper, but it was a big old house, hard to maintain amid pain and depression. Upstairs, the four bedrooms collected dust, and the litter box overflowed in a small bathroom. Downstairs, the carpet needed vacuuming in the little space behind the steps, where Arnie calculated on tiny memo notepads his "figures" of wheat prices, cattle prices, cost of equipment repairs, hay sold to passersby. The kitchen needed sweeping, and so did the adjoining laundry room and the "extra room" off the porch with a deep freeze packed full of meat we'd wrapped. The downstairs bathroom needed to be scoured, and the dining room with all its cabinets needed dusting. So did the living room. Then there was the damp basement, which wound in the shape of a U. It was full of canned vegetables and Kerr jars of sand-plum jelly covered in gray dust and cob-webs.

Arnie would come in after finishing chores. Betty would drag herself downstairs to peel potatoes, then bread and fry the pack of homemade pork chops bleeding through white butcher paper after thawing all day in the kitchen sink. As she made din-ner, not speaking, she was preoccupied.

She and Grandpa had started bickering, as they rarely had before. Their twentieth wedding anniversary was approaching, and Camp Fun Farm, as Aunt Pud used to call it, was less fun than it once was. Arnie was in his midsixties and still tending the farm, because cattle need fed whether a farmer has bad knees or not. He had a new scar above one eyebrow where a deep hunk of skin cancer had been removed. They were both tired and cranky.

I often heard them fighting in the kitchen, a new sharpness in Grandma's voice. Maybe their age gap hadn't seemed so wide when she was thirty-two and he forty-five, but the distance between forty-nine and sixty-two seemed much greater. Arnie's legs, which had knelt so many times to fix so many pieces of machinery and tie so many fences, ached, and he struggled to get up the stairs to his bedroom.

Grandma had been drinking a lot of beer and taking a lot of medication since her mom's death. One afternoon, she took me through the entire farmhouse, both stories and the cavernous old basement, to show me where she had hidden things: a wad of cash in a jar, her .38 pistol, exotic trinkets Aaron had collected in the 1940s as a soldier overseas.

"Just in case," she said, and I groaned.

"Grandma, it's not like you're *old*!"

"Hey, I won't be here forever," she said.

She told me seriously that she wanted to be buried without a bra.

"I hate the damn things," she said. "You can burn 'em at my funeral."

That was the unsentimental power that came with the struggles of a poor woman's life: a dry humor rather than a sense of victim-hood, an unemotional appraisal of your own inevitable death and the coins you want to make sure your granddaughter finds. In their most sober, aligned moments, the women before you carried that grave strength like queens.

Dorothy, Betty, Pud, Polly, Jeannie — the psychological weight of their lives forced them into profound awareness. It was a way of experiencing the world that higher education has a way of erasing on campuses founded by men who exalted logic and intellect as the only path to knowledge. They had a confidence in their own intuition, a sort of knowing deeper than schooling can render and higher than the dogma of a church. If they could bear the pain of experiencing their world long enough, without numbing themselves, they had what you might call "powers."

Dad and Grandpa Arnie were mystics, of sorts — a private spirituality that existed apart from their Catholicism. They communicated with livestock, felt a foundation problem in an apparently sound structure, had correct hunches about where water was in earth.

Something about being a woman, though, came with an old wisdom that I feel fortunate to have inherited. Mom could extend her arm over a neat stack of waxy apples in the produce section and feel in her hand, tipped by long fingernails the color of the fruit, which ones were most crisp. It was the energy in them, she said. Betty swore she had psychic dreams as a child until she prayed that they would go away. Pud and Polly talked about good vibes and bad vibes. They all liked the Eagles song "Witchy Woman" and cracked up when it came on, like they had a secret, and in the end the joke was on the rest of the world.

It was real, August. It was a blessing of class, even, in that the academic and professional worlds they couldn't access would have frowned on it. It was a power no one could take from them. It was a way of seeing the world that they crafted themselves.

7
THE PLACE I WAS FROM

My life has been a bridge between two places: the working poor and "higher" economic classes. The city and the country. College-educated coworkers and disenfranchised loved ones. A somewhat conservative upbringing and a liberal adulthood. Home in the middle of the country and work on the East Coast. The physical world where I talk to people and the formless dimension where I talk to you.

Stretching your arms that far can be painful. As a permanent resident of Grandma Betty's relatively stable household, I found myself coming and going across miles of highway, hoping never to lose ties with my parents and brother. Most weekends in high school, once I had my learner's permit, I drove away from the farm on Friday evening. Then, on Sunday, I hugged my immediate family goodbye to drive west down a straight, flat stretch of asphalt back to my dirt-road life with my grandparents. I felt that if I didn't hold my family together, even as economics tore it apart, no one else would.

I often cried when I drove from one home toward another. In the dark, I rolled down the dirty window of Grandma's old car, shaking violently at highway speed. I felt a promise to my family: Somehow I'd do well in the world, not just with my heart but with my bank account. I'd pay off all their debts. I'd buy for them what they couldn't buy themselves, even if it was just a day off work. The idea made my eyes fill with the tears that maybe, on another highway in another youth, Dorothy, Betty, and Jeannie had not let themselves cry.

I stuck my head out the window to see the stars more clearly, to feel the thrill of a cool evening whip my hair away from my face. I felt young and old at once. I felt large in my own skin but small beneath the black sky.

That powerful sky I was under has a lot to do with Kansas culture and its economy. Wichita would become an airplane-manufacturing hub; one of our most famous daughters was Amelia Earhart; our other most famous daughter, of course, is a fictional farm girl who got pulled into another world by a tornado.

Kansans groan when people bring up that movie. If you're traveling and someone hears where you're from, they often joke, "You're not in Kansas anymore," as though they're the first person who thought of it.

Yet it is true: I was a Kansas farm girl with wanderlust who watched many storms blow the shingles off our roof. Every spring and summer, heavy air masses moving in opposite directions clashed above us. The horizon was a strip of pink sky between the brown earth and a rolling black wall of cloud. We needed to worry when the sky took a green tint, the air became still, and the cattle huddled against the fence, looking concerned.

We were too far from Kingman to hear the sirens, but when the words crawled across the bottom of the TV screen with a beep, I'd run upstairs to get my boom box, typewriter, journals, and photographs. I'd stash them in the basement with the canned corn and cobwebs, and climb back up the damp steps to run outside and watch the sky.

Grandma Betty would be smoking calmly, watching the Doppler radar report on the evening news. Grandpa Arnie would be worrying about the wheat and trying to get the tractors into the shed before the hail started. About once a year we'd all go to the basement and ride out the storm with candles and a weather radio, then emerge upstairs to see what God had done this time. A tall fence would be floating in the swimming pool, or an uprooted tree would be leaning against the grain bin.

One storm, in particular, stands out in memory. I was a teenager. I ran outside to watch from the north side of the house, between the water faucet and the rosebush ripe and fragrant with pink and white blossoms against the garage where we butchered hogs and cattle. The hail had stopped — the moment of stillness when the trees seem to hold their breath and you can hear a cow shift its hoof in the mud.

The swirling clouds were just above my head, reaching down with little arms of gray, white, black, orange, and green, so low they might touch my face. They spun around a middle void, stretched and grabbed at one another, pulling back into themselves — the beginnings of a funnel.

A supercell, as meteorologists call it, swirling over the plains is still the most beautiful thing I've ever seen. That day was the closest I'd ever been to the center of one. I loved such storms in the way I had loved the dangerous spillway that opened the dam of Cheney Lake and let water crash through while I clung to the safety fence alone as a child. Some sort of pressure was breaking.

No tornado sucked me into the sky, but like so many young Americans in those years I would have no choice but to leave home if I was going to thrive. To do so suited me, I guess. I had long been doing, learning, writing, thinking things that set me apart from the women in my family. But that widening distance sometimes hurt. I had overheard Grandma on the telephone one night, talking to a friend, when I was still just a kid.

"I don't understand half of what she's saying," Grandma told her friend.

Her words were confirmation of what I'd known my whole life: that I was somehow strange to the place I was from. I had fit my origin like a baby fits a womb — awkwardly, nourished by both the good and the bad until she outgrows the space.

Around that same time, I dreamed that Grandma Betty and I were in a 1950s convertible, blue and white like Ed and Irene's Chevy was in stories. She was driving. It was a warm, sunny day. Grandma pulled up next to a park, where adults and children were buzzing around playground equipment. We got out of the car and walked to the playground. A little girl, about two or three years old, came to me and looked up. I saw her face and realized that it was me as a child.

I looked at Betty. Next to her stood her tiny childhood counterpart, with white-blond hair and big cheeks, wearing a little dress. Amazed, I looked out across the playground and saw that every adult there was accompanied by the child version of herself.

When I woke up, I knew just what I was trying to tell myself. Whatever childhood I'd had was over, whether I liked it or not. I wasn't a woman yet, but I had been my own mother for a long time. I was old enough to become pregnant with you, but I was also old enough to drive. Old enough to swear that I would never suffer the way the women before me had — not at the hands of a man and not at the hands of an economy.

Those women knew struggle along highways as a way of life, and as their immediate descendant I felt their destiny pushing itself onto me. Now those women I loved, once seeming forces of power above me, had been revealed as hurt little girls. No matter how much I loved them and the home we had shared, I was getting out of their goddamn car.

■ ■ ■ ■

Economic inequality is one cultural divide that causes us to see one another as stereotypes, some of which allow the powerful to make harmful decisions in policy and politics.

That separation is experienced intimately, though, as distances we might not realize are related to class. I grew up seeing, in particular, how it rips at the bond between children and the people who might have taken care of them. The struggling divorcée, lacking means to provide a proper home, loses custody of her child; the poor teenager puts her baby up for adoption; the meth addict tells her kids to hide when state child-welfare agents knock on the trailer door; the alcoholic, unemployed father knows his children will be better off without him and drives away with a broken heart. The young woman I once was longed to have you but knew she couldn't do right by you or herself if she did.

By the time I was in high school, I had figured out that Betty had a son. We had never talked about it. All I knew of him were a couple black-and-white photos in which a mysterious blond baby sat next to my four-year-old mother in living rooms I'd never seen. I recalled whispers, cryptic conversations between Grandma and her sisters about a boy named Bo.

One day when I was in high school, I came home to find a list, in Grandma's handwriting, near the cordless handset that had replaced the rotary phone next to the bathroom door. It was a list of phone numbers for private investigators.

When Grandma got home with sacks of groceries, I told her I thought she should find her son. She let out a loud sigh, the way she always did after I had badgered her enough about something she didn't want to think about. She told me about when Bo was nine or ten, just before she lost in court for good and decided it was best for him if she stayed away, when she drove to Colorado and got to spend a few hours with him.

"I told him I'd see him again soon, and that I'd have a bicycle for him," she said, her voice shaky. "He wanted a bike real bad. He was so excited. But I didn't have any money. I was dirt poor. Christ, I was just a kid. So I never got him the bike. That's the last I seen him. He probably grew up thinking, 'Wow, what a lousy mom, she lied to me and split.'"

Her face was wet. She turned back to the

sink. I sat there thinking about how I should get up and give her a hug, but I didn't.

"I think he's lucky to have you for a mom," I said.

"Thanks, Lou."

Soon, in the fall of 1996, during my junior year of high school, Grandma asked me to go with her and Grandpa Arnie to Denver to meet her grown son. Mom didn't come with us — maybe because of work, maybe something more.

Driving along the highway, Grandma smoked even more than usual. I asked her to crack the window. The sound of wheels on the highway and the wind of western Kansas was better than a cloud of smoke. I stretched out across the back seat of the Toyota minivan that Grandma had bought used so that I could drive the 1986 Corolla every day to and from work and school.

Grandma didn't speak after we left the farm with an Igloo cooler of canned pop and plastic baggies of licorice. She was usually quiet on the road but not this quiet. It was a ten-hour drive to end a nearly thirty-year separation.

Grandpa Arnie snored in the passenger seat. He had never met Bo and didn't know the details of that story from Grandma's past. But he had a way of understanding

381

things without needing to discuss them. He had left the farm in someone else's hands for the weekend — the first time I'd seen him do so in my entire life — and that told me how much he cared.

Arid western Kansas is even drier than our southern part of the state. Tumbleweeds blew in the dirt that the highway cut through. A few trees marked the flat space between horizons. It was hard to see autumn with so few changing leaves.

We crossed into Colorado and soon saw the faint outline of mountains on the horizon, always thrilling to us. We pulled into Uncle Carl's driveway in the winding streets of a Denver suburb in early evening. He and Aunt Pat lived in a big, nice house with new carpet and a neat garage full of golf clubs and bicycles in a winding suburb. Carl had come a long way from his and Betty's poor childhood.

It was weird that he ended up here, I thought, from Kansas to Texas to Michigan to, by chance, the same city as his long-lost nephew. He had offered his home as a place for the reunion with Bo, who was now thirty and working as a cable-TV installer, climbing poles to connect wires. He had been a Marine in the 1980s and was newly married.

Uncle Carl looked more like Dorothy than ever with his shiny, round cheeks and bumpy nose. He gave us a tour of the place, and Grandpa Arnie inspected all that was growing in the backyard. Betty wandered around the house like a wild, frightened animal. Or she went to the bathroom to comb her hair or make sure her shirt was evenly tucked into her pants, a larger size than in years past.

We finally heard a car pulling into the driveway. Betty moved toward the window to peek outside, and Pat opened the door. A blond man stood there with his young wife. Betty's chest had been puffed out since she left the living room, like she'd taken a deep breath and not let it go. The instant she saw her son, she turned quickly and looked at me with huge eyes and a half smile.

"God, you look just like your father," she told him.

Bo sucked in a shaky breath, like maybe that hadn't been the best thing to say. After all the introductions, he turned to her with a pained look.

"Why do you keep calling me 'Bo'?" he said. "My name is Robert."

Betty blinked. "Okay," she said.

They stayed in touch after that. A couple times a year, he would make the ten-hour drive to the farm or we'd drive to Denver. He and my mom ended up being close; she even moved to Denver some years later to be near him and his young family. It was a reunion owed in large part to what Betty had made of her life — the confidence she had gained working in "the system," as she called the criminal courts, the steadiness and sanity that she ultimately found in spite of her chaotic past, the mere fact that she had survived.

Perhaps most important to our family's happier endings was that, while Betty had plenty of good excuses to become a bitter, cynical person, she had somehow preserved her natural outlook on the world: that justice is worth fighting for, and the notion of a better life is always worth a shot.

Just as Betty and my mom were reuniting with Robert, I was getting ready to leave home. The specifics were unclear and fell to me to organize and decide, as is usually the case for a college-hopeful teenager whose family never went.

The Marines set up a table in the lobby of my high school and said they'd pay for my college. I took their information packet home and read every word. Shelly had gotten involved in ROTC at her high school in

Wichita. My new uncle Robert had appreci-ated his time in the Marines, he told me. A couple younger cousins of mine, Polly's teenage sons, would soon join the Army and Navy.

Dad had barely missed going to Vietnam. He turned eighteen two years before the draft ended, and Grandpa Chic told him he would turn recruiters away if they knocked on the door of the farmhouse. Both of his older brothers had been in the National Guard. But Dad didn't think much of the military and wasn't sorry he missed going overseas. He thought the United States had done terrible things with its armed forces over the years, back to its crimes against the American Indians whose arrowheads he'd found in the dirt when he built our house in 1984. You didn't need a college educa-tion to know that, he said.

All the same, the prospect of getting an education for "free" made me lie awake at night, listening to the bullfrogs outside and the fan whirring in the window and pictur-ing myself as a soldier. It would all depend on what sort of scholarships I got, I decided. I prayed.

The teachers at Kingman High said it wasn't necessary to take the SATs, which were required for admission to most major universities across the country, so I didn't. Kansas universities required only the ACT, they said, so I took that test.

I'd previously taken the PSATs while seated on a folding chair in our gymnasium. I was exhausted from waiting tables at a Pizza Hut on the highway the previous night and, thinking it inconsequential practice — the "P" stood for "preliminary" — I answered questions with uncharacteristic carelessness. Weeks later, the guidance counselor, who was also the boys' track coach, approached me in the hallway.

"You only missed National Merit by a few points," he said.

"What's National Merit?" I asked. It was, it turned out, an academic honor that would've paid my way at many elite universities. Kansas public education was excellent on a national scale, but my years in rural schools didn't come with the same opportunities as Wichita districts.

Still, I started getting brochures in the mail from colleges across the country. We didn't have a computer at home, and my high school had just one computer online; it wasn't yet the "digital age" for most people, so our rural mailbox was the only way for universities to reach me. Their brochures included pictures of happy kids my age walking across campuses of trees and old stone buildings with happy parents who had sweaters tied around their shoulders.

The pile of recruitment materials outgrew the folder I kept them in, then outgrew a box, until finally I kept them in big bags in my bedroom. I had no idea how to process them, other than to keep the ones from universities famous enough that I'd heard of them.

Many of the letters named visiting days for touring the campus. I didn't know that visiting colleges together was a rite of passage for many families. The cost of travel would have been unthinkable, anyway. Grandma had a small stash of cash from her years of working at the courthouse while living in Grandpa's paid-off farmhouse. I didn't know exactly how much it was, but it was there when friends and family needed bailed out of a bind. I never thought to ask her to pay for campus visits. I understood college as a wholly independent endeavor — one my parents and grandparents vaguely supported but became nervous and even self-conscious discussing. They knew even less about the process than I did.

On graduation day, I looked out at my class of sixty or so graduates in red caps and gowns, lined up in folding chairs on the small-town gym floor painted with a red eagle. My family was all there, proud. They had not been to many high school graduation ceremonies. But I felt less satisfaction than I did relief. There was a diploma in my hand, a scholarship with my name on it, and no baby inside me. I thought, *No matter what happens now, I made it.*

There was a great deal of work ahead of me, but I had passed the first gauntlet in escaping a probable version of my life — one where all my hopes and dreams were compromised by the necessity of caring and paying for your life.

College applications require an application fee, so I had ended up applying to only one school, the University of Kansas. I knew I liked the hilly town where it was located, since I'd attended an honors academy on scholarship there a couple summers prior, and it had a good journalism school. Most of my friends were going to the historically agricultural college or small university outposts in windblown western Kansas. KU in liberal Lawrence was thought of by most people in Kingman as a snobbish place. I experienced my enrollment there as an unimaginably fancy achievement.

I received merit-based and geography-based scholarships that covered my tuition and then some, so I dropped the idea of enlisting in the military. I didn't get Pell Grants, though. While I'd moved out years earlier and they didn't pay for most of my upbringing, Mom and Bob still claimed me as a dependent for the deduction on their taxes. Since my grandparents had not legally adopted me, I had to list Mom and Bob's joint income on my federal aid application. So while my actual need qualified me for Pell Grants that wouldn't have to be repaid, Bob's modest income meant I received only federal loans with subsidized interest.

That excruciating experience was a formative one, I see now. I started my college career needing something I didn't get because the need went unacknowledged on a form that didn't ask the right questions. Most people who write laws weren't raised by their grandparents due to economic hardship, and the federal aid formula is based on the assumption that parents help pay for college.

I ended up doing an investigative story about the issue for the student newspaper. It was the first thing I ever wrote that was picked up by the national wire to run in papers across the country. So many students thanked me for writing it that I never stopped thinking about the distance between how poverty is handled in public policy and what it looks like in human lives.

Before I got to campus, though, I spent the summer after graduation saving up money for a car. I'd been in a bad wreck and totaled Grandma's old Corolla on the last day of classes. I borrowed her van to work the wheat harvest at the grain co-op in Kingman. At the old elevator at the end of Main Street, a high school friend and I weighed wheat trucks when they rolled onto the scale. I ran out the door to hand farmers tickets printed with the weight of their load, the price of wheat that day, and how much money was going into their account.

"You're Nick Smarsh's girl, aintcha," some of them said, and I smiled. I hadn't lived with my dad in almost ten years, and he'd been gone from the country for just as long. But out there a person is forever known by what family she belongs to.

We wore hard hats when we went in and out of the mill with sacks of feed. A tall, poorly ventilated column full of dusty grain in the Kansas summer is a volatile thing. While I worked there, a grain elevator to the east blew up and killed seven men working inside it.

Once the June harvest was done, I worked

fifty miles away at a hotel reservations call center on the far east side of Wichita. College hadn't even started yet, and I'd been exhausted for years.

In August, I handed a man $3,000 in cash for a small brown sedan with a good engine and a deep gash in the driver's seat. A few days after I turned eighteen, I loaded the backseat of my car and said goodbye to Mom in the driveway of a suburban town house into which she, Bob, and Matt had recently moved. Bob was proud of me and excited for my upcoming adventures. He looked at my mom.

"You're not going to help your daughter move to college?" he said. He'd done so with his own three kids in recent years, as I recall.

Mom looked embarrassed, like it had never occurred to her. It hadn't occurred to me either. We all hugged, and I drove away with my map.

I wonder now whether she didn't go with me because the thought of a college campus — and all that she wouldn't know to say and do there as my mother — intimidated her. She wasn't one to act intimidated, of course. But when I got older I'd see how uncomfortable my family sometimes acted in places that had become natural to me.

From the farm to campus, the journey was eight counties, two hundred miles, three hours of prairie. I drove northeast through the heat on the tall golden grass, up through the Flint Hills toward the Kansas River. August was a wealthy month for wheat farmers, recently paid for the grain they'd spent all year farming. August was also the month when I harvested a lifetime of hard work and left.

In college, I began to understand the depth of the rift that is economic inequality. Roughly speaking, on one side of the rift was the place I was from — laborers, workers, people filled with distrust for the systems that had been ignoring and even spurning them for a couple decades. On the other side were the people who run those systems — basically, people with college funds who end up living in cities or moving to one of the expensive coasts. It's much messier than that, of course. But before arriving on campus, I hadn't understood the extent of my family's poverty — "wealth" previously having been represented to me by a friend whose dad was our small town's postmaster and whose mom went to the Wichita mall every weekend.

Even at a Midwestern state university, my

background — agricultural work, manual labor, rural poverty, teen pregnancies, domestic chaos, pervasive addiction — seemed like a faraway story to the people I met. Most of them were from tidy neighborhoods in Wichita, Kansas City, the greater Chicago area. They used a different sort of English and had different politics. They were appalled that I had grown up with conservative ideas about government and Catholic doctrine against abortion. I was appalled that they didn't know where their food came from or even seem to care since it had always just appeared on their plates when they wanted it.

There was no language for whatever I represented on campus. Scholarships and student organizations existed to boost kids from disadvantaged groups such as racial minorities, international students, and the LGBTQ community. I was none of those things, and professors and other students often assumed from looking at me or hearing me speak that I was a middle-class kid with parents sending me money.

To pay my room and board during my freshman year at college, I worked as a tutor for poor middle-school kids in nearby Kansas City and Topeka in the afternoons, as a stage technician for a performing arts center in the evenings, and as my dorm's front-desk attendant overnight. During spring break, I was the trail boss for an environmental cleanup crew. I waited tables, too, late-night shifts worth a forty-five-minute drive to Kansas City because the tips were better there. I knew other kids with jobs but not many who had no choice but to work.

A young woman in poverty, vulnerable twice over, I was mistreated at many of those jobs. I thought of you often, then — that question, *What would I want for my daughter?* The answer was always to quit and find another job, so I would. I felt the tension between my need and my dignity every day. Some days I went hungry because I refused to work somewhere a male boss looked at my body.

There are many complicated reasons why so few people cross a socioeconomic divide in any lasting way, but one of the reasons is simple: It is a painful crossing. Those were the hardest years of my life.

When I called home, I heard the familiar stories: My thirty-year-old cousin Candy didn't know how she'd pay her hospital bills, but she'd survived colon cancer. At a party Grandma threw at the farm, Arnie's daughter-in-law rifled through unlocked parked cars to steal cash — to buy drugs, my mom speculated — and in the process took Candy's last $20. Well, Candy had had it, so she beat the shit out of her while my mom cheered her on and Arnie's son Tom tried to pull them apart.

After the party, Mom figured out that her wedding band, which she'd stopped wearing but kept in her purse, was missing. A few days later, she drove an hour from Wichita to her stepsister-in-law's house in rural Kansas and pounded on the door. Mom sat on the porch for hours and hours until she finally came to the door and handed over the ring, miraculously not yet sold for drug money. Meanwhile, Dad was on a new job site. Chris was having more health problems, in and out of the hospital with a stomach burned through by painkillers. Bills bills bills.

Then I hung up and went to class.

Few people knew how much I was struggling both emotionally and financially, because I didn't talk to anyone about it or even understand how bad off I was. Knowing I'd never ask for it, my high school cheerleading coach mailed me $300. I put it in a thank-you card and mailed it back. Like the conservative laborer who spurns the idea of "handouts," my pride was bigger than my need.

I didn't know the term "first-generation student" and didn't grasp yet that I had in fact "grown up poor" and was still very much "living in poverty." The best I could come up with for describing my situation was that I was a "financially independent student" and tell people that "I grew up on a farm."

I once took a roommate, a funny, sharp girl raised in lower-middle-class Wichita, to the farm and was stunned to see it through her eyes. Everything was worth exclaiming about — the cows, the pigs, the chickens, the butchering shed, the cow tongue pickling in a jar in the refrigerator, the way every single adult was drinking alcohol.

Tom and his wife were living at the farm since they had no money and Grandma would take needy people in whether she liked them or not. This was before the ring theft, I guess.

My friend's mouth fell open when Tom boomed through the front door, carrying a plate of flayed raccoon meat to put on the stove.

Eating raccoon was remarkable even for us. The occasional turtle or rabbit ended up in the kitchen as novelty, maybe, but raccoon seemed plumb trashy. I was embarrassed when my friend told the story again and again back on campus — a situation I found I could control by telling the stories myself.

"Cows are more pleasant than goats," I'd say to explain why we had one and not the other, and my college friends would crack up like it was an amazing joke. Grandpa Arnie had bought a few goats when I was little, and they had turned out to be a menace.

"Why did he buy the goats?" they would ask, as though the answer were complicated and perhaps had something to do with personal fulfillment.

"Because they are cheap and eat weeds," I'd say, and they'd bend over laughing. By then I'd be laughing, too, because I was amazed it was so funny to anyone.

In those moments I saw that mine wasn't as much a sad story as it was a rare one, that better-off people's fascination was not just derision but, sometimes, honest awe. The distance between my world and my country's understanding of it had been growing because so few people from my place ever ended up on a college campus and beyond to tell its stories. It was a distance I wanted to make smaller.

During the fall of my sophomore year in

college, Grandpa Arnie was diagnosed with pancreatic cancer. He briefly received hospital treatment, but the cancer had progressed too far for anything to save him. Grandma Betty took care of him at home. He died in six weeks.

I'd been to a lot of funerals by then. Arnie's brother, who had colossal hands. Ray's mother, whose face was shaped like mine. The sixteen-year-old girl I'd roomed with at cheerleading camp who lost control of her truck and was buried in a blue sweatshirt that read CHEERLEADER. My high school's middle-aged athletic director, who was so tall he must have needed a special casket. Grandpa Chic, who looked old, the way a dead body ought to look. Wrinkled Judge Watson, in whose chambers I'd played while he and Betty smoked between hearings. My great-grandma Dorothy, who was buried in a satin nightgown that Pud had bought.

I wasn't prepared for Grandpa Arnie's wake, though, which for me fell during a busy week of college exams and deadlines. I took a test, got in my car, and sped south. As trees gave way to grassland and the sky got bigger, I spent the three-hour drive thinking about Arnie. How I would get off the bus and see him high off the ground, resting easily atop his white Case tractor, rolling out of the big metal shed pulling a disc plow. I would feel relieved that he was still doing chores and not already sitting at the kitchen table with a big glass of tea, because I hated how he greeted me.

"Juh learn anything?" he would say.

Not wanting to bother explaining the complicated lessons I had mastered in the classroom — algebraic formulas, three-point essays — to a grandfather who hadn't gone beyond sixth grade, I always replied sullenly, "No."

We both knew I was leaving soon, not just from the farm but from the only way of life Grandpa had ever known. It was a separation born of class, that a child might lose a sense of belonging within her own family for going to college.

When I got home to find Grandpa driving machinery, he did not ask about my studies. There were more important things to do.

"Girl!" He would holler down at me over the huge engine. "Close the gate behind me!"

The deep voice, full of power and phlegm, was lost to the churning equipment, but I had learned to read his lips — thus avoiding misunderstanding his directions and the red-faced explosion that followed. I would nod, and he would wheel slowly across the gravel that was our front yard as dogs, cats, chickens, and the odd piglet scattered from the painful roar.

Once he turned toward the field, Grandpa Arnie would look back at me. Through dust, he would raise one index finger, which is how farmers wave to say hello, goodbye, and thank you. Then he would surge forward, pulling the green plow out to the quarter where Jerry the farmhand was already turning the earth.

I arrived in Kingman underdressed and late for the wake. Having raced out the door back at my apartment, I still was wearing jeans and a Nike windbreaker as I ran across the street to the mortuary near my old high school.

Dad and Chris, always late, got to the door the same time I did. Dad put his hand on my shoulder as I hurried him inside. He was walking like he was old, although he was just forty-four. He was wearing his snakeskin boots with a suit that was too big.

"I'm going to need you to help me get through this," Dad said, his voice low.

His hairline was nearly halfway back on his head now, and his light brown beard was going gray. He had known Arnie even before he'd known my mom. But, having lived with him for much of my life, I'd surely been closer to Arnie, and it didn't feel right to be summoned as Dad's shoulder to lean on. I turned from Dad to go alone toward the chapel.

The people inside were already halfway through the Rosary. No seats remained in the main area, so I knelt in the last pews of a side room set off by a tall partition. I couldn't see past the make-shift wall to the casket and the pulpit and my family. I could hear but not see Father John, the priest who had married my parents and grandparents and presided over all my sacraments. The people near me were Arnie's distant friends, long-lost cousins, and members of the farming community reaching halfway across Kansas. Some turned and recognized me as immediate kin who belonged in a closer seat. I wondered whether Grandma Betty was crying.

I squeezed my hands together and tried to concentrate on counting the Hail Marys but could think only about how Arnie's big, leathery hands that swatted wasps and tied fence were lying somewhere in the other room, and why didn't I bring a Rosary, how did the people who weren't Catholic know what to do, where was Grandma Betty, couldn't I have changed clothes at an intersection coming through Wichita, what kind of person takes a college exam after her grandpa dies, and how was Grandpa Arnie dead?

I looked at the funeral program the mortuary had printed and for the first time registered Grandpa's middle name, August. He had been born that month in a farmhouse a few miles away in 1932, the worst year of the Great Depression. I didn't think of you right at that moment, but the name stuck in my brain for several years until I realized it was your name, too.

After the prayers, people filed into the chapel to view the body. I felt hands on my back ushering me ahead in the line. I came around the partition and saw the dark brown coffin with engravings of wheat stalks. It was a perfect coffin, if a coffin can be perfect. Arnie's first wife and her husband were bent over the body. I always forgot about the first wife.

I saw Grandma Betty standing on the other side of the casket with a few members of our family. She had been crying. She looked at me with a sad smile, and Shelly walked over to take me past the body.

"Hey. You okay?" she said.

"Yeah. I was late," I said, looking down at my jeans.

We stepped up to the open casket. I felt like I was going to fall down for a moment. I tried to think about how it wasn't really him lying there. His jaundiced skin had been poorly concealed by thick, tan makeup. He was wearing his brown polyester suit, with his wide maroon tie, and the coffin was brown, and Arnie was a little bit brown, and everything was brown like the earth. A stalk of wheat lay across his chest. He wore his Tony Lama boots that I used to run and get from his closet so he wouldn't have to climb the stairs with his bad knees. I looked at his face, sinking into the folds of skin pushing up from the collar around his remarkable neck. Betty never could find collars that fit him. I thought his whole body was sinking. I noticed a bit of hair coming out of his right ear.

"Hey," Grandma Betty said, rubbing my back with her hand, which held a wadded tissue.

"Hey," I said.

We hugged right there with a line of people behind us waiting to look at the body. Then Betty leaned into the coffin and stuck her pinkie in his right ear. It didn't seem right to me to go burrowing into the crevices of a corpse. But she dug around inside the ear and pulled out a clump of wax, which she rubbed into her tissue. Shelly and I looked at each other.

"Hey, Betty, what's on his tie?" Shelly whispered close to Betty's ear.

"What?" Betty said.

I had noticed, but not really noticed, a small metal pin in the middle of his necktie. We leaned closer to examine it. It read FORGIVEN.

"I think his ex-wife put it there," Shelly said.

"I thought that bitch was up to something," Betty said. Her voice sounded like it might break soon.

As she undid the pin, she started to cry, just barely, and moved away from the casket. I said a prayer and sent a message into space for Grandpa Arnie or his soul or whatever might be around, and stepped past.

On the way out, I saw Jerry, who was approaching middle age and had been Arnie's farmhand since he was a teenager, wearing the look of a son who had lost his father. Tall and skinny, he seemed suddenly like a scarecrow. He looked me in the eye while a crowd of people scooted around us.

"Hello, Sarah," he said, and somehow we were giving each other a long hug, though he was always so shy, and we never talked much through all the years of him hammering in the shed or drinking iced tea at the kitchen table with Grandpa. He cried a little bit, too. "He was real proud of you," he said.

Leaving the mortuary, I was anxious to see the farm for the first time in months. I drove past the wheat fields that looked cold and dead but were alive underneath. Green sprouts would appear soon. I turned onto the long gravel driveway and saw the square white house that I'd left behind for college the year prior.

When I opened my car door, the farm didn't seem to be there. The cows and pigs made no sounds in the darkness, and I couldn't smell them, because the November air was frozen. There already was talk of a farm sale. There was no one left to keep the farm alive. Jerry had his own family and acreage now. Arnie's grown children lived in other places. Betty was depressed and still sick with chronic fatigue. I was in college. Matt was a teenager and had grown up mostly in the city anyhow.

I grabbed my backpack, full of heavy textbooks, and crunched across the earth, past the cars that had beaten me home. I opened the metal gate, then the metal screen door, then the wooden front door that opened into the kitchen with its wooden chair where Arnie drank iced tea after his chores, when I got home from school.

"Juh learn anything?"

It was a question impossible to answer, and his tone struck me as skeptical. But there was a vulnerability in his question. Whatever the gift of school was, he didn't possess it, and he knew that. He made the inquiry less because he cared about the answer than because he cared about me — Sarah Lou, the baby he'd held, the child he'd taken along on countless happy chore excursions across his land, the teenager for whom on dark winter mornings before school he had scraped ice from the windshield of a beat-up car parked next to his farmhouse's chain-link fence. He'd seen himself in the way I smelled the air for rain, and he quietly admired the way I checked on newborn animals every day, without fail. We both had 20/10 vision. We exchanged glances when Grandma Betty got drunk during weekend farm parties and climbed onto the kitchen counter to dance.

During his fast decline, I visited him in a Wichita hospital. We knew he was going to die and that I might not see him again. I held his big hand as I stood next to the bed, where he was smaller than normal under a white sheet. We hadn't talked as much since

I'd become a teenager and made big plans to leave and go places he would never see.

"Grandpa, I —" I had a lump in my throat too big to talk.

He patted my hand. His hand was enormous and brown against my small pale one. His fingers were thickened by work.

"We know how we feel about each other," he said.

Soon there would be an auction. Grandma Betty would keep the house, outbuildings, and some acreage. She got money from the government for letting some of the land sit still and regenerate. Other acres she shared with Arnie's old friends, who would tend crops and give her a piece of the profit. But the farm as we knew it was dead. There was a lot of equipment to be sold.

On a frigid weekend, we covered a couple hayracks in antique gadgets dug from the recesses of our barns. Farmers from around the county stood spitting and kicking the dirt and waiting for the auctioneer to get to the big stuff, like the tractors and combines. The big sky was white and gray.

To keep the cold off my skin, I had on the 1970s insulated coveralls I used to wear for chores. It felt good. An auctioneer faced the house from atop a hayrack that Grandpa used to pull us through fields on starry nights for fun. Men and women in coveralls, stocking caps, and work boots held thermoses of coffee. Their kids huddled next to them.

"Arnie was a good man," the auctioneer said, his breath a white puff in the air. "Let's give 'm a good sale."

Then he said numbers quickly, and the people in the crowd raised their hands to bid. They bid on things they didn't need, because they knew the man they had belonged to and they knew his family who stood next to them now. In the greatest gesture of respect, they bid high.

"SOLD!" the auctioneer said before his young helper lifted up the next item. They moved through the small things first and then auctioned off the combines, tractors, plows, and other big machinery.

The country people pulled cash out of their billfolds with cold fingers. In a rare act, they had driven a price up, rather than down, and intentionally paid more than market value. They knew Arnie had done the same at other farm sales. They nodded at us as they helped one another load the pieces of our farm into their pickup beds. They knew what a person's life was worth.

About a year after Grandpa Arnie died, during the autumn of my junior year in college, I was editing a story in the campus paper's newsroom on the night of the 2000 presidential election. The whole staff was on duty, watching election returns on a boxy television mounted to a wall above a Rosie the Riveter poster and a fax machine that press releases came across. Earlier in the day I had cast my first-ever ballot in a national election, for George W. Bush. A friend and fellow editor with reddish-brown dreadlocks, a head scarf, and plugs in her earlobes sat down next to me at my computer, looked into my eyes, and asked, "How could you vote for him?"

Something had changed my people politically in the twenty years since my mom had voted for Jimmy Carter when I was an infant, the year Reagan won. There I was to prove it — a liberally minded young person from the rural working class who had somehow voted Republican.

Whatever caused the change, it crystallized with the popularity of a new conservative cable TV network. We didn't have cable at the farm, but in Wichita Mom had started listening to conservative talk radio. She'd nod along in the car as a host spewed venomous attacks on liberalism. Something in his apparent outrage about "government handouts" appealed to her. She was open-minded and progressive on most social issues but raised a defiant middle finger to the idea of so-called assistance, so I did, too. I voted for Kansas native Bob Dole in my rural high school's 1996 mock presidential election. Mom and I cheered when the GOP retained a majority in both houses that year. During my senior year, I wore a sticker on which I'd written IMPEACH CLINTON in all my student-organization group pictures on yearbook photo day.

Aunt Pud was the only one in our family who I recall refusing to budge from older affiliations between class and party. "The Democrats are for poor people, and the Republicans are for the rich," she would declare and slam her beer on the table.

"No," Mom would reply. "Democrats help people, and Republicans help people help themselves."

People on welfare were presumed "lazy," and for us there was no more hurtful word. Within that framework, financially comfortable liberals may rest assured that their fortunes result from personal merit while generously insisting they be taxed to help the "needy." Impoverished people, then, must do one of two things: concede personal failure and vote for the party more inclined to assist them, or vote for the other party, whose rhetoric conveys hope that the labor of their lives is what will compensate them. It's a hell of a choice, and initially I made mine based on my mother's ideas. My liberal peers were no different in that respect, for the most part having shown up on campus with their parents' beliefs.

It was a sociology course the spring of my junior year that dismantled my political views about fiscal policy. Study after study that I found in my research for the class plainly said in hard numbers that, if you are poor, you are likely to stay poor, no matter how hard you work. As I examined the graphs over and over, my heart sped up with shock and anger. On the matter of my own country's economic system, for all my family wisdom about what something ought to cost and who was peddling a con, I had been sold a bill of goods.

The people I'd grown up with were missing that information. But the liberal people I met in college often were missing another sort of information: What it feels like to pee in a cup to qualify for public benefits to feed your children. A teenager's frustration when a dilapidated textbook is missing a page and there's no computer in the house for finding the lesson online. The impossibility of paying a citation for expired auto insurance, itself impossible to pay despite fifty hours a week holding metal frying baskets at KFC.

It wasn't that I'd been wrong to be suspicious of government programs, I realized, but that I'd been wrong to believe in the American Dream. They were two sides of the same trick coin — one promising a good life in exchange for your labor and the other keeping you just alive enough to go on laboring.

Meanwhile, as college experiences took me outside my home state, I realized that Kansas as a whole suffered from a similar disconnect with power. The broader country viewed states like mine as unimportant, liminal places. They yawned while driving through them, slept as they flew over them.

If you're cast as a stereotype enough times — as a poor person, as a female, as the native of a place most people have never been — you might feel who you truly are fortify in opposition to it. Where the shame I sometimes felt as a child in poverty had once been, as a young woman in a new setting I felt a quiet pride about that place thought forgettable or populated by trash.

We were the "breadbasket"; I'd helped harvest the wheat that fed the world. Wichita was the "air capital"; my grandmothers had assembled warplanes there in the same factories where my aunts and uncles now worked. We were in "tornado alley"; we had ridden out storms in trailers and farmhouse basements and lived to describe the softball-size hail and the hay straw driven by the wind into a tree trunk. Whether or not I got a college degree, those experiences would always be my first education.

I ended up being admitted to a federally funded program that encouraged minority, first-generation, and low-income students toward graduate school. The small handful of white kids already in the program, I found, had given us a nickname: "White Trash Scholars."

In the late '70s, just after she divorced Dean, the guy with the squeaky voice who took her to Sears, Betty started thinking of Arnie again. She'd never forgotten that dance at the Cotillion. She drove past two or three country-western clubs where she knew Arnie hung out, hoping she might see his truck: The Wagon Wheel. Frankie's Lounge. Then at a stoplight where West Street intersected Kellogg, which turned into Highway 54, Betty looked up in her Corvette, and Arnie was sitting there in his brown GMC.

She honked and waved. They pulled into Gerrard's truck stop and talked over coffee. Thus, the highway women of my mother's family spent the next quarter century moving in and out of Arnie's farm.

Now that Arnie was dead, they all hit the road again. Within two years, Betty remarried and moved to Iowa to be with a rancher she met when he saw our hay-bale rows from the highway and stopped to ask about the price. Pud, Larry, and Candy moved to Florida to escape the Kansas winter. Shelly moved to Louisiana to be with a man she'd met on the internet. Mom divorced Bob and moved to Kansas City.

Even though she had moved north, Grandma had kept ownership of the farmhouse, outbuildings, and a few surrounding acres. The machinery and most of the land had been sold off, but the heart of the place still belonged to her.

The house sat unoccupied for seven years but still held furniture, televisions, clothes, photo albums. Nearby farmers stored their machinery in the Big Shed east of the house and their hay bales in the Little Shed near the cattle pen to the north. They kept their livestock in the pasture and rented acreage from Betty to grow wheat and milo.

The farmhouse itself began to fall apart

with no proper keeper, though. Windows cracked, the basement flooded, the chimney that had crumbled over my childhood bedroom crumbled further.

Betty had been reluctant to sell the place, because it was hard telling how long her Iowa marriage would last, and she might want to move back. Plus, her family members might need a place to stay, as they often had. So she left the water service running and, in winter, kept the furnace on a low setting to prevent frozen pipes. It was an expensive solution for anyone, especially the woman who taught me how to haggle garage-sale prices from a dime to a nickel. Eventually, she stopped ordering propane and let the house go cold.

By then, a decade had passed since I'd left the farm. I'd finished college, worked at a newspaper in Kansas City, moved to New York and back, worked as a grant writer for nonprofits, taught writing at universities, and bought a small house in Lawrence. Along the way, I'd visited the farm whenever I could. Bumping down the dirt road off the two-lane blacktop, I would roll down my window to smell the earth and the air, as Dad and both my grandfathers had done when I rode along to help feed the cattle or count the kernels on heads of wheat.

Once up the gravel drive and out of my truck, I'd trace familiar outdoor tracks and sensory memories: At the chicken coop, holding a warm egg for the first time. At the tin-roofed Cat Barn, Grandma's shrill *keeeee keeeee* as she walked from the house carrying metal pans of cat food, a dozen farm cats jumping from cobwebbed corners of old horse stalls. At the hay shed, now collapsing, dusty straw bales scratching my shins. At the tree row to the north, the evergreens where Shelly and I played, the sting of horsefly and mosquito bites, the discovery of deer ticks and ringworms burrowed into our skin. At the big metal shed, the smell of dust and oil — still present — and of Grandpa Arnie's sweat through a thin snap-up shirt, long gone. At the swimming pool behind the farmhouse, now filled in with dirt and weeds, the smell of chlorine and the slick skin of a frog I tried to save.

In its current condition, the place warranted a low price, but Grandma balked at most offers and periodically unlisted the property to save the fee and rely instead on word of mouth. In early 2008, she finally sold the house and sheds by auction. After a bit of business wrangling, the farm had a new owner, and Betty needed to clean the place out by March.

"God, I dread it," Betty told me. She was only sixty-two but had been diagnosed with emphysema and arthritis. She found the task of clearing out the farm both emotionally overwhelming and physically daunting.

The house was brimming with the bounty of her many Walmart sale raids and weekend garage-sale escapades, the acquisitions of a woman who grew up with next to nothing and thus relished the act of accumulating the cheap somethings she could afford. These items overflowed from upstairs closets: bath salts made in China, faux-leather wallets, electronic language translators, fuzzy slippers, Life Savers candy. She wrapped them as gifts for grandchildren.

The kitchen, where Betty had fed so many family and friends, contained dinnerware, measuring cups, casseroles, heart-shaped cookie cutters, pancake makers, juicers, grease-splattered cookbooks, and no fewer than three garage-sale blenders.

Betty was the keeper of a few family heirlooms — her grandma Irene's nineteenth-century mirror, her grandfather's heavy iron tools, an orange highway cone my parents had stolen as a prank when they were in love thirty years earlier. These resided in the basement, which also contained shelves of decades-old canned jelly and garden vegetables, boxes and plastic tubs filled with crafting supplies and mouse droppings.

Back upstairs: the china cabinet full of my great-great-grandma Irene's crystal and silver, inherited from women too far back for me to name; the built-in cabinets full of miscellaneous tools and games; shelves lined with knickknacks; four bedrooms full of furniture. They all provoked Betty's anxiety.

The February night when Betty and I arrived to spend a weekend cleaning out the farmhouse, the place lacked running water and was freezing cold due to an empty propane tank. So we shared a cheap motel room ten miles down the highway in Kingman.

"God, I dread it," she said again. "Part of me would just as soon light a match and burn the damn thing down."

The next day, Betty's younger sister Polly and her husband showed up to help us. They lived in Kingman then but for years had lived in an old two-story house Betty had bought as a rental a few miles south of the farm, close to Murdock.

The gray, late-winter morning had the wet, Midwestern cold that can freeze the inside of your nose if you step outside and breathe too quickly. Betty turned on and opened the electric oven to warm up the kitchen. She had called someone to partially fill the propane tank so that we might get the furnace going. We began our work in the old butchering garage. It was supposed to rain that afternoon, and we meant to get the outdoor sorting done before tackling the house.

Polly and her husband helped us hoist a broken garage door onto its crippled tracks. Brittle old glass from the garage door windows rained on our heads. I held the door up while they pushed out the dead Toyota pickup I'd driven for several years after Betty moved to Iowa.

They went about sorting fishing poles, wagons, and tools, and I climbed into the rafters to pull down Betty's old warsh bins. She wanted to keep them in honor of her grandma, who first used them in the 1920s. They were thick with dust that coated my throat.

"If I were you," I told her, "I would ask myself, 'Will I use it? Does it have extreme sentimental value?' If both answers are no, get rid of it. It will just weigh you down." Grandma nodded but didn't listen.

I spotted a bucket deep beneath a butchering table and yanked at the handle. Polly helped me pull it free, and we both covered our mouths from a horrible odor. The bucket contained a few small tools, which were stuck to the bottom by thick, dark goo — the decomposing juices of an animal no longer recognizable. I held my breath and hurried across the gravel yard with the bucket. I set it between the cattle pen and the Cat Barn and ran back to the garage. An eastern gust occasionally placed us downwind from the bucket, gagging us with the reek of death. We finished sorting the garage, sheds, and barns just as it started to rain.

The house stunk of mice, alive and dead, but we were relieved to get warm. It had been the wettest winter in recent memory, and we were cold in a deep way. All day we had to squat outside the house to pee, since the water was turned off and we couldn't flush the toilets.

At Betty's suggestion, Polly and I took things for ourselves. I loaded my pickup bed with gardening items, kitchenware, and a few antique tools, the cracked and rusty sort of things that were in style in home decorating as "shabby chic" farm-life knockoffs at department stores but to us were practical possessions. For more sentimental reasons I took our old egg sign, a sharp, rusted square of corrugated tin onto which Betty had painted EGGS 1.00 DOZEN and placed at the corner of our dirt road and the blacktop. Polly took their mother's purse, which no one had sorted through in the fifteen years since Dorothy's death.

I was relieved to discover that our task was merely to glean from the house desired items, rather than to properly empty and clean the place — a job that would require weeks, not a weekend. Still, I was uneasy about leaving such a mess for the new owners and about having pieces of my childhood handled without reverence by strangers.

"That's how auctions work," Grandma said. "As is."

I took the things I cared strongly for but left behind much with mixed feelings: the decorative ceramic cats my mom bought me when I was small, the marked-down teal dress I'd worn as homecoming queen candidate. I followed the sorting advice I had given my grandmother, but not without pause.

Jerry the farmhand stopped by to help. A high school friend of mine visited with her baby. Polly's daughter and her young family came for the kitchen table. It was funny how the casual swirl of visitors so easily resumed at the farm.

Then it had been dark several hours, and the truck was full of things, and everyone but me and Grandma Betty was gone. It was our last moment on the farm. I needed to pee before we hit the road. In the black country night, Betty waited in her truck, smoking with the heater on and the windows up, heavy rain glistening past the headlights. I unbuttoned my jeans and squatted next to a walnut tree.

People have asked me many times, "How did you get out?"

It is a deeply flawed question. But if I indeed "got out" of something, what was it? It was many things, mostly red ones:

The tiny red shack on a prairie that my parents first brought me home to. The giant glass bottles emptied of blended whiskey and filled over the years with red pennies, the collection of which proved what we didn't have. My red neck, blistered from selling Chinese fireworks out of a tent in a field. The red dirt under my fingernails. The red meat we dug knives into as we butchered the cattle whose muddy corral we could smell from our front door. The red blood on Jesus's hand that promised my sacrifice would be rewarded. The red nail polish my mom wore when physical appeal was one of few available privileges. The ideological confines of "red state" politics that didn't get the chance to be challenged.

Now I am in a different place. But have I really gotten out of those red places? I've seen something of the world, but I still live in my home state. I have a good leather bag, but I love it most for the fact that it cost $3 at the Goodwill. I have a cell phone, but I get voice mail messages from collection agencies looking for my immediate family members. I have a graduate degree but a heap of debt acquired in obtaining it.

If there was something to get out of, some place or class, in many ways I am still there and perhaps always will be. I am there by choice, to some extent, appreciating its riches that shaped me — the wildness of a childhood untended, freedom from expectation, a robust, learned understanding of my own capabilities.

To experience economic poverty in a country famous for its abundance is to live with constant reminders of what you don't have, like running a hot marathon next to a cool reservoir from which you're not allowed to drink. In the absence of certain securities, I had no choice but to go down, down, down, down, down to a taproot and then further down into places material wealth is less likely to force you. There I often heard a voice. It was yours, which is to say that it was mine.

I did not leave one world and enter another. Today I hold them simultaneously — class being a false construct, like any other boundary or category we impose. You don't really climb up or down, get in or out. Mine isn't a story about a destination that was reached but rather about sacrifices I don't believe anyone, certainly no child, should ever have to make.

Those sacrifices leave scars. My mom sometimes left the tags on the things she bought, preferring to display them unopened rather than enjoy using them up. Even if your situation improves or never needed improving, you can go on feeling destitute at your core. Class is an illusion with real consequences.

Economic destitution is just one of many possible poverties, of course. People of all backgrounds experience a sense of poorness — not enough of this or that thing that money can't buy. But financial poverty is the one shamed by society, culture, unchecked capitalism, public policy, our very way of speaking. If you're poor in a wealthy place, common vocabulary suggests that economic failure is failure of the soul.

The term "poor" is used to represent those without money, and it also is a descriptor meaning outright badness, as in "poor health" or "poor test results." In a country where personal value is supposed to create wealth, it is easy for a poor person to feel himself a bad one. Many of the people who raised me believed themselves to be bad. I know because they often treated me like I was bad.

The greatest fortune of my life is that I knew they were wrong. What I truly got out of is a sense of lack — a feeling that knows no socioeconomic boundary. You were the one who helped me do it, your presence telling me you deserved happiness and therefore so did I.

It's no surprise, then, that the moment I let you go was the moment America would say I made it.

The night we separated, I felt you go like a hand slipping out from mine after we'd held each other for lifetimes. I was around thirty years old but felt like I'd lived a lot longer. It had been that sort of life.

People sometimes say they feel something in their bones. There's probably a chemical component to it, but we call it intuition. Often it's about whether something is right or wrong, whether someone is lying. But sometimes it's about an entity changing form. Before they got the call, they looked at a clock the moment a loved one died. Or they knew they were pregnant before they missed a period or took a test.

That night, I was lying in my bed in a big house I had recently bought. It was so beautiful — a huge, thoughtfully built structure with vaulted cedar ceilings in the great room, which alone had more square footage than most places I'd lived. It sat on a forested hill and had wraparound windows with a western view of the Kansas sky and my nice college town.

I was a young professor. I had worked so hard and fast that by my late twenties I had already reached the top of my American climb from childhood trailers and farm-houses to waiting tables to college degrees to unfulfilling but good jobs to, finally, work in which I made a decent salary for my knowledge and creative passion. I had remained partnered with my high school boyfriend all those years, even though he had never developed physical desire for me — a situation that was painful at the time but that I now see served my intentions perfectly. To ensure that nothing knocked me off my path to a more stable life, I had sacrificed even more than I realized.

When I'd gotten the tenure-track job at a small university, I called Dad from the porch of my first, modest house.

"You've given 110 percent your whole life," he said. "From now on you can give 70 percent and it will still be better than most people."

He knew that I would never stop working hard, though. It was deep in me, deeper than religion, to strive. But what I'd strived for, that amorphous goal I'd set as a child — to break the painful cycles I'd been handed by my family before I had any child of my own — had been reached.

Perhaps sensing this, though we'd never discussed it, around that time my mother surprised me with a toy xylophone, its gift tag marked in her elegant script: "from Grandma Jeannie," "to future grandchild." I put it in a storage tub with the dresses she had sewn me when I was a baby. I wrote on the lid BABY, then paused with the marker and added a question mark. BABY?

When I sold my first place and bought the next one, that dream house on a hill, I put the tub in a closet and got to work on renovations and repairs.

I loved the place for the strength in it. It had spent forty years on a hill, and its foundation hadn't slid an inch. But once I fixed it up with my dad's help and guidance, I quickly became uncomfortable with how other people saw it and what they thought it meant. Affluent people gasped when they walked in and saw the cedar beams, the big windows, and the treetop view. I had gotten it for a steal, but the fact was that I somehow lived in one of the most beautiful houses worldly people had ever seen. They wanted it for themselves.

It was the first time I'd ever had a material possession that inspired envy in others. I hated how it felt. To alleviate their fantasy that it was a paradise there, I'd point out how hard it was to clean and mow the whole place myself, how strenuously we had worked to refinish the ceilings. To relieve their confusion about how I afforded it, I'd tell them the purchase price, well below what humble little houses were going for.

The issue was that I needed to square where I was with the story about where I came from — a seemingly great distance to reconcile.

I was lying there in my bed, and suddenly I sensed you in the room. It was the same presence with whom I'd spoken for so many years but closer and more specific, like a real person. I closed my eyes and saw you for the first time as a clearly defined image — a child's form. You didn't look like me, but I knew who you were. And I knew why you were there: to say goodbye.

You were the poor child I would never have — not because I would never have a child but because I was no longer poor.

Until then, my transition into a life so different from the one I began with was still tenuous, and thus you remained as a flicker — a would-be child born into poverty — even after I got a graduate degree or my first salaried job. At those moments I was still "poor" by a lot of people's standards. But that title of "professor," that beautiful house on a hill — I could no longer think of myself as a sunburned toddler in a hot trailer.

I could still have a child, so far as I knew, but I understood that you would no longer be waiting to enter me. If I were to become pregnant from that moment on, it would be a different soul, a different person. I would keep the storage tub marked BABY? with the gift inside from my mother to a future child. That child would never come from where I did, though, because my surroundings and I had so thoroughly changed. A cycle had been broken, and the place it tore was between me and you.

I felt you leave like a soul that had waited around in my room for a thousand years. Thank God, but how it hurt.

I had done what I set out to do, and I was glad. I made a decision at a young age and followed through with ruthless conviction. I kept you at arm's length so long that the window for physical connection passed.

I cried in my bed. I cried so hard that the pillowcase looked like the ones beneath my head when I was a child — wet orbs, cold against my cheek. That I couldn't have you meant I'd left where I was from and who I once was in irreversible ways, no matter where I chose to live or how I did it.

I cried to mourn a loss in success, then. I was so grateful to have known you and to feel you leaving that I cried from amazement, too.

That night, I felt the separation from you in my bones — the physical you that would never exist. But the invisible connection that had existed all along, prior to that night, still exists, which is why I can talk to you now.

You will never feel the Kansas wind in your hair, August, and for that I am not glad. But you will never have to fight like my family did. For that I am grateful.

You never needed a world to respect you.

Your worth was unto itself. Betty was right: A penny is a penny.

Jeannie used to hint at that same gulf between my value and the way I'd be appraised, even in those years when she was angry and cruel. If a high school teacher picked on me for who my family was, Mom would raise her eyebrows just a bit, as if to say that woman's opinion was hardly worth getting ruffled over.

"She senses greatness," Mom would say, as though that were the final verdict.

An august thing is impressive and dignified, and beneath my mother's pain she saw me and perhaps herself just that way. Maybe it was that undercurrent in her, subconsciously felt if rarely evidenced, that allowed me to quiet the world and hear you speak.

You weren't my daughter, of course, but my highest self — less a guardian angel than my own power emanating, necessarily disembodied from a body and mind I had been told by society had little worth.

"Stop breeding," society had said about my people.

I laughed recently when I realized that's exactly what I did but for reasons precisely opposite their hateful ones. I listened to a different voice.

You are priceless, the voice said. It was

431

my voice, and it was yours.

I heard you, August.

My life's work was to be heard, and the poor young mother will have a hard row at that. No child of mine would ever have to do what Dorothy, Betty, Jeannie, or I did. Or what Teresa or so many poor women from different places did. I loved us both so much that I made sure you were conceived only in my mind. A little sad for the woman in me, but great for the god in you.

I realized recently that if I had given physical birth to you at the age Jeannie gave birth to me or Betty gave birth to Jeannie, your first election as a voter would have been in 2016. That was another big turning point in America, like when Jeannie cast her first vote for Carter in 1980 and I cast mine for Bush in 2000. Soon after that election at the turn of the millennium, when Jeannie also identified as conservative, her and my politics both changed a lot. Like the rest of my close family members, we ended up as progressives who agreed on just about everything. So I don't know how you would have voted.

I do know that you would have been vulnerable to an election's outcomes, to sociopolitical shifts that inevitably hurt the poor first. I know you would have been a child of the working class, probably white, maybe already a mother yourself. I know I would have prayed for you to be known not by your status or education level but by the obvious value of your merely being. Maybe, too, by what you would have given your country: a lifetime of true labor that fed and moved the world.

This country has failed its children, August, failed its own claims about democracy and humanity. The American Dream, in particular, sometimes seems more like a ghost haunting our way of thinking than like a sacred contract worth signing toward some future.

Maybe what holds a society together in a lasting way isn't a calculated trade involving sacrifice, currency, and power — a wobbly claim that you get what you work for — but something more like a never-ending spiral of gifts.

An honest economic system might still come to fruition in this place, whose most noble ideals are always available to us. That's a dream worth having, I think. That's a goal worth working toward.

The best version of so many things has been conceived but remains unborn — like the girl you might have been and the country I trust your spirit is helping to create somewhere: America in high summer, tired from a season of fieldwork but clear-eyed and full of promise under the harvest moon.

ACKNOWLEDGMENTS

Thank you to my agent, Julie Barer, and my editor, Kathryn Belden, for shepherding this book with not just intellect and skill but the rarer wisdom and knowing. Without their support during the last few years of its gestation, it would be a much different and less realized thing.

Thank you to the Scribner publishing team. Among them, special thanks to publicist Kate Lloyd, who immediately understood the story, and to Nan Graham, for editing the memoirs of poverty and labor that shaped me as a budding journalist drawn to personal narrative. Thanks, also, to legal counsel Elisa Rivlin, whose expertise resulted in important improvements to the manuscript.

Thank you to Carrie Frye, for a bright editorial push when I was finishing an important draft, and to Maud Newton, whose friendship as a fellow writer appeared at critical junctures in my publishing journey. Thank you to Andrew Spackman, whose presence helped me across the finish line.

These Midwest-affiliated women stood by me when I took the personal and professional risks that allowed the book to finally manifest: Michelle Hubicki, Melanie Burdick, Marguerite Perret, Stephanie Lanter, Simran Sethi, Tara Neill, Mary Quinn, Courtney Crouch, and Amy Martin. When difficult circumstances took me to Colorado, Pat Cox opened her home to me so that I could continue working. Later in the process, these Texas writers and friends welcomed me when I moved away from Kansas for perspective: Michelle García, Alyssa Coppelman, Bryan Mealer, and Hillery Hugg. Thank you to all of them.

During my fifteen years of research and writing, many people read, critiqued, and encouraged earlier pages that laid a foundation for these, now so different yet the same. Thank you to Patricia O'Toole, Honor Moore, Richard Locke, Lis Harris, Frank McCourt, Lauren Hoffman, Rhena Tantisunthorn Refsland, Aura Davies, Annie Choi, Gina Kaufmann, Michael Noll, and others who touched the oldest passages here.

Thank you to the English teachers of Kansas public schools, who told a child from a family of laborers that she was a writer who deserved to be heard: in elementary school, Val Cheatham; in middle school, Patty Strothman; in high school, Stacey Walters and Lawna Bass Kurtyka; at a state university, Mary Klayder and Tom Lorenz.

With deepest reverence, thank you to my family for surviving, with humor and dignity, the difficulties that allowed this book to exist. When I asked for their blessing to tell our shared past, they bravely answered yes. Their reasons for standing behind my work, as they sometimes told me: Because it might help someone else, and because it is true.

ABOUT THE AUTHOR

Sarah Smarsh has covered socioeconomic class, politics, and public policy for *The Guardian, VQR,* NewYorker.com, Harpers .org, *The Texas Observer,* and many others. She is currently a Joan Shorenstein Fellow at Harvard University's Kennedy School of Government. A former professor of nonfiction writing, Smarsh is a frequent speaker on economic inequality and related media narratives. She lives in Kansas. *Heartland* is her first book.